MW00627255

1 July 2021
Madzie, our (somewhat) famous forebear,

love from Charles.

PESHTIGO 1871

Peter Pernin's Peshtigo Fire Memoir *The Finger of God Is There*!

Translated and edited by Charles E. Mercier

TBR Books
New York

TBR Books is a program of the Center for the Advancement of Languages, Education, and Communities. We publish researchers and practitioners who seek to engage diverse communities on topics related to education, languages, cultural history, and social initiatives.

CALEC - TBR Books
750 Lexington Avenue, 9th floor
New York, NY 10022
www.calec.org | contact@calec.org
www.tbr-books.org | contact@tbr-books.org

Front Cover Illustration: Peshtigo Harbor 1871, Peshtigo *Times*. Wikimedia Commons.

Cover Design: Nathalie Charles

First Edition: *Le doigt de Dieu est là! ou Episode émouvant d'un événement étrange raconté par un témoin oculaire* by Jean-Pierre Pernin. Editions Eusèbe Senécal, Montréal, 1874.

ISBN 978-1-636070704 (hardback)
ISBN 978-1-636070643 (paperback)
ISBN 978-1-636070650 (eBook)

Library of Congress Control Number: 2021935531

Praise

In one volume Charles Mercier has provided a valuable service to three arenas of history: fire in the Great Lakes region, the state of Wisconsin in the 19th century, and Roman Catholic ecclesiastical/missionary activity in North America. His resurrection of Father Peter Pernin's remarkable account of the Great Peshtigo Fire of 1871, accompanied by Mercier's trenchant introduction and commentary, is a fine example of the historian's art.

> — Peter M. Leschak, author of *Ghosts of the Fireground: Echoes of the Great Peshtigo Fire and the Calling of a Wildland Firefighter*

A sizzling memoir of the Great Peshtigo Fire of 1871 by Father Peter Pernin, a French missionary in Green Bay, Wisconsin, has been given a new, sensitive translation by Charles Mercier, the author's great great grand-nephew, who meets the exacting standards of a classical scholar while drawing on a deep well of Catholicism. Miraculous.

> — Mary Norris, author of *Between You & Me: Confessions of a Comma Queen* and *Greek to Me: Adventures of the Comma Queen*

Natural disasters have a way of revealing the religious reflections of those who suffer. Charles Mercier's new translation of a French Catholic priest's account of the Great Peshtigo Fire of 1871 brings to life the horror and hope that came with the deadliest fire in American history. Combined with a rich and rigorously researched introduction, Mercier's translation brings readers into the world of a foreign missionary on the American frontier, resulting in a valuable contribution to our understanding of Catholicism in the United States.

> — Michael Pasquier, Jaak Seynaeve Professor of Christian Studies, Louisiana State University, author of *Fathers on the Frontier: French Missionaries and the Roman Catholic Priesthood in the United States, 1789-1870*

Contents

Preface

In 1874, Jean-Pierre Pernin (1822-1909) was a priest of the Roman Catholic diocese of Green Bay, Wisconsin, 52, who ten years before had come from the diocese of Autun (Saône-et-Loire) in France as a diocesan missionary to the United States. He was missionary rector of two parishes, Peshtigo and Marinette, in the northeast corner of Wisconsin, and had survived the Great Peshtigo Fire, October 8-9, 1871, which burned the whole town to the ground and killed some 2,000 people, the deadliest wildfire in American history. As a fundraiser to support the rebuilding of his two churches, two houses, and a school building lost in the fires, and as a way of finding some meaning in what had happened, Pernin produced an 18,000 word memoir of the experience.

He wrote the memoir in his native French and published it in Montreal with Eusèbe Senécal as *Le doigt de Dieu est là! ou Épisode émouvant d'un événement étrange raconté par un témoin oculaire*. He published it simultaneously in English translation with John Lovell as *The Finger of God Is There! or A Moving Episode of a Strange Event Told By An Eyewitness*. This edition makes the work, intended as bilingual, fully available for the first time since its original publication.

For a hundred years now, Pernin's fire memoir has steadily found readers as a gripping survival story and as fundamental documentary evidence for the Peshtigo fire, even recently among wildfire professionals and writers on forest ecology. Yet the French original has never before been republished and the work has been known only in three incomplete reprintings by the Wisconsin Historical Society of the 1874 Lovell translation, which was not entirely adequate anyway. This edition provides a critical edition of the original French and a fresh, complete English translation with introduction and notes, material condensed from my critical biography of Pernin (in progress), that attempt to locate the work in its social and theological context. In the Appendix are found several writings relevant to *Finger of God*.

The Wisconsin Historical reprintings omitted passages "dealing largely with matters of Catholic faith" and pertaining "to the religious reflections and ideas of the author," thus robbing the work of some of the significance its Roman Catholic missionary priest author intended. Pernin's *Doigt de Dieu* emerges here as an estimable work of North American francophone literature, whose style reflects both the humane Classical studies and amateur science of a mid-19th century French Collège and the humor of Wisconsin lumberjack culture; as a work of popular theology and theodicy; and as an important document of French missionary experience in a multi-religious America. Pernin's assimilation as an American went so far as a Catholic priest's enthusiastically amplifying his Catholic understanding of natural disaster with Calvinist theology.

Furthermore, for a year in 1868-1869, Pernin had pastored the French Belgians of Robinsonville, Wisconsin, on the Door Peninsula east of Green Bay. Among his parishioners was Adèle Brice (1831-1896), who had been inspired to establish there a religious community and school in response to a vision of the Virgin Mary she experienced. In *Finger of God* Pernin risked his diocesan standing to argue that the wildfire had miraculously passed over Brice's community to vindicate the truth of the apparition. *Finger of God* became the first published source for those events and a document therefore essential to a critical history of the Robinsonville Mariophany, declared "worthy of belief" by Green Bay Bishop David L. Ricken in December 2010, the first in the United States so declared.

Full disclosure: this effort began as a work of family history. I am a great grandson of one of the nieces Pernin brought with him to Illinois in 1864. I am nevertheless as ready to explicate my great great granduncle's shortcomings as I am pleased to perpetuate his literary work, especially in observance of October 8-9, 2021, the 150th anniversary of the Peshtigo fire, an event awesome both in its destructive power and in the resilience and determination to rebuild that it summoned of its survivors. Pernin observed that already in 1874 the fire was an event "more and more forgotten each day," yet his work has contributed to what Stephen J. Pyne called its "cachet as 'forgotten,'" which "has paradoxically helped make it better known than almost any other rural conflagration," a paradox that would have amused and delighted him.

Charles E. Mercier
Borough of Woodmont, Milford, Connecticut
February 11, 2021

Introduction

E arly on the morning of October 9, 1871, Father Peter Pernin found himself submerged in the cold Peshtigo River of Peshtigo, Wisconsin, together with hundreds of fellow townspeople and parishioners, as a fathomless wildfire surged above them. A cow swam by. Their hair caught fire if they stood up too tall. It was absurd, but by staying in the river more than five hours they saved their lives. Seven years before, Pernin had come to the United States from France as a Catholic missionary priest. He had asked for the absurdity: the enormities of North America — the blizzards that maimed and killed, the mosquitoes and rattlesnakes, the rainwater that poured down on those being ordained in an unfinished cathedral, wine frozen in the chalice in the middle of Mass — had been part of the romanticized appeal that called forth the French foreign missionary's heroism.

What Pernin experienced he felt extraordinary, scientifically, even spiritually. God had intervened to save him. And having been educated in Classical humanities at a rigorous French Collège, he was a writer capable of communicating what he felt. He decided to write a short memoir of his experience of surviving the fire. He wrote it in French and traveled to Montreal to publish it and at the same time to arrange for an English translation. The effort was a part of his multifarious program to raise funds to rebuild the facilities of the two parishes he pastored, Peshtigo and Marinette, Wisconsin, all of which had burned. As a man of the nineteenth century Pernin had some understanding of the uses of mass media.

The life and times of Peter Pernin

Jean-Pierre Pernin had grown up in Flacey-en-Bresse, an agricultural village of population 1200 in Saône-et-Loire in east central France, not far from the Swiss border. He was born there February 22, 1822. Bresse is known for its chickens and also for the distinctive arrangement of its farms into houses and outbuildings, in which a household of as many as 15 to 20 might have lived. Jean-Pierre was the seventh of nine children and part of an extended family of at least 50 members who lived near one another.

Jean-Pierre might have been a shepherd as a young boy, become a farmer and carter in Flacey like his father Benoît, or even aspired to be a sabot maker like his eldest brother and godfather Jean, 14 years older, who moved on to make shoes in the bigger town of Poligny (Jura) and eventually Lyon. Instead, his half first cousin, a Catholic priest, intervened and invited him 135 miles away to a pre-professional humanities education at the Collège de Meximieux (Ain), where he was superior, and to a start along the career path of a Roman Catholic priest.

Pernin's hometown, Flacey-en-Bresse: Church of St. Martin of Tours.

The cousin was Denis-Joseph Maîtrepierre (1800-1872), who grew up six miles south of Flacey in Cormoz (Ain). When Maîtrepierre arranged for young Pernin to begin clerical studies and deprive his family of his labor, he understood how that might provoke resistance. His father had opposed his own beginning at Meximieux at 15 in 1815. Maîtrepierre would become a figure significant to the history of the Society of Mary, the Marists, a Catholic religious congregation founded in Lyon in 1816. He was in the group of the first twenty Marists, who made religious profession in 1836, and became the congregation's first novice master.

Meximieux, founded in 1803, directed by Maîtrepierre from 1833 to 1845, was an institution important to the post-Revolution

Catholic restoration in France. It developed from a clandestine seminary conducted in the 1790s, whose students showed themselves as agricultural workers by day and read Caesar and Vergil by night as an act of political defiance. Meximieux was a *petit séminaire* (minor seminary), a place where students experienced rigorous physical discipline, learned bourgeois manners if they came off a farm, and were imbued with Classical humanities study as propaedeutic to philosophy and theology.

A farm outbuilding en colombage *(half-timbered), Flacey-en-Bresse.*

It was a Collège, which in French academic culture at the time comprised what in modern America is, roughly, the eight years of middle school, high school, and first two years of college. Collège began with the rudiments and at its completion was to have prepared students for advanced studies in a professional field. Those training for Catholic priesthood would go on to study philosophy and theology, but as a pre-professional Collège, Meximieux did prepare those who chose otherwise for other career paths. A young man would not of course enter Meximieux without a spiritual interest or an openness to being on track for the Catholic priesthood, though it was a unique educational opportunity for many who would not become priests.

Pernin completed seven forms at Meximieux and graduated in a class of about 30 in August 1842. For four years he continued with philosophy and theology at the *Grand séminaire* (major seminary) of Autun (Saône-et-Loire), his home diocese, then in the seminary chapel was ordained a Catholic priest by Autun Bishop Bénigne-Urbain-Jean-Marie du Trousset d'Héricourt on an Advent Ember Day, Saturday, December 19, 1846.

Pernin studied humanities 1835-42 at Collège de Meximieux (top, Imp. Française Paris*) and was chaplain of Collège d'Autun 1851-54, where Napoleon had learned French (bottom,* Wikimedia Commons*). Pernin's college chapel was the church at left, forming a wing of the Collège courtyard, now Église Notre-Dame.*

    Pernin was a diocesan priest of Autun over the next 18 years. His earliest appointments signaled a promising career. His first was as *vicaire* of St. Pierre, Mâcon, one of two downtown parishes of the city that was the Saône-et-Loire prefecture and center of the wine business, under a *curé* who was a diocesan luminary, Claude Tailland (1799-1854). After four years in Mâcon, December 1846 to January 1851, he was appointed chaplain of the Collège d'Autun. Pernin returned to the city of his seminary training, having in common with the students the Collège education he had received at Meximieux.

The Collège d'Autun had a tradition of more than 230 years and of distinguished alumni that included three Bonaparte brothers (Napoleon learned French there) and was an institution to which leading families of Autun and environs sent their children. A student who overlapped the last year of Pernin's chaplaincy was Louis Renault, the 1907 Nobel Peace laureate.

After 1853 Pernin was no longer chaplain of Collège d'Autun. He does not reappear in diocesan records until February 1863, when Autun Bishop Frédéric de Marguerye appointed him *curé* of St. Just, Rancy (Saône-et-Loire), a rural village like Flacey, though less than half the size. Why after two prominent appointments out of seminary and then a gap of nine years Pernin reemerges to history in a tiny village curacy I cannot say. But wherever he had been, Pernin lived the life of a village *curé* for less than a year. He resigned on February 6, 1864 and was off for Iroquois County, Illinois, in the diocese of Chicago.

Pernin was not alone in leaving France. By the end of the nineteenth century almost two thirds of the 6100 Catholic missionary priests working abroad were French. In an 1850 issue of *Annales de la Propagation de la Foi*, a Lyon publication with news of Catholic missions worldwide, Pernin might have read the letter from Chicago Bishop James Van de Velde on the need for priests on the Illinois prairie, to which he himself would be responding in 14 years' time. Through his cousin and seminary superior Denis Maîtrepierre, Pernin had constant acquaintance with Marist missionaries, which included at least five of Pernin's 30 or so Meximieux 1842 classmates.

Against the background of international French missionary movement, Pernin took his place within a tradition that for 50 years brought Catholic priests from Meximieux to the American mid-west. These included Mathias Loras (fourth superior of Meximieux, 1817-1824, first bishop of Dubuque, eventually Iowa, 1837-1858); Joseph Crétin (attended Meximieux in the 1810s, first bishop of St. Paul, Minnesota, 1851-1857); and St. Paul archbishop John Ireland. Maîtrepierre himself and a group of friends who were Meximieux classmates, then fellow Marists, had resolved to follow Mathias Loras to America. One of them was Bressane Pierre Chanel (1803-

1841), eventually canonized a Catholic saint, who grew up within a few miles south of Flacey and Cormoz, went to Oceania instead of America, and met death at the hands of the Futunas in 1841. Pernin was in second form at Meximieux when he heard; Maîtrepierre had been named heir in Chanel's will. If Maîtrepierre and friends went elsewhere than America, Pernin went off in their stead to seek more bourgeois forms of martyrdom.

As Tangi Villerbu, author of *Les Missions de Minnesota* (2014), has emphasized, French diocesan missionaries could not have been recruited nor departed for North America without the networking of friends and former students, who might have responded more to immediate, specific needs, than a broad missionary vocation. Pernin came to Chicago at the invitation of its fourth Catholic bishop, the personable and energetic James Duggan (1825-1899, bishop 1859-1880). By 1864 Chicago had developed from French fur trading center into multi-ethnic American city where French-speaking Catholics had been resenting perceived mistreatment for thirty years. In the 1860s Duggan, who himself spoke French, was recruiting French-speaking priests for two immediate, specific, and interrelated reasons: he wanted to affirm and reconcile French-speaking Catholics in Chicago, who in 1857 had published a manifesto in the Chicago *Tribune* denouncing his predecessor Anthony O'Regan for having annihilated their community, and to support those of downstate counties against defections to Charles Chiniquy, a figure both symptomatic of and in part fueling that resentment.

Chiniquy (1809-1899) was a Catholic priest, once of the diocese of Quebec then of Montreal, turned anti-Catholic polemicist and pastor, formally from 1858, of First Presbyterian in St. Anne, Iroquois County, Illinois. His drama was freighted with national and international significance: a new Martin Luther was leading francophone America and even Quebec into a new Reformation. Pernin's first assignment was to St. John the Baptist, L'Erable, Iroquois County, Illinois, 15 miles southwest of St. Anne. He began there October 16, 1864 and lasted three years and five months.

Pernin had brought with him two nieces, daughters of his eldest brother and godfather Jean, Zoé, 21, and his own goddaughter Maria-Berthe, 16. The two were leaving behind in Lyon their father, stepmother, two brothers, a younger sister, and a ten-year-old half sister. Zoé's daughter, in an oral history recorded in 1968, remembered the two were "heart-broken" to leave France, but there must have been necessity. His nieces helped him keep house in L'Erable, supporting his ministry and serving frequently when needed as baptismal sponsors and marriage witnesses, even traveling with him to his missions, stops south on the Illinois Central Railroad.

James Duggan (1825-1899) became the fourth Catholic bishop of Chicago (1859-1869) at age 34. George P. A. Healy painted him in 1862 at the height of Duggan's energies, when his initiative brought Pernin and Philibert Crud to the diocese. At the time Duggan was chairing an effort to purchase a collection of Healy paintings as the nucleus of a civic art gallery. Archdiocese of Chicago.

Duggan extended the invitation to Chicago through an intermediary, Philibert Crud, another French missionary priest, who must have known Pernin in the networks of Marists and Meximieux alumni and became his close friend in America, someone mentioned twice in *Finger of God*. Crud (1828-1913) grew up in Ain, attended Meximieux, joined the Marists, was ordained in 1854 in Belley, taught six years at Marist institutions, left the congregation in 1861, left France for North America for a year in the diocese of Quebec and two years, 1862-64, in Iroquois and Kankakee Counties, Illinois. On arrival in November 1862 Crud spent a few days in Chicago with Duggan, who asked his help recruiting French-speaking priests, either Marist former colleagues or any of his friends. Crud did so and Pernin was the one fruit of his effort. The thought of securing Marists for Chicago was plausible, given that the first two Marists to come to the United States (one of them Pernin's Meximieux 1842 classmate Joseph-Marie Gautherin) arrived in February 1863 to tend French-speaking Catholics in Louisiana, then under federal occupation.

Philibert Crud (1828-1913), here in the early 1870s, was Pernin's best friend in America. Diocese of Green Bay.

Before 1908, when the Vatican administratively declared the United States no longer missionary territory, Roman Catholic canon law common to the wider church did not apply there. That legality informed Pernin's missionary career: he was never legally a "pastor" (when we use the term here, we are using it informally as to church law). He was a "missionary rector" in charge of a "quasi-parish," without the canonical rights accorded pastors under common church law. Nor was he entitled to canonical due process if ever accused of impropriety. American bishops at the time, in the opinion of critics of the canonical situation, were a law unto themselves and were obliged neither to offer a hearing to a priest they might discipline (or a Marian visionary for that matter) nor to take responsibility for a priest's welfare after dismissing him. They could be contemptuous and disinclined to draw distinctions between personal slight, mendacious intrigue of a clerical enemy, small indiscretion, and serious crime. Missionary diocesan priests coming to America depended personally on the good will of their bishop in a way they had not experienced before in the diocesan bureaucratic settings of Europe.

Late in 1866, within two years of having sponsored Pernin's mission in Illinois, Bishop Duggan began to exhibit signs of mental illness. The Chicago diocese thereafter was in some administrative chaos until Duggan's removal as bishop in April 1869; his absences for health reasons and abrupt and erratic decision making, including peremptory dismissals, created immense bad feeling. In the midst of all that, Pernin found it opportune to move to a new diocese, broken off from that of Milwaukee, that of Green Bay, Wisconsin, canonically established March 3, 1868. Again Philibert Crud was the intermediary. After dismissal from the diocese of Chicago in October 1864, he was received by the diocese of Milwaukee and pastored French-speaking Belgians on the Door Peninsula east of Green Bay. He summoned Pernin to replace him for a year as he made a return trip to France.

Pernin's two nieces stayed in Illinois, making their own arrangements and beginning their own lives. In November 1868, with Pernin presiding, Maria-Berthe married a French Belgian Catholic farmer, Pierre Berger, and spent the rest of her life in Clifton, Iroquois County, Illinois. One of their four children would marry into a Presbyterian family of St. Anne. Zoé moved to Chicago, taught French at Dearborn Seminary, a college preparatory school for women, then about 1869 married a Frenchman from Bagnols-sur-Cèze (Gard), Victor Lassagne, a fruit dealer with decades of commercial experience in Louisiana and Arkansas. Over the next 20 years in Chicago the two would establish businesses in French luxury goods, jewelry, lace, a Restaurant Français and hotel. Pernin would love his nieces and their children as daughters and grandchildren.

Pernin spent ten years in the diocese of Green Bay, assigned to five parishes:

- St. Joseph's, Robinsonville, December 1868 to September 1869, where one of his parishioners was Adèle Brice, the Belgian woman who had experienced a vision of the Virgin Mary and in response had begun a shrine, religious congregation, and school. Pernin would write about her in *Finger of God*.

- St. Peter's, Oconto, August 1869 to December 1869, where he would return for a weekend of recuperation after the fire.

- Assumption of the Blessed Virgin Mary, Peshtigo and St. Patrick's, Marinette, December 1869 to September 1875, an assignment that early on included attending Menominee and Cedar River, Michigan, across the Menominee River in the diocese of Sault Sainte Marie and Marquette. As he was proud to write about, Pernin renamed St. Patrick's Our Lady of Lourdes when he rebuilt the Marinette church after the fires. He was suspended from ministry October 1874 to July 1875 on his return from Montreal, where he had arranged to publish *Finger of God*.

- Sts. Peter and Paul, Grand Rapids (now Wisconsin Rapids in the diocese of La Crosse, Wisconsin), September 1875 to October 1878, where Pernin was reassigned after being reinstated to ministry.

Pernin's Green Bay years were difficult: he survived the fire in 1871, recuperated, for two years visited lumber camps in winter and put on church fairs to raise money to rebuild two churches and a school at a time of national economic downturn, fought with enemies in his parishes over rebuilding priorities, in December 1873 lost Joseph Melcher, the bishop who had brought him to Green Bay and had supported him, faced the opposition of diocesan authority over the Marian apparition that he believed in, fended off public accusations of embezzlement in the fall of 1874, and was suspended from ministry ostensibly for having spent too much time away arranging *Finger of God*. After all the disruptions and controversies, Pernin again transferred dioceses and in November 1878 was welcomed by that of St. Paul. He would spend the last 30 years of his life in Minnesota.

The bishop of St. Paul, John Ireland (1838-1918, coadjutor from 1875, bishop from 1884, archbishop from 1888), was himself a francophile Meximieux alumnus, class of 1857, 15 years behind Pernin, and adulated his Collège with loving nostalgia. "Meximieux is ...closely knitted into the history of the Diocese of St. Paul," he wrote in 1916. Pernin left behind Bishop Franz Xaver Krautbauer and the heavily German ecclesiastical culture of Wisconsin for a diocese that French priests, many of them Meximieux alumni, had played an honored part in building up. He would find peace more than controversy and ecclesiastical preferment rather than censure.

For the next 16 years Pernin worked in Houston County, the southeast corner of Minnesota, along the Mississippi, pastoring Church of the Crucifixion, La Crescent, 1878 to 1886, and St. Patrick's, Brownsville, to 1894. His last four years of parish work took him west, to St. Bridget's, Simpson, Olmsted County, to 1897, and St. Joseph's, Rushford, Fillmore County, to February 1898.

In 1889, Ireland won Pope Leo XIII's approval of an ecclesiastical reorganization that made Ireland the metropolitan archbishop over five new episcopal sees in Minnesota and the Dakotas. Winona became the episcopal city for a new diocese comprising the southern strip of Minnesota from the river to the South Dakota border (in 2018 renamed Winona-Rochester). After a decade in the diocese of St. Paul, Pernin was taken into that of Winona. In the fall of 1891, first Winona bishop Joseph Cotter (1844-1909) chose Pernin for the first vicar general of the new diocese. Pernin thereby held the highest office in the diocese after the bishop and authority to administer in the bishop's name. He was that unusual vicar general who had once been suspended from ministry by another. He would be in office six years.

Pernin turned 76 in February 1898 and retired as diocesan vicar general and regular parish pastor. Cotter then named him,

April 1, 1898, the first regularly appointed resident chaplain of St. Mary's Hospital, Rochester, from which would emerge the institution now known collectively as Mayo Clinic. This was the only hospital in the United States owned by a religious congregation, the Sisters of St. Francis of Our Lady of Lourdes, that partnered with non-sectarian doctors. Pernin lived at the hospital with the Franciscan sisters, who founded and sustained it. The day Cotter introduced him as new chaplain Pernin told the Sisters, "He has brought you an April Fool."

Pernin's last birthday: Pernin from Rochester, Minnesota to his grandniece Zoé Lassagne in Chicago, March 8, 1909, mentioning William Worrall Mayo. "My celebration of birth day has been grand. I had the old (ninety years old) Mayo father at dinner with me, and lots of wishes, cards, and so on."

Peter Pernin,
Detroit, ~1890.

William Worrall Mayo, founder of St. Mary's together with Mother Mary Alfred Moes, OSF and his two sons William and Charles, attended the party that the Franciscan Sisters gave Pernin for his 87th, and what would be his last, birthday, February 22, 1909. Pernin died at St. Mary's, Saturday October 9, 1909, at 8 AM, 38 years to the minute of his rude expulsion from the survivors' tent on the Peshtigo River the morning after the fire.

Pernin had lived a 19th century life: he grew up tending animals amid the *colombage* of Flacey-en-Bresse and died at Mayo Clinic. He watched steamboats, then railroads, then motorcars change Mâcon, Marinette, Rochester. When needing to fundraise or play diocesan politics, as we will see, it occurred to him to avail himself of national mass media (though *Finger of God* itself was never a commercial success). If the title page of *Finger of God* proclaimed him "Missionary to the United States," by the time Pernin started in Illinois at age 42 in 1864 and got as far west as southeastern Minnesota in 1878, the frontier had already passed him by.

Pernin was a transitional kind of post-missionary missionary, a Catholic diocesan priest in the expanding American towns of the post-Civil War Gilded Age, when recently built railroads were giving convenient access to parishes on a line rather than a circuit. He filled the more routine need for Catholic diocesan personnel to serve growing numbers of French-speaking Catholic immigrants to the United States, particularly from Canada and Belgium, a foreigner staffing a regular parish in an established but understaffed diocese. He brought Catholic sacramental ministry to immigrants and settlers already Catholic, working to raise the material and devotional standards of his parishes and to develop the bureaucratic infra-structure of a new diocese.

The Finger of God

It was in St. Louis that Pernin first felt encouraged to write what became *Finger of God*. To clear his head and recover his health after the fire he decided to travel, which would also give him an opportunity to raise funds for the rebuilding of his parishes. He intended "to go all the way to Louisiana and return from the east (79)," but this plan proved too ambitious: he got as far east as Terre Haute, Indiana and as far south as St. Louis, Missouri. Bishop Melcher must have smoothed Pernin's way in St. Louis: coming from Vienna and northern Italy at the invitation of its first Catholic bishop Joseph Rosati, from the mid-1840s for more than twenty years Melcher had worked there, eventually as vicar general for German-speaking Catholics.

After half a week of work in devastated Peshtigo, a weekend in Oconto, and a visit with Melcher in Green Bay, Pernin returned to Marinette the week of October 16 and over the next eight days performed five baptisms of recently born infants. October 24 was his last Marinette record, after which he wrote in his register that he left on his travels. Since he had to pass through Chicago anyway, it is hard to think that he did not check in with his niece Zoé, husband Victor, and their one-year-old son Victor, his grandnephew, to hear their story of surviving the Chicago fire. He could well also have returned to Iroquois County to visit his niece Maria-Berthe and family in Clifton for a few weeks of quiet recuperation on their farm.

It was "two distinguished bishops," one American, one British, who "urged" him to write (7). These likely were Archbishop Peter Richard Kenrick, who welcomed Pernin to St. Louis, and Herbert Vaughan, bishop of Salford, England from September 1872, eventually Cardinal Archbishop of Westminster. On a trip through the American south to support Catholic missionary outreach to African-Americans, Vaughan visited St. Louis in January 1872 and would have met Pernin. Kenrick, who had held slaves, discouraged Vaughan's initiative and disallowed him fundraising in St. Louis.

Pernin was embarrassed and defensive about how long it took the memoir to appear, more than two and a half years after the fire. With the speed of a journalist, within months of the fire Frank Tilton, editor of the Green Bay *Advocate*, had already published *Sketch of the Great Fires* with "thrilling and truthful incidents by eye witnesses." By spring 1874 Pernin was finally ready to arrange publication of the manuscript. As a replacement, he secured a German priest, Nicholas Gällweiler, 32, who arrived by April 17 from the diocese of Vincennes. Gällweiler had been pastor of the

German parish St. Benedict's, Terre Haute from March 1871 to February 1872, where he apparently met Pernin in December 1871 when Pernin stopped in Terre Haute on his way to St. Louis. Pernin's last sacramental record in Marinette was April 26 and after that, in "the very last days of April 1874," he was off to Montreal, an opportune place in which to arrange the publication of his memoir in both French and English.

8-10 Rue St. Vincent, Montreal, once the offices of Eusèbe Senécal.

Pernin wrote the memoir in his native French. He called it *Le doigt de Dieu est là! ou Episode émouvant d'un évènement étrange, raconté par un témoin oculaire.* The book's 18,000 words in 104 pages were published in trigesimo-secundo format (3 ½ x 5 ½ inches) in late spring 1874 by Eusèbe Senécal, one of the largest printers and publishers in Montreal. A Conservative and Catholic who had spent a year in *petit séminaire*, Senécal published periodicals for both the government and the religious congregation of the Sulpicians and in the mid-1860s began to publish literary works with the aim of stimulating French Canadian literature.

Simultaneously the work was translated into English (by someone uncredited) and appeared as *The Finger of God Is There! Or, Thrilling Episode of a Strange Event Related by an Eye-witness*, published, also in 32mo, 102 pages, by John Lovell. Lovell was an Irish immigrant and devout Anglican, who among many printing and publishing interests committed himself to supporting Canadian literature. In their salon, Lovell and his wife Sarah Kurczyn, who conducted a young ladies school, included Ignace Bourget, Catholic bishop of Montreal.

Bourget (1799-1885) proved another episcopal supporter. In summer 1874 he was 74 and toward the end of his 36 years as Catholic bishop of Montreal (1840-1876), perhaps the greatest builder of Catholicism in the province of Quebec, conservative, saintly, "authoritarian, uncompromising, intolerant," today a polarizing figure. Pernin had Bourget's personal imprimatur within weeks of his arrival in Montreal. If Lovell followed his usual procedure for something not a money-making novel, a sponsor, like Bourget, had paid for the production of the English version.

Bishop Ignace Bourget (1799-1885), photographed in 1862 by Montreal photographer William Notman (1826-1891), supported the production of Pernin's book. Musée McCord.

Bourget and Pernin had interests in common. Bourget had received Charles Chiniquy into his diocese from that of Quebec and authorized him as a temperance crusader from 1848 to 1851 (partly because it was a value concomitant with willing submission to ecclesiastical authority), the same Chiniquy who led the schism in Illinois that Pernin in 1864 was brought from France to help address. Also, Bourget had a personal devotion to Notre-Dame de Bon Secours to whose intercession he attributed his surviving typhus during the 1847 Montreal epidemic and was pleased to support Pernin's claim of a miracle at the first Shrine of Our Lady of Good Help in the United States. To have dated his approbation May 24, 1874, the day Bourget had designated as the patronal feast of Notre-Dame de Bon Secours in Montreal (Our Lady Help of Christians on the Catholic calendar), was sympathetic symbolism and a link to the religious community of Robinsonville, Wisconsin.

Pernin, St. Louis, 1872, within months of surviving the fire. He had his carte de visite *made at Cramer, Gross & Co.*

In preparation for publication Pernin sat for the frontispiece portrait made by Jules Marion, the 23-year-old designer at Conservative *La Minerve*, considered among the best woodblock engravers in Canada. Both versions of Pernin's little book must have been issued not long after May 24.

Woodblock portrait by Jules Marion (1851-1878), 1874. for the first edition of Doigt de Dieu.

Pernin's work never sold well and passed into obscurity even if he was mentioned occasionally for the rest of his life in newspaper items as its author. The French original *Doigt de Dieu* has never been republished before this. The Lovell English version was rescued from oblivion by the State Historical Society of Wisconsin. In 1918-19 *The Wisconsin Magazine of History* republished most of it for the first time, serialized in two parts, as edited by Joseph Schafer. Schafer was a Wisconsin native, University of Wisconsin PhD under Frederick Jackson Turner, who became Oregon's first academically trained historian and the author of the fundamental *History of the Pacific Northwest* (1905).

"Fortunately for us," Schafer wrote, "the Peshtigo fire produced a capable historian in the person of Father Pernin, the village priest," who records the story in "enduring form." The State Historical Library learned of the book only in 1915 and located a copy, the only then known. Schafer also found the republication timely: on October 10-12, 1918 a wildfire in Carlton County,

Minnesota, known now as the Cloquet Fire, killed 453, the most lives lost on a single day in a natural disaster in Minnesota history, and destroyed 38 communities over 250,000 acres under conditions reminiscent of Peshtigo in 1871.

Schafer's edition preserved Pernin's original title, chapter headings, and subheadings and made a few minor adjustments of spelling, usage, and paragraphing, while omitting the passages dealing with Pernin's visit with Bishop Melcher, inability to keep a preaching date for Philibert Crud, and trip to St. Louis, in the words of the editor, the "personal doings of the author during the following weeks." Schafer did mention the first publication in Montreal, Bourget's approbation, the book's intended benefit of the Marinette church, and its preface and appendix, but omitted to reprint them as "dealing largely with matters of Catholic faith" and pertaining "to the religious reflections and ideas of the author."

The Historical Society in 1918 gave the memoir an enduring place in Wisconsin history and lore. At the same time it partially obscured its Catholic setting and its place in French-American Catholic heritage. To have removed the Robinsonville material in the Conclusion, in embarrassment about such things as an appearance of the Virgin Mary, was to remove one of Pernin's important historical claims. Those were not unreasonable editorial decisions, but ever after they influenced how the book would be received, even by Catholics.

To observe the 100th anniversary of the fire in 1971 *Wisconsin Magazine of History* again incompletely reprinted the Lovell English version of the memoir, also republished as a separate booklet, edited and with an introduction by William Converse Haygood, the *Magazine*'s editor from 1957 to 1975. The title now became "The Great Peshtigo Fire; An Eyewitness Account." Haygood's introduction, notes, epilogue, and bibliography up to 1971 integrate Pernin's personal story into the history of the Peshtigo fire, and in his view "no writer has yet to equal in vividness, imagery, or sheer drama the contemporary account of Father Pernin." He restored the "personal doings" passages Schafer excised and offered a brief reconstruction of Pernin's career. Haygood's 1971 edition was reprinted in a second edition in 1999.

Amateur scientist, ironist, theodicist

In *Finger of God* Pernin combined the curiosity of an amateur intellectual with a French ironist's taste for the absurd (also characteristic of Wisconsin lumberjacks), the technique of a Meximieux-trained Classical rhetorician, a French Catholic pious belief in Mariophanies and Eucharistic miracles, and a Calvinist theology of natural disaster.

Pernin attempted objective observation of events in the manner of the circle of committed Catholic antiquarians and amateur natural scientists he had known in Autun as seminarian and Collège chaplain, who, from the 1830s, explored the ancient history of Autun, the most Romanized Celtic capital city in Gaul. They identified the site of the native Aedui's hilltown of Bibracte, eight miles to the west on Mt. Beuvray, which Julius Caesar took in 58 BCE and where he started writing the *Gallic Wars*; discovered and published the early Christian Greek Pectorius inscription; restored the tympanum sculpture of St. Lazare Cathedral, now thought a masterpiece of Romanesque carving.

Pernin attempted accurate computation of the speed of the firestorm, two leagues (six miles) an hour and an accurate estimate, from both experience and his reading, of the area burned and of casualties. He estimated from southwest to northeast of Peshtigo the area burned was 15 to 20 leagues (some 45 to 60 miles) wide and five to six (15 to 18) long. He estimated at least 1000 casualties, half of Peshtigo's population, and recognized that transients and recent arrivals could never be counted. (We would say today an area 80 by 30 miles, not counting the area on the other side of Green Bay, and 1500 to 2500 victims.)

Classical writing like Pliny on the eruption of Vesuvius and Thucydides on the Athenian plague, Meximieux humanities reading, informs Pernin's approach to prodigious natural disaster and its effects. In the manner of Herodotus or Pliny the Elder, he identifies four "extraordinary phenomena (80)" as if scientifically noteworthy: the force of the firestorm, the intensity of the heat, a strange "gas," and a "miraculous... balloon," though with the death-balloon Pernin reaches the limits of his science. Even so, about the fire generally

Pernin wrote with accuracy and insight enough as to have interested even present-day fire and forest ecology professionals.

Chemistry at Meximieux, a course added to the curriculum as a modernizing innovation in 1840 for Pernin's second form, had only gotten Pernin's science so far. But even as Meximieux had taught a Catholic farm boy bourgeois standards to aspire to, its humanities curriculum had prepared Pernin to be a writer. Six years of French composition, together with three of Latin and one of Greek, emphasized prose narrative and description. Pernin was among the better students during his last two years at Meximieux, winning class prizes for runner up in French description, literary analysis, and Latin and French oration.

Pernin was steeped in Classical rhetoric. His use of the Classical historical present for vividness in narration is a mannerism that jars readers of modern languages, as does his occasional asyndeton. Techniques such as tricolon and antithesis came easily to him as organizational and interpretive tools. The whole work is organized as a tricolon in three chapter headings, Before, During, and After the Catastrophe, echoing Meximiard Classicism (Aristotle *Poetics* 1450b: "A whole action has a beginning, a middle, and an end."). Antithesis can serve moral instruction, as in the chapter sub-headings "Some were insufficiently serious" and "Others were foolish," two distinct deviations from the virtue of prudence (Aristotle *Nicomachean Ethics* 1106b: "virtue is a mean.")

Describing his first view of ruined Peshtigo Pernin writes as gravely as he can:

> It is sad to have to speak of that which no one can express and no expression can portray... I no longer found anything of that which, three days before, had existed, not trees, not fences, not houses. All had been consumed. Some charred debris remained standing, to show the fury of the devastation that had passed by this place. (62-63)

Here he varies the inadequacy trope with a double antithesis between silence and speech and between speech and effective speech and uses tricolon ascending in its content (trees, fences, houses).

His pre-fire conflictedness between irrational fear and rational confidence he appropriately formulates in antitheses worthy almost of Seneca:

> These two conflicted feelings, of which one intruded on me in spite of myself and over which the other had no influence, even though it was the product of rational argument, threw me into a kind of moral lethargy and paralyzed all my energy. (30)

Pernin's occasional success with formal techniques of Classical rhetoric is something to which the 1874 Lovell English translation is utterly tone deaf.

As had students of rhetoric in the ancient Mediterranean 1500 years before, young Meximiards exercised their rhetorical skills by developing commonplace scenarios, *amplification*. The homework handed in by one of Pernin's classmates for a French composition class in 1841 survives in a later publication of his collected verse, "The Sailor and the Fisherman," a work of 45 rhymed alexandrine couplets. A shipwrecked sailor washed ashore receives hospitality in a humble fisherman's cabin. When he recovers and wants to return to a life wandering the seas, the two compare the joys of adventurous danger and obscure security.

As a heritage of that training, Pernin enjoyed writing dialogue and often in *Finger of God* overlays the sound of several voices. With dialogue he dramatizes important moments like that of learning of the loss of his facilities in Marinette:

> "And my church?"
> "It burned."
> "And my nice rectory?"
> "It burned."
> "And my school?"
> "Burned too." (60)

Or like that of leaving his house for the last time and bidding farewell to his lamps: "'Soon,' I told them, 'you will see a light that will overshadow your own.' (41)" Accordingly, accurate marking of quotations, careless in the original publications, must be an important editorial priority for *Finger of God*.

Three times Pernin pastes the voices of newspaper clippings into his narrative. Not to have recognized this technique has occasioned some inaccuracy in writing the history of the fire. The "I" of the Green Bay *Advocate* story that Pernin included on the fire in Peshtigo Sunday morning, September 24, is the story's correspondent, not Pernin, as Gess and Lutz, authors of a standard work on the fire, took it, reading too quickly and ignoring the indentation in the 1999 Wisconsin Historical edition.

Pernin's most ambitious use of dialogue conveys bits of the conversations he had with fellow survivors after his post-fire return to Peshtigo, representing impressionistically reports scattered in time and space (66-67). Accurate quotation marks and paragraphing, imperfect in the French original and mostly abandoned in the 1874 Lovell, are essential to make clear the distinction between what Pernin sees and does and what he is told by others. Pernin is not everywhere, but he is hearing reports from everywhere as he walks along Oconto Avenue. "Down there, in this well, we recovered 16 bodies," for example, in the original occurs within quotation marks. Pernin is not here part of the "we." It is an interlocutor who speaks.

Pernin hears of a familicide and the next sentences are his gloss on the story from his own knowledge: "This man was named Towsley. He had indeed, it's true (*en effet*, confirming the story he had heard), worked on my church the whole summer..." Haygood's note 8 in the 1971 Wisconsin Historical edition (repeated in the 1999 edition) corrects Pernin's "implication here that the bodies were found in Peshtigo." (The Towsleys in fact lived and died in the Lower Sugar Bush.) But that implication arose only from the inaccurate use of quotation marks.

The 1874 Lovell sometimes makes Pernin sound like a bumpkin, but from the French original emerges a droll ironist capable of laughing at himself and deconstructing a cliché: "sometimes I could even see the comic side of this strange show and laughed at it to myself (48)." From Bressane chicken casserole cookery he draws a simile to describe the subtle destruction of the altar linen he had buried to preserve before the fire: "when I touched it, it fell apart, it could no longer hold together, as if the heat had cooked it *à l'étouffée*. (65)"

"The way is open, go!" was a French spiritual cliché, words with which one might encourage a departing missionary. The spiritual director of Maurice Bellière invited him with those words to a mission in Malawi, as he wrote to his correspondent Thérèse of Lisieux in 1897. When on his way off his property the approaching firestorm removed as an obstacle his gate and fence by blowing it away in the air, Pernin found that the metaphor had become unexpectedly literal, as if in an Aristophanic comedy or a nightmare: "'The way is open,' I said to myself, 'let's go!' (42)."

When at the riverbank Pernin's neighbor was annoyed to be pushed into the water for his own good, Pernin advises nevertheless "it was better to moisten than to burn (*mais il valait mieux se mouiller que de brûler*)." This was a playful variation on 1 *Corinthians* 7.9: "It is better to marry than to burn (*il vaut mieux se marier que de brûler*)," a text he must have heard a thousand times as a seminarian considering a commitment to celibacy against the baleful compromise of marriage.

Pernin manages an urbane humanism, but his primary aim in *Finger of God* was devotional and theological. By omitting Pernin's "religious reflections and ideas" the Wisconsin Historical editions annulled its central meaning as Pernin conceived it. John Lovell had begun to publish religious writers in the 1850s and 1860s including Montreal's Sephardic hazan Abraham de Sola and two Catholic missionary priests who worked among the Mohawk and learned their language, Quebecois Joseph Marcoux and Sulpician Jean-André Cuoq from Haute-Loire. The title page of both French and English versions announces Pernin as "missionary to the United States," in a way parallel to that in which that of Marcoux's *Lettres aux Chefs Iroquois* (1869) calls him "*missionaire du Sault*" or that of Cuoq's *Catéchisme Algonquin* (1865) calls him "*masinaigan gaie aiamie nikamanon.*" *Finger of God* has its proper place among such works. The 32mo format of *Finger's* publication further indicates its genre: pocket size is convenient for carrying a Biblical or devotional work.

Pernin's very title, *The Finger of God Is There!*, alludes to Scripture and announces a theological purpose. Pharaoh's magicians acknowledge Aaron's power to effect the plague of gnats as the "finger of God" (*Exodus* 8.19). The "finger of God" wrote the ten commandments (*Exodus* 31.18, *Deuteronomy* 9.10). It is "the power of God in action" by which Jesus casts out demons (*Luke* 11.20). To Pernin, the finger of the Blessed Virgin is "her intervention to grant favor to those who put their confidence in her. (91)" Claude Tailland, the pastor under whom Pernin served his first parish in Mâcon, used the words to mark an intervention by God to reveal himself in a way that cannot be mistaken because evidence is overwhelming.

> As God is the truth and as he must for his own sake as for ours teach with certitude and remove from us every danger of error and illusion, the character which will accompany the manifestation of his will will be clear, striking (*frappant*, another word on Pernin's title page), plain, of the sort that each can say without fear of being mistaken, The finger of God is here!

A paraphrase of Pernin's rebarbative title (so rebarbative that not even I use it for this edition) more accurate than "The Great Peshtigo Fire" would be "An Unmistakable Intervention of God's Power."

Finger of God was written primarily as a work of theodicy, justifying the ways of God to man. Fire, in *Sirach*, was created to calm the anger of its Maker (39.28-9); it goes before God and burns up his enemies in *Psalm* 97. To interpret the fire, Pernin amplified the Old Testament understanding of God as avenger with the theology of Calvin, the stark combination espoused to this day by anti-science fundamentalists. God's finger punishes the wicked and saves the good. Pernin concludes with the sort of material that Schafer first found unreprintable. Peshtigo, a town of saloons and brothels accommodating lumbermen on the frontier of the Wisconsin logging boom, "is the modern Sodom meant to serve as an example to all. (90)" The Peshtigo fire was God's fire and brimstone on a sinful city. If we wonder why chastisements, precursors to the final dissolution, fall "so unequally on nations equally guilty," the only answer is, "Who can fathom the designs of God? (88)" Terror of fiery death united Protestants and Catholics. "No reasoning succeeds so quickly in making men comprehend the greatness of God and their own insignificance. (Marinette addition)"

In discussing the historicity of Christian Gospel miracles, the scholar of the historical Jesus John P. Meier usefully distinguishes between what history can say and what theology can say: "a positive judgment that a miracle has taken place is always a philosophical or theological judgment. Of its nature it goes beyond any judgment that a historian acting as a historian can make." Green Bay *Advocate* editor Frank Tilton spoke similarly when he wrote about the 1871 fires as to God's interventions in history, "Whether we were all unrighteous, or lacking in faith, or doomed to chastisement for our sins or for a solemn warning to the world, we leave to others to decide." He was just a journalist.

By that standard, Pernin is at his most theological when he claims in *Finger of God* that two events that occurred on the night of the fires were miracles, that is, works of God's power and intervention. These two, to some degree potentially explicable in natural terms, were the preservation of his church's tabernacle in the Peshtigo River and the survival of the religious community of Robinsonville, both personally and in its property and facilities, which the fire unexpectedly bypassed.

A tabernacle in a Roman Catholic church is the ceremonial box, traditionally with a veil or curtain, in continuity with the tent and the bread of the Lord's presence in Hebrew Scripture, which contains inside the Blessed Sacrament, the real sacramental presence, in Catholic belief, of the risen Jesus under the appearance of unleavened hosts of bread. When in panic Pernin couldn't open it to save the Blessed Sacrament the night of the fire, he pulled it along with him in his buggy and submerged it in the Peshtigo River. Pernin and his parishioners judged miraculous that the tabernacle survived undamaged inside and out. Secondly, when the fires of October 8-9 destroyed parts of Brown, half of Kewaunee, and most of Door Counties on the east side of Green Bay, the Shrine of Our Lady of Good Help in Robinsonville — chapel, convent, and school on the site of the appearance of the Virgin Mary to Adèle Brice in 1859 — should also have burned. But the fire passed it by with great precision. Pernin's account in *Finger of God* (98-99) is an important contemporary witness for the Shrine's survival that night.

From our vantage of 150 years we recognize the limitations of Pernin's scientific and theological perspective. Wildfires are ecologically necessary and beneficial, regenerating forests and renewing soil. Natural causes explain the Peshtigo fire. Stephen J. Pyne, environmental historian once a forest fire fighter, in a forward to the 1999 Wisconsin Historical edition of Pernin's memoir, posited an ecological "Peshtigo paradigm" at work all over the world, wherever conditions are less than fully suburbanized: "A prolonged drought, a rural agriculture based on burning, railroads that cast sparks to all sides, a landscape stuffed with slash and debris from logging, a city built largely of forest materials, the catalytic passage of a dry cold front — all ensured that fires would break out."

It was hardly a miracle that the Peshtigo tabernacle survived, since Pernin himself put it in the water to preserve it and under the circumstance could have exaggerated its watertightness. In any event, his irresponsible (by Catholic standards) Eucharistic custody made an intriguing backdrop for claiming a Eucharistic miracle. Pernin was prepared to credit a miraculous preservation of the Eucharist from fire by the famous event in 1608 Burgundy at the Abbey of Faverney (now Haute-Saône), the "Hosties miraculeuses." A monstrance containing two consecrated hosts displayed for adoration on the eve of Pentecost, May 24, survived a fire that destroyed much of the abbatial church that night and was said to have been subsequently suspended in air for 33 hours. The miracle had recently been officially recognized, by Pius IX, in May 1864.

The sparing of the Robinsonville community as claimed was without question miraculously precise. And the fire did rage on the 12th anniversary of Adèle's colloquy with the Blessed Virgin on October 9. But Catholics can be superstitiously impressed by numerological coincidence and there were other structures that survived the fire, either anomalously or through non-sanctimonious hard work.

One still stands in Peshtigo, a house under construction in October 1871, 150 S. Beebe, whose green wood perhaps saved it, an anomaly not a miracle. There were those who took practical steps beyond prayer to save their property. An experienced 20-year-old Irish logger named John Nelligan from New Brunswick by way of

Pennsylvania spent the night of the Peshtigo fire stranded on a farm along the Oconto River. The Frenchman in charge on the farm, "hysterical with fear and sobbing out of his belief that the place would be burned to the ground ...soon forgot his fears and tears under pressure of hard work, hauling barrels of water." Together they fought the fire and saved the farm buildings. Abram Place, fur trader, among Peshtigo's largest landowners, together with his Ojibwe in-laws knew to anticipate the fire and dig a firebreak that saved their farmhouse, uniquely in the Upper Sugar Bush, and provided life-saving sanctuary to many. What are we to conclude about the sanctity of Marinette's residents from the fire's unexpected passing over Marinette while burning Menekaunee and Pernin's St. Patrick church?

Physicist Steven Weinberg has written, "Questions like 'What is the natural place of fire?' or 'What is the purpose of the moon?' are bad in themselves, leading away from real under-standing." It is sanctimonious to build a town of wood in a forest, be careless with fire in a drought, then attribute the wildfire that results to a vengeful God. The Peshtigo fire in itself had no moral sig-nificance. By attributing the Peshtigo fire to a God avenging himself on his guilty creation, Pernin in *Finger of God* was influenced by Calvinism: "all prosperity has its source in the blessing of God, all adversity is his curse." At the time of the fire, Pernin had been marinated in the preaching of itinerant Protestants urging repentance to avert the wrathful God. Congregational and Lutheran pastors in Peshtigo preached fire and brimstone amidst the smoke of the Sunday morning fire of September 24, 1871.

A lecture that Pernin happened upon in Terre Haute, Indiana on his way to St. Louis had confirmed him in a Calvinist approach to understanding the fire (87). This was "Great Fires of the World and Their Results," Friday evening, December 15, Dowling Hall, given by Rev. John L. Gay, rector of St. James Episcopal, Vincennes, Indiana. Pernin's fifty cents admission benefited an Episcopal church for young men in Bloomington. Gay (1809-1904) was an "old school" Southerner from North Carolina who had a long, diverse career in America and Canada as priest of the Protestant Episcopal Church: missionary, scholar, professor, intellectual, slaveholder, and contrarian eccentric. The historical and moral significance of the 1871 fires was of course a topic of conversation, writing, and preaching that fall. Gay spoke of the 1666 London and 1812 Moscow fires as background to those in Chicago, Wisconsin, and Michigan, as well as of contemporary techniques of fire prevention and containment, the prevalence of drought, and the end of the world. But what stuck with Pernin was Gay's idea that what had happened was an "image of the fire that must devour the earth at the end of time. (87)"

The audience of only 40 was a disappointment. The Terre Haute *Gazette* was pleased that townspeople recognized that newspaper reading obviated paying money to hear a lecture, though also blamed the popular preference for "minstrelsy, black crooks [that is, musicals like the 1866 *The Black Crook*], circuses, or masquerade balls." "Terre Haute yearns for elevated heels much more than for elevated morals." This was what Pernin concluded as well: "so true it is that people today are as they were in the time of Noah and as they will be in the last days, indifferent to all the warnings of heaven. (87)" But the authority of this "learned lecturer" confirmed Pernin in the theological understanding he would bring to interpreting his experience and writing his memoir.

The only known photo of Dowling Hall, Terre Haute, Indiana, in 1867, where Pernin heard John L. Gay's lecture "Great Fires of the World" on December 15, 1871. Vigo County Public Library.

Balzac had earlier in the century identified and mocked as banal and bourgeois the theology of the justiciary God implicit in Pernin's title and in the notion of "the finger of God." The dedication of *La Rabouilleuse* (1842) promised a work "filled with these deeds far removed from the reach of law by the closed doors of private life, but as to which the finger of God, so often called chance (*hasard*), takes the place of human justice, and where the moral is none the less instructive and striking (*frappante*) for having been spoken by someone in mockery." In it a hypocrite doctor says to his patient: "There's a God after all, my child, do you see? You have been the cause of a great misfortune, it must be put right. The finger of God is in this (it is inconceivable not to find the finger of God in everything!). Religion is religion: submit, resign yourself, that will calm you first of all, that will cure you almost as well as my drugs."

So too, with irony slightly less delicate, could a Wisconsin lumberjack laugh at the sanctimony. John Nelligan's hotel room bed was once set on fire by a practical jokester while he slept in it. He explained the circumstances to the salesman across the hall who helped him put the fire out: "It must have been a visitation of Divine Providence on a wicked soul and nothing less!" James McMaster, proprietor of the *New York Freeman's Journal*, the leading national Catholic newspaper, in the issue of October 21, 1871 called the idea that Chicago was "a modern Sodom" and burned for its wickedness the "snufflings of the pietistic hypocrites," rightly ridiculed.

The New Testament itself can challenge simplistic belief in a justiciary God: "Do you think that they were worse offenders than all the others who dwelt in Jerusalem? I tell you, no... (*Luke* 13.4-5)" Thomas Aquinas, whose nineteenth century revival came too late for Pernin's seminary studies, might have provided him with a more nuanced Catholic understanding of what is traditionally called natural evil: natural disasters are not evil in themselves, but only for the unfortunates caught in them. God endowed creation with its own laws. Events in it occur within a concatenation of causes. In God's permissive will, as distinct from his acting will (a distinction lost to the theology of Calvin), a good thing (like fire) can act so effectively as to cause another good thing to lose its form. Pernin had already become so acculturated an American as to sound more like Cotton Mather — "how fearfully did we see the Heavens blazing over us, with Coruscations that fill'd People with a fearful Expectation of the fiery Indignation which is anon to devour the Adversaries of GOD!" — than Thomas Aquinas — "*Divina providentia non excludit contingentiam a rebus.*"

Yet Pernin is inconsistent in *Finger*, even self-contradictory. While discerning the finger of God, he stresses his own efforts to save himself and others and recognizes how chance, together with effort, was a factor in survival. When he says, "For survivors it was only a matter of chance. No one could boast of having had more presence of mind than anyone else. (83)," he comes close to the Balzacian remark that the finger of God is only another way of saying *hasard*.

Pernin can also be a realistic and merciful pastor. Nelligan had scoffed: "There was a general impression that the world had come to an end and in the villages surrounding Peshtigo many people committed suicide, evidently desirous of being among the first to greet Gabriel." But Pernin confronted a pastoral problem. To his parishioners' obtuse question, "is this the end of the world?," understandable while engulfed by fire, Pernin's answer was more gently equivocal than sanctimonious: "I don't believe it is, but if all countries have been burned like ours seems to have been, it won't be long before the end of the world comes for us. (52)" If Pernin means, "it's not the end of the world, but it's the end of our world," that is a realistic, sensible, and gentle answer.

Pernin mercifully excused Towsley's suicide and familicide for his loss of reason. He realistically understands that people turn to prayer in disaster and forget God afterward. Alluding to the theme of the Mariophany, he finds an excuse for Belgians' negligence in teaching their children catechism that the Virgin Mary, as reported in the official history of Robinsonville, did not find: "They are a religious people, simple and hard-working, but for the most part quite remiss in giving their children the religious instruction that they never received themselves. (92)"

The pastoral mercy Pernin could show was in part an influence of the humane ideal of Denis Maîtrepierre's personal motto, drawn from the Roman comedian Terence: "*homo sum.*

humani nil a me alienum puto. I am a human being. I deem nothing human foreign to me." Another influence was Alphonsus Liguori (1696–1787), whose pastoral moral theology, steadily made canonical in the Catholic church during Pernin's lifetime, emphasized warm devotion to the Virgin Mary and sought to mitigate traditional rigorism. In his years at Meximieux, Pernin had been under the authority of Alexandre-Raymond Devie, bishop of Belley 1823-1852, the first French bishop to adopt Liguorian pastoral thought for his clergy and one who saw to it that Marist founder Jean-Claude Colin adopt it for the Marists.

Liguori's *Sermons in time of Calamity* (1758, French 1836) preached that God's chastisements are not punishment but merciful invitations for sinners to repent. Sins should excite dread less than confidence in divine mercy. God can want only to bless and never to punish, an opinion distinct from Calvinism. Pernin echoes that: "Nothing [other than danger] detaches souls so completely from earth and raises them towards him on whom we all depend. (Marinette addition)" *Finger of God's* insistence that "the catastrophe seems to have enjoyed ...multiplying its warnings (13)" and that "all the alarms that preceded appeared as warnings of a great catastrophe for which [God] wanted us to be prepared. (24)" is understandable in light of Liguori's "When it is a question of punishing, he waits, he warns, he multiplies his warnings: *the Lord God has done nothing without having revealed his secret. (Amos 3.7)*"

Yet in the end, for Liguori God is merciful only "up to a certain point, beyond which he lets his justice go to work." (Comparison with Pope Francis in *Evangelii Gaudium* (2013), "God never tires of forgiving us," is one way to formulate development in Catholic theology of mercy.) When he tires of mercy, God will punish sinners, but then it is not God who punishes, but sinners punishing themselves. Liguori's *Sermons* were meant as pastoral exhortation and not a consistent theology of natural evil and Pernin reflects their contradictions. His sense of pastoral realism only incompletely balanced the theology of the vengeful God that informs *Finger of God,* but Pernin's harsh Calvinism was itself a flexible accommodation to his American milieu.

In *Finger of God*, even while far from hostile to scientific analysis, Pernin proposed his own "Peshtigo paradigm," a theological framework within which the fire was God's punishment on the sins of Peshtigo and the preservation of the Peshtigo tabernacle and of the community in Robinsonville were miraculous vindications of God's power. Unearthing Pernin's Peshtigo theological paradigm here is worthwhile less to advocate than to examine. In American culture Pernin's sanctimony still comes easily to anti-science Christian fundamentalists when confronted by the effects of ecological abuse and disasters natural and otherwise. Is the covid pandemic of 2020, I wonder as I write under quarantine, a sign of the end of the world or does that fear seem as provincial as that of the people of Peshtigo trapped by a wildfire in a tiny corner of Wisconsin in 1871? The resilience of Pernin and his townspeople in rebounding after a disaster is perhaps the better Peshtigo paradigm to perpetuate.

The theological shortcomings and inconsistencies of Pernin's *Finger of God* trivialize the most sensitive questions one could ask about how ecological and human autonomy might function under divine sovereignty, about subsidiary causation, God's mercy to sinners, and God's purposes, if God exists, in allowing evil. If Pernin's prose style is more supple than his thought, perhaps that delineates the strengths and weakness of a mid-nineteenth century seminary education disproportionately focused on Classical humanities.

Diocesan and parish politics

With the death of Green Bay Bishop Joseph Melcher, December 20, 1873, lamented in *Finger of God*, Pernin lost a cordial supporter. Pernin's published advocacy in the summer of 1874 of the Robinsonville Mariophany now put him at odds with Edward Daems, Melcher's vicar general, who administered the Green Bay diocese for nineteen months before the installation of a successor. Edouard Daems, OSC (1826-1879), from Flemish Brabant, a priest of the Order of Canons Regular of the Holy Cross, was a figure foundational to the diocese of Green Bay, who had brought Belgians to settle the Door Peninsula and built churches for them. An exacting pastor and administrator, he had been long suspicious of the Mariophany and the Robinsonville devotions. Pernin's provocative support of the alleged fire miracle at Robinsonville made the more acute the unpredictable challenges a Mariophany, with its independent parallel authority, might bring to good diocesan order.

Edouard Daems, OSC (1826-1879), vicar general and sometime diocesan administrator of Green Bay 1868-1879, disciplined Pernin and Philibert Crud in 1874-75. Diocese of Green Bay.

Already from December 1872 Pernin had had to negotiate parish and diocesan politics in the Peshtigo fire aftermath. In Catholic parishes of the 1870s there was nothing unusual in ethnic hatred among communicants, before a parish might become prosperous or populous enough to divide into new ethnically discrete parishes, nor in slander as public sport, particularly in a stressful time of rebuilding after catastrophe. Pernin faced enemies in his parishes who alleged he had misappropriated funds he had raised. To protect himself in response to the allegations, Pernin obtained a letter from friends in St. Louis, who attested that the money they had donated was given to him personally, to be used at his discretion. He would file this letter for public scrutiny in the offices of the Marinette and Peshtigo *Eagle* and refer to it as a part of the comprehensive self-defense he would offer two years later.

When reorganizing and rewriting in fair copy his Marinette/ Peshtigo parish registry, something he put off completing until as late as 1886, Pernin began to add material unconventional for a sacramental register: he felt free to annotate it with diary-like remarks and comments. He placed the first of his post-fire autobiographical remarks in the blank space underneath the record of his five October 1871 baptisms: "I left unfortunately for St. Louis, Mo. in order to recuperate health and means to rebuild with, giving chance by my absence to very bad tongues to hurt me badly at Peshtigo especially."

Another initiative Pernin took to shore up his position was to promote himself in the national Catholic press, articles to which he would later call attention in *Finger of God*. On June 8, 1873, Trinity Sunday, Pernin made a civic event and fundraiser of the cornerstone ceremonies for the new Marinette church, whose name he was changing from St. Patrick's to Our Lady of Lourdes. Beside Bishop Melcher, Pernin's invited dignitary was William Corby, Holy Cross father, who famously as chaplain gave general absolution to the Irish Brigade at Gettysburg in 1863 and was just then serving as founding president of University of Our Lady of the Sacred Cross (eventually Sacred Heart College) in Watertown, Wisconsin, in between two terms (1866-72, 1877-82) as president of University of Notre Dame. Corby sermonized at the afternoon ceremony and lectured in the evening.

An article about the day was placed in the June 28 *Freeman's Journal*, "Filling Up the Waste Places." The article had an insistently pro-Pernin tone: "...our esteemed pastor... All [the festivity] is an index of the endeavors of our esteemed Pastor, Rev. Pernin, to promote the welfare of his people. The parish... promises, under his energetic direction, to be one of the most flourishing... With his zeal and labor he cannot fail to win the love and esteem of his parishioners, and advance the cause of holy religion in this place." In whatever collaboration Pernin and his parish supporters wrote the article and attributed it pseudonymously to "Witness," self-promotion helped his survival. In his own name at the end of the article Pernin published, both in Latin and in English translation, the dedication document he had written to set his achievement, the first Catholic church in the United States dedicated to Our Lady of

Lourdes, in its historical circumstances. (The complete article is found in the Appendix).

Again, for a second time in seven months, Pernin and parishioners caught national attention with another self-promotional event publicized in the *Freeman's*: a tribute to Pernin's "silver wedding" on Tuesday January 6, Epiphany day. The 25th anniversary of Pernin's ordination to the priesthood had occurred December 19, 1871, more than two years before, while he was on his way to St. Louis, and perhaps he felt he had not had a spare moment since. Perhaps his parish supporters thought he needed a timely demonstration of the "spirit of appreciation manifested by the congregation for their Pastor" regardless of literal chronology, all the more needfully now that the bishop who had brought Pernin to the diocese had died.

The *Freeman's* article, January 31, 1874, "Catholicity in Marinette, Wis.," attributed again to a pseudonymous "Witness," had polemical purpose similar to the earlier one about Cornerstone Day, supporting Pernin against his enemies in the parish. The article, like the silver wedding celebration itself, had two themes, the difficulties of Pernin and the triumph of Pernin: "Their good Pastor has been working very hard, and with the limited means at his disposal... although laboring under many disadvantages... strenuous efforts... numerous congratulations from his parishioners..." If even Protestants supported his efforts, why were there Catholics resisting him? On the happy day ten neighboring clergy joined Pernin, who celebrated a Solemn High Mass with deacon and sub-deacon. Three sermons in three languages were preached.

Festivities continued the next day Wednesday, January 7, with the Indian Dinner, an annual Marinette tradition recently imagined so ancient as to go back to early French missionaries, in the very ancestral home of the Menominee. When the Menominee reservation was established in 1856, many Menominee moved to Keshena Falls, but some stayed in their old homes from the Illinois border to the Upper Peninsula with a concentration in the area of Marinette and Menominee, Michigan. Among those who stayed were the fifty Indian Catholic families of Pernin's parish, "good, simple, pious people," who attended the dinner. Menominee were exceptionally devout and gracious, particularly by contrast with some of Pernin's Irish-American and French-Canadian-American parochial antagonists. The Indian Dinner was usually January 6, but the Menominee had put Pernin first. As paternalistic and racist as this celebration could be — the dinner dramatically reenacted the submission of the Indians to the Black Robes — devout Menominee were also seizing on the meaning of the Epiphany in Catholic theology: a gathering of all nations to worship the newborn redeemer. (The complete article is found in the Appendix).

Six months proved too long a time for Pernin to have spent away from Marinette publishing two editions of *Finger of God* in Montreal, though he had been away for seven while recuperating from the fire. Perhaps he had agreed with diocesan administrator Daems to be away only for three months. By August 15 Daems treated Pernin as absent without leave and appointed in his place William J. White pastor of Marinette and Peshtigo. Between August 15 and October 4, White conducted 18 baptisms and was listed in the Marinette and Peshtigo *Eagle* as the Catholic pastor.

In October 1874 Pernin finally returned from Montreal (and wherever else he had been) to an unhappy homecoming. He found himself locked out and in trouble, as he wrote in the parish register:

> Leaving Rev. father Galweiler in charge of Marinette and Peshtigo with the agreement of Rev. Daems administrator, the very last days of April 1874 I left for Canada, in order to work hard, and I did too, to push on the work on my Church of Marinette. I was very unwise to do so.

> During my absence human passions were excited against me by circulating false rumors. Clouds were gathered little by little. at last the cyclone burst. my property was taken from me. the key of my Box P.O. seemed to keep all informations to be inquired and answered. I came back in October and found all upset. My successor, father White temporally sick in the room of the Administrator's. I found the parish all divided. the party made up against me opposing. the faithful friends fighting against them at the door of the Church to open it to me... went to G. Bay and came back the following

day... with a letter stating that my "faculties were taken from me for having been too long in Canada."

Unauthorized absence was a serious offense. Curbing clerical absenteeism had of course been an emphasis of the Council of Trent, which held that unauthorized absence from a diocese should be punished by interdiction from sacred ministry, and Edward Daems was a stickler for regulations. But in America in October 1874 Pernin had no canonical recourse by which to clarify any misunderstanding or to appeal his suspension. He would have to wait for that for nine months. In 1869 a Cleveland diocesan priest, Eugene O'Callahan, in the *Freeman's* (as "Jus") had notoriously found a double entendre in the notion of 'suspension' without due process or right of appeal. A priest's innocence, he wrote, can be established "only after you are hanged (suspended)..." Pernin was not in danger of becoming homeless: he had a house to live in and could maintain the hope that the incoming bishop would resolve his situation. He also had ties to the community, including the support of *Eagle* editor Luther Noyes. From October 1874 to July 1875 Pernin stayed, as he put it, in his "house as a simple citizen."

Suspension gave Pernin time to draw up an accounting of money he had raised over the previous three years and the *Eagle* gave space to publish it as two pieces of polemical self-defense. In his absence he had again been accused of embezzling funds collected for fire relief. "An Answer to a Three-Year Old Scandal" ran in the *Eagle* on November 14 dealing with Peshtigo and "Father Pernin's Marinette Account" on November 21.

Eagle editor Luther Noyes, who had supported Pernin's rebuilding efforts all along, reporting warmly on the two church constructions and the school ("it will be a benefit...," "the name of Pernin alone...," "one of the most beautiful churches in the northwest..."), supported Pernin now under accusation by publishing him at great length. Calling attention to his November 21 Marinette accounting Noyes wrote: "As the Rev. gentleman has been assailed by some and charged with dishonesty, we have allowed him the use of our columns for him to vindicate himself." As Pernin's accusers declined the opportunity to make their evidence public, Pernin seemed to have won the exchange. On February 12, 1875 Pius

IX appointed Franz Xaver Krautbauer bishop of Green Bay, a Bavarian who had worked in the dioceses of Buffalo and Milwaukee. He was ordained bishop and installed in Green Bay on June 29. Within a month he restored Pernin as pastor in Marinette.

Parochial and diocesan disputes are background to *Finger of God*, but if the official reason for Pernin's suspension was his overlong absence, or if rumors of embezzlement and unpopularity had reached diocesan administrator Daems and influenced his disciplinary action, what most exacerbated relations between Daems and Pernin would have been that *Finger of God* declared forthrightly a belief in Adèle Brice's visions, the Robinsonville fire miracle, and the value of pilgrimage there at a time when Daems opposed that belief. Any well-intentioned visitor would accept Robinsonville, or so declares the final sentence of *Finger of God*. Daems' opposition to devotions at Robinsonville is also, then, important background to *Finger of God*.

Pernin wrote cautiously about the Mariophany. He felt it necessary to "abridge details and be prudent in what I say so as to preserve the modesty of some and the sensitivities of others among the living of whom I must speak and who might read these lines. (91-2)" He naturally respected intimate details of Adèle's spiritual life, but there were other eggshells to walk on. As the official history of the Robinsonville Shrine puts it, "Dear Sister had a great deal to suffer from some misunderstandings, especially from some of the clergy." While leaving final judgment to Catholic Church authority, *Finger's* concluding "Important reflection" backtracks on what he had already presented as miraculous: "By relating the preceding event I have absolutely no intention of calling it a miracle, any more than I am calling a miracle the preservation of my tabernacle in the midst of the Peshtigo fire. Each of these events edified me and as I retell them here, I have no other aim than to edify others. (99-100)"

Within weeks of taking office, Bishop Krautbauer, apparently accepting the advice of Daems, who continued as vicar general, made it a priority to discipline the Robinsonville Shrine. The two visited the Shrine unannounced and rudely caught the sisters off guard. The next day, on July 20, 1875, Adèle and seven sisters wrote to Krautbauer to clarify and apologize:

Robinsonville July 20, 1875

Right reverend bishop,

Some people came here this morning when they heard about your visit yesterday, and there was a kind of excitement when they knew that your Lordship was accompanied by rev'd father Daems instead of the good pastors who could give better informations. They were talking about writing to your Lordship in our favor. If your Lordship receives some letter less respectfull, don't impute to your poor servants any kind of irreverence, for if the last of your children, we will be also the most respectfull and the most obedient of all, even in case of a condemnation by your Lordship.

There must be some charges against us, Monseigneur, since we have been excommunicated. Oh! in the name of our dear Mother, let us know what crime we have committed. Before condemning, please let the accused defend themselves.

If we are allowed to continue the hard task we undertook with the approbation of two right reverend bishops [Henni and Melcher] and under the direction of several good pastors [including Pernin and Crud], we will try to do just as well as before our sad misfortunes. We don't dare to promise better. Now, dear and right rev'd bishop, if your Lordship wants some explanations about the apparition of our dear Mother in this holy place, about the many miracles wrought in the Chapel, about the immense crowd of pilgrims who came to pray with us, we are ready to give them.

Some people warn us to complain about the ill treatment we received from the reverend father Daems and [Rev. Erasmus] Leccia [pastor at the time of St. Joseph's, Robinsonville] but we don't like to accuse anybody unless ordered by your Lordship.

Excuse the impoliteness we may have committed yesterday at your visit, it was so unexpected that we were not ready at all to receive your Lordship as he deserves.

Your very respectfull and humblest servants in Jesus and Mary,
Sisters Adele Brice   Mary Gagnon   Maggie Allard
Catherine Lambert   Elizabeth Gagnon   Ada Allard
Zoé Allard   Louise Thurber

The official Shrine history cannot tell the full extent of the discipline or when it was rescinded. But a year later the school was in session and pilgrimages had resumed. Krautbauer never officially recognized the story of Adèle's visions or the miracles, but did allow to be built a new larger chapel, school, and convent and presided over the dedication of the chapel in 1881.

According to Philibert Crud's 1912 memoir (full, to be sure, of self-serving misinformation), Daems' opposition to pious activity at the Shrine went back to its beginnings after the claimed apparition in 1859.

> This extraordinary movement of the Catholic population throughout the whole area attracted the attention of the Bay Settlement missionary, Rev. Father Daems, charged with the Robinsonville mission. He knew that episcopal authority was unaware of the existence of the pilgrimage for which no authorization had been requested. He thought it necessary to intervene to stop what he considered an act of revolt against authority. Without taking into account that this people lacked knowledge of the canonical regulations that it would have been wise to suppose that they left to themselves, he treated them with a severity that could only imagine that it was an act of conscious revolt. This was not the case. Enthusiasm and piety had inspired these ignorant people in everything they had done. They were scandalized that the missionary reproached them for building the chapel and the doubt he cast over the reality of the apparitions. Discontent flared violently when Father Daems chose a feast day [1864 or earlier] to come and forbid the pilgrims to pray in the pilgrimage chapel built by Satan as a standard against that of Christ and when he announced that the visionary would be excluded from the sacraments for as long a time as she refused to retract her lies.

To avoid further scandals, Adèle stopped going to Bay Settlement, according to Crud, yet her standing only grew in the community and she continue to pray with pilgrims and to instruct children. Crud, according to Crud, intervened with Bishop Henni (Robinsonville being in the diocese of Milwaukee until 1868), defeated Daems, and became Adèle Brice's supporter in her mission.

Against this background we recognize how provocative was Pernin's *Finger of God*. He was advocating the authenticity of the Mariophany and the validity of pilgrimage to the site, popular manifestations that Edward Daems had been long suspicious of and sought to contain. With the words "the finger of God is there!," in September 1665 in what is now the department of Hautes-Alpes in southeast France, Antoine Lambert, vicar general of the then archdiocese of Embrun, recanted his previous skepticism and affirmed his belief in the validity of the apparition of Our Lady of Laus and a miraculous healing. Pernin's very title is a declaration of belief in the Mariophany and confirming miracle for anyone who catches the reference. And to further challenge Daems' authority, Pernin had even won the support and patronage of Bishop Bourget of Montreal.

Tension between Daems and Pernin is clear from the disappointment Adèle and the sisters felt "when they knew that your Lordship was accompanied by the Rev. Daems" and the distinction they drew between the hostile and ill-informed Daems and "several good pastors," like their supporters Crud and Pernin, "who could give better informations" to the new and uninformed bishop. That distinction mirrors Pernin's in his "Important reflection" between those who would go to the Shrine with good intention, such as pilgrims or visitors open to the truth, and those with bad. Anyone well-disposed would come away from a visit to the Shrine at least edified and perhaps even convinced of the validity of the apparition. Pernin and Crud could well have been among the "some people" who came to Adèle's support and warned them "to complain about the ill treatment."

Karen Park, author of a 2012 article on the Mariophany, took as "fact undisputed by the official account" that Bishop Melcher once excommunicated Adèle after she refused to recant her story and commanded her to dismiss the children from the school, but, ultimately impressed by her zeal and obedience in turning over to him the keys of her school, reversed his decision. Yet this is substantiated only by Sister Dominica's vague "it is said" and refer-

ences to the thirdhand oral tradition of Milo P. Smits, O. Praem., a
Norbertine Father, pastor of St. Joseph, Champion (Robinsonville)
from 1908 to 1951.

It is intriguing that these reported sanctions by Melcher
against Adèle are the same that Philibert Crud claims Daems
confronted Adèle with in the early 1860s. It is possible that these are
actions and attitudes of Daems from the early 1860s displaced by the
oral tradition onto Melcher in the late 1860s/early 1870s. In any
event, Adèle's July 20, 1875 letter to Bishop Krautbauer groups his
two predecessors, Henni of Milwaukee and Melcher of Green Bay,
by contrast with him, as having given approbation to her work.
Furthermore, Melcher's putative dread of francophone Mariophanies had not precluded his presiding over the cornerstone ceremony of Pernin's new church in Marinette, which he was renaming
and dedicating Our Lady of Lourdes.

In fact, *Finger of God* tells an early version of the story of
turning over the keys, emphasizing less Adèle's obedience than her
disinclination to hold property independently of the bishop at a time
when trusteeism was an issue (a point to which Pernin was particularly sensitive having lived in Iroquois County as a neighbor of
Charles Chiniquy): "Around the two structures stretch six acres of
land, which were given over to the devout woman and which she
herself gave over to his Excellency the Bishop of Green Bay. (97)"

These tensions were surely a factor in Daems' decision to
discipline Pernin in late summer 1874. Not only did Daems replace
Pernin in his absence with William White, but White felt thereby
empowered to change the name of the parish once more from Our
Lady of Lourdes to Sacred Heart of Jesus. This was an act of stepping
away from devotion to Mariophanies, the two of which Pernin had
linked in his mind and in his memoir. In the diocese of Green Bay he
was perpetuating Lourdes as he was advocating Robinsonville.
(Sacred Heart would become the name of a Polish parish founded in
Marinette nineteen years later, in 1893.)

Likewise provocative was Pernin's republishing in *Finger of
God* excerpts from the two self-promotional *Freeman's Journal* articles.
The first of them republished the document of dedication of the new

church to Our Lady of Lourdes, which Bishop Melcher had presided over. This he did at the very time, summer 1874, when diocesan administrator Daems was allowing William White to remove the name Our Lady of Lourdes. The articles had once fortified Pernin against inimical parishioners and by republishing them excerpted in *Finger* he intended to "make sufficiently clear the nature and the difficulties of my enterprise," among which was Daems' unfriendliness. If Pernin was again seeking support from the independent, national Catholic press, it was another reason for Daems to feel displeased.

Pernin's tabernacle on display in its own tabernacle at the Peshtigo Fire Museum, Peshtigo.

As it happened, Daems also suspended Philibert Crud from ministry on March 5, 1875 amid difficulties between Crud and the trustees of the parish of which he had been pastor since August 1870, St. John's, Green Bay. So had Pernin and Crud, the two pastors associated with Robinsonville and known as supporters of the Marian visionary Adèle Brice, both been suspended by administrator Edward Daems during the *sede vacante.*

Both Crud and Pernin were restored to ministry by incoming Bishop Krautbauer in July 1875. Crud was reassigned to St. Hubert's, Rosière, on the Door Peninsula, and Pernin, in September, to Sts. Peter and Paul, Grand Rapids, Wood County. In the next year, 1876, John Chebul, Pernin's successor as pastor, presided over the dedication of the completed church of Our Lady of Lourdes that Pernin had built and that *Finger of God* had been written to support.

In 1959 Pernin's Lourdes parish moved from the Menominee riverfront to the more suburban west side of Marinette when a new church was built on Taylor Street. Pernin's facilities became Marinette Central Catholic High School in 1958. Pernin's Lourdes church was razed in the summer of 1978. The name of Lourdes church survives within Holy Family parish, consolidated from four ethnic parishes in 1989. Thanks to Pernin the only Roman Catholic diocese in the United States to have approved a Marian apparition was the first to have a church dedicated to Our Lady of Lourdes. Pernin Street in Marinette, which runs from Cleveland Avenue to Main Street and terminates at the Catholic block in front of what is now St. Thomas Academy, remembers his time there.

The church Pernin built in Peshtigo stood until it burned down in 1927. The parish replaced it that year with a Congregational church building moved from the east side of the Peshtigo River to sit on the same foundation. A new St. Mary's church building opened on South Wood Avenue in 1956 and the old became the Peshtigo Fire Museum in 1963.

The Peshtigo tabernacle remained in the Marinette church for a time, but eventually was replaced and lost track of. Green Bay auxiliary bishop John B. Grellinger rediscovered it in the 1970s after a long search, stored on top of an old cabinet in the sacristy of St. James, Amherst, 90 miles from Peshtigo. The tabernacle he identified survives today, displayed May through October in the Peshtigo Fire Museum and the rest of the year in a side chapel of the current St. Mary's Church in Peshtigo.

In an American missionary career that lasted 45 years, Pernin had of necessity been flexible. When a church burned down, he built a new one. When accused of impropriety, he campaigned in the media. Brought over as a French specialist, Pernin learned English and learned to minister to indigenous and European Americans of various ethnicities, eventually becoming part of a deliberately diverse mix of officials of the new Americanist diocese of Winona. He learned the American kindliness to family members no longer Catholic. He eventually became proud chaplain of St. Mary's Hospital, Rochester, where, thanks to the Mayos and the Franciscan Sisters, secular science and Catholic faith cohabited peaceably.

Pernin shares an intersection in Marinette, Wisconsin with Frederick Carney (1835-1899), wealthy Marinette lumber business man and community pillar.

Finger of God reflects that flexibility, having attracted for 150 years readers from different perspectives. Pernin won for his memoir the encouragement and readership of slaveholder Peter Richard Kenrick and African-American rights campaigner Herbert Vaughan, and at different times had the episcopal support of ultramontane conservative Ignace Bourget and Americanist liberal John Ireland. For different reasons Pernin appealed to both Bourget and an eventually post-Christian wildfire fighter Peter Leschak.

In his memoir *Ghosts of the Fireground: Echoes of the Great Peshtigo Fire and the Calling of a Wildland Firefighter* (2002), Leschak became Pernin's most appreciative and professionally attuned reader, following Pernin imaginatively, "trying to learn more about this enemy/friend, adversary/mentor—good and evil fire." At 18 in 1969 Leschak had converted from cradle Catholic to evangelical Protestant after a transforming encounter with Jesus Christ more vivid than what he had experienced in the "bland pages of the Baltimore Catechism." The Catholicism Leschak grew up with in Minnesota was a heritage of Ireland's and Pernin's era there. But if Leschak found its rigorism insufficiently charismatic, because of the editorial excisions of the Wisconsin Historical editions he never had to confront the rigorous Calvinism that had ecumenically influenced the Catholicism of the fire memoir.

Leschak ended up post-Christian. But the humane value of the wisdom in action of a Catholic missionary trained not by firefighting science but by the wisdom of humanities study, diocesan seminary, and Wisconsin lumberjacks remains unsanctimoniously worthwhile even without the Catholicism. Leschak recalled James Russell Lowell: "All the beautiful sentiments in the world weigh less than a single lovely action... On the banks of the Peshtigo River, on the verge of bursting into a human torch, Father Pernin was lovely and magnificent."

Editing the French text

The text is based on the 1874 Senécal. Original punctuation and usage is mostly kept. The original comma usage, heavy handed by modern standards, allows us to hear Pernin's spoken rhythms (occasionally influenced by his student experience of Latinate periodic style): comma for a speech break, semi-colon for a bigger break. Pernin sometimes uses ellipses to be expressive. Original paragraphing is mostly kept, sometimes important to Pernin's meaning, as when he assigns a brief sententious observation to a whole paragraph. A few overlong passages are paragraphed. Dashes in the original (—) sometimes indicated a paragraphing intended and not made.

Original indications of quotations in dialogue, however, whether by dashes or quotation marks, are inconsistent and careless. Since dialogue is essential to Pernin, correcting the quotation marks was an important editorial task. Inconsistent original capitalizations are made consistent. *Compagnie* always capitalized for the Peshtigo Company and *Digue* for the Mill Dam; always uncapitalized: days of the week, months, words for the four directions, pronouns for the name of God, *belge* as an adjective, *église* for the local church building, and the words *tabernacle* and *ciboire*. Numerals and some abbreviations are spelled out. Pernin's versions of place names are kept: Ménominie for Menominee, *Rivière aux cèdres* for Cedar River, and *Baie Verte* for Green Bay (inconsistently). Routine correction of spelling, accentuation, gender, and number is not noted in the list of corrections to the text.

LE
DOIGT DE DIEU
EST LA !

OU

EPISODE EMOUVANT

D'UN ÉVÈNEMENT ÉTRANGE RACONTÉ PAR UN TÉMOIN
OCULAIRE,

L'abbé PERNIN,
MISSIONNAIRE AUX ETATS-UNIS.

Avec Approbation de Mgr. l'Evêque de Montréal.

———

Au profit de l'Eglise de Notre-Dame de
Lourdes, à Marinette, Etat du Wisconsin.

———

Transivimus per ignem et aquam,
Et eduxisti nos in refrigerium." (Ps. 65.)
Nous avons passé à travers le feu et à travers l'eau,
Mais vous nous en avez retirés pour nous donner le repos.

———

MONTREAL
EUSEBE SENECAL, IMPRIMEUR,
Nos. 6, 8, & 10, RUE ST. VINCENT.

1874.

Title page of the French first edition, Doigt de Dieu, *1874.*

Corrections

8 20 Juin, 1873   28 juin, 1873

8 add A. Druiding, St. Louis (Mo.), architecte,

20, 25, 54 sceaux   seaux

31 qu'il avait Lovell 1874 "there was abundance of water" qu'il y avait

32 Dress   Drees

39 †2e magasin†   Lovell 1874 supplies "neighboring store."

51 J'assayais   J'essayais

55 n'avait pas n'eût pas

60 [no quotation mark before] Est-ce possible!... à Marinette!" "Est-ce possible?... à Marinette!"

61 pentalon   pantalon

[Lovell 1874 Marinette addition] *Dunlop   Dunlap*

65 omit —Plusieurs en effet remarquèrent un tremblement de terre au moment où tout tremblait à la surface sous la fureur du tourbillon.—set apart by dashes, after "...si quelque courant électrique l'eut traversé." 1874 Lovell 67 "Whilst touching on this subject we may add that many felt a shock of earthquake at the moment that ever[y]thing on the surface of the earth was trembling before the violence of the hurricane."

66 leurs os, me dit l'un d'eux, mais le vent   leurs os," me dit l'un d'eux, "mais le vent

67 Ils me montrèrent les places où ils avaient retrouvé des tels et des tels. "Là une mère trouvée couchée sur la figure avec son enfant cachée dans son sein, qu'elle avait vainement essayé de soustraire au feu — ici toute une famille, père, mère et enfants tous calcinés et raccourcis par la chaleur. "Dans les ruines de la pension de la compagnie, il y avait près de 70 personnes tellement détruites qu'on ne pouvait reconnaître ni sexe, ni âge. Là-bas, dans ce puits, nous avons retiré 16 cadavres. Un des ouvriers de notre église avait son couteau à la main, son cou était coupé, 2 de ses enfants avaient aussi

le cou coupé ; mais non sa femme, morte et rôtie près d'eux." Cet homme s'appelait Towsley.

Ils me montrèrent les places où ils avaient retrouvé des tels et des tels. "Là, une mère trouvée couchée sur la figure avec son enfant cachée dans son sein, qu'elle avait vainement essayé de soustraire au feu."

"Ici, toute une famille, père, mère et enfants tous calcinés et raccourcis par la chaleur."

"Dans les ruines de la pension de la Compagnie, il y avait près de 70 personnes tellement détruites qu'on ne pouvait reconnaitre ni sexe, ni âge."

"Là-bas, dans ce puits, nous avons retiré 16 cadavres."

"Un des ouvriers de notre église avait son couteau à la main, son cou était coupé, deux de ses enfants avaient aussi le cou coupé ; mais non sa femme, morte et rôtie près d'eux."

Cet homme s'appelait Towsley.

68 vile vil

77 Ocouto   Oconto

90 *erudimi   erudimini*

92, 93, 94, 97, 100 Brisse   Brice

100 en à la facilité   en a la facilité

The English translation

The English translation of *Doigt de Dieu* published by John Lovell in 1874, though not an unfair representation of the whole, was inadequate. The editorial principles Lovell could bring to translations had once provoked controversy when he published Andrew Bell's tendentious translation of Garneau's *Histoire du Canada* (1860, 1862) and allowed a "free, rather than a slavishly literal translation" and "such modifications as would make it acceptable to the entirety of our people, whether of British or French origin." Pernin's uncredited translator likewise often tried to make a Catholic priest sound more plausible to English-speaking Protestants, the sort of editorial favor the *Wisconsin Magazine of History* bestowed when editing out the religious ideas of a Catholic missionary.

While making this new translation, I considered every word of the 1874 Lovell, especially for its 19th century English vocabulary. Pernin conceivably contributed to it himself and it certainly represents the reactions of a bilingual Quebecois anglophone. I have hesitated neither to appropriate and perpetuate what I thought felicitous in it nor to correct what is negligent. While having at hand the first editions that belonged to Pernin's niece, my grandmother's aunt, Maria-Berthe Pernin Berger (1847-1941), I also gratefully made use of the first editions of *Doigt de Dieu* and *Finger of God* digitized on Internet Archive at archive.org.

VERSION FRANÇAISE

Le doigt de Dieu est là !
ou Episode émouvant d'un événement étrange raconté par un témoin oculaire

L'abbé Pernin

Missionnaire aux États-Unis

Avec approbation de Mgr. l'Évêque de Montréal

Au profit de l'église de Notre-Dame de Lourdes
à Marinette, État du Wisconsin

Transivimus per ignem et aquam

Et eduxisti nos in refrigerium (Psaume 65)

Nous avons passé à travers le feu et à travers l'eau

Mais vous nous en avez retirés pour nous donner le repos

Montréal Eusèbe Senécal Imprimeur

Nos. 6, 8, & 10, Rue St. Vincent

1874

Table Des Matières

Approbation

[5] Nous soussigné, évêque de Montréal, avons lu l'opuscule intitulé : *Le doigt de Dieu est là*, etc., par l'abbé Pernin, et nous en avons été vivement ému.

Comme nous avons l'intime conviction que cet ouvrage ne peut qu'intéresser les fidèles de notre diocèse dont les entrailles s'ouvrent à toutes les misères, nous leur en recommandons instamment la lecture. Nous croyons même devoir leur conseiller de conserver chez eux un exemplaire de cet opuscule, afin de pouvoir le lire et relire souvent en famille, pour avoir continuellement sous les yeux des exemples frappants qui montrent combien Dieu est bon pour ceux qu'il veut sauver et combien en même temps il est terrible, quand il est forcé d'appesantir son bras vengeur sur ceux qu'il doit punir.

D'ailleurs la vente de ce livre, devant être au profit de l'église de *Notre-Dame de Lourdes*, qui se bâtit à Marinette, chacun se fera sans doute un devoir, en l'achetant, d'encourager cette excellente œuvre, qui tournera à la gloire de Dieu et au bien des âmes.

Montréal, le 24 mai, jour consacré dans l'église à honorer Notre-Dame de Bonsecours, en l'année 1874.

+Ig. Ev. de Montréal.

Avant-Propos

[7] Pourquoi ne publier ce récit que deux ans et demi après la grande catastrophe ?

Pour deux raisons principales :

1o. Affaiblie par l'épreuve, ma santé a été très chancelante depuis cette époque funeste, et ne m'a pas permis de m'occuper de ce travail.

2o. Les préoccupations nombreuses aux-quelles j'ai dû me livrer pour subvenir aux besoins spirituels de mon peuple privé de tout, et les troubles par lesquels j'ai passé, m'ont absorbé en ne me laissant aucun loisir.

Pourquoi écrire aujourd'hui ce récit, qui, quoique étant l'épisode d'un des plus émouvants phénomènes de notre époque, commence à être un fait du passé qui s'oublie de jour en jour ?

Pour deux raisons aussi :

1o. Plusieurs personnes éminentes, entr'autres deux évêques distingués, l'un aux Etats-Unis et l'autre en Angleterre, m'ont pressé d'écrire ce récit qu'ils ont jugé capable de faire du bien à plusieurs âmes. C'est un devoir pour moi de céder à ces conseils de personnes qui ont toute mon affection et toute mon estime.

[8] 2o. En publiant ces lignes, je me propose aussi d'intéresser à mon œuvre plusieurs personnes charitables, et de recueillir d'elles des secours pécuniaires pour m'aider à mener à bonne fin mon œuvre de restoration à Marinette.

Les deux extraits suivants que je traduis de deux articles publiés dans le *Freeman's Journal* de New-York, feront suffisamment comprendre la nature et les difficultés de mon entreprise.

New-York, 28 juin, 1873

"Un désert qui refleurit de nouveau"

Dimanche, 8 de juin, fut un jour dont les catholiques de Marinette se souviendront longtemps. C'était un jour de visite de la part de leur évêque, Mgr. Melcher, de Green-Bay, venu pour bénir la pierre angulaire d'une nouvelle église destinée à remplacer celle qui avait été détruite par le feu dévastateur de 1871, qui couvrit de ruines cette partie du pays.

La cérémonie fut imposante, etc...

Voici le document renfermé dans la pierre angulaire :
Sous le Pontificat de Pie IX, pape,
Joseph Melcher, étant évêque de Green-Bay,
U. S. Grant, président des États-Unis,
C. C. Washburn, gouverneur de l'état du Wisconsin,
A. Druiding, St. Louis (Mo.), architecte,
L'abbé P. Pernin, pasteur de l'église catholique de Marinette,
Et l'abbé W. Corby, de la Société de la Ste. Croix, prédicateur de circonstance.

En présence de plusieurs prêtres et d'un vaste concours de peuple, cette pierre angulaire a été bénie par l'Ordinaire du Diocèse de Green-Bay, pour cette église qui doit être bâtie en l'honneur de *Notre-Dame de Lourdes*, et pour le Salut de plusieurs.

[9] Tout ceci montre le zèle de notre Pasteur Bien-aimé et la peine qu'il se donne pour le bien-être de son peuple. Sa paroisse, quoiqu'écrasée par les pertes énormes que lui a causées le feu, promet d'être bientôt, sous l'influence de sa direction énergique, l'une des mieux organisées dans cette partie de la contrée. Avec de telles preuves d'intérêt et de dévouement, le zélé pasteur ne peut manquer de conquérir l'amour et le respect de ses paroissiens, et d'avancer la cause de la Religion dans cette place.

Le deuxième extrait du même *Journal* de New-York est du 18 janvier 1874. Il fut envoyé au rédacteur du *Freeman* à l'occasion de mes noces d'argent, c'est-à-dire, du 25ème anniversaire de ma prêtrise.

Je ne citerai que la partie qui concerne mes reconstructions.

Les catholiques de Marinette ont cruellement souffert des feux terribles qui, il y a deux ans environ, dévastèrent le nord du Wisconsin. Leur église, leur presbytère et leur école furent détruits complètement, et ils s'efforcent depuis ce temps-là de remplacer ce qu'ils ont perdu. Leur Pasteur, M. l'abbé Pernin, a travaillé beaucoup, mais ses ressources étant très limitées, il n'a réussi jusqu'il présent qu'à rebâtir la moitié de son église.

Le Père Pernin, malgré le désavantage des circonstances, n'a pas oublié les enfants confiés à sa charge, et après de courageux efforts il a réussi à élever une école paroissiale. Le zèle du Pasteur a été généreusement assisté non seulement par les catholiques de Marinette, mais aussi par la partie protestante de ses habitants. Cependant ils n'ont encore accompli qu'une partie de leur tâche. L'école n'est pas encore ouverte, faute de ressources, mais on espère recevoir avant longtemps une assistance de quelque côté inconnu.

[10] J'ai dédié mon église à *Notre-Dame de Lourdes*, aujourd'hui célèbre dans l'univers entier par les merveilles d'amour et de miséricorde qu'elle répand partout.

C'est, je crois, la première église des États-Unis consacrée à la Ste. Vierge sous ce nouveau vocable. Mon intention, en choisissant une semblable patronne, a été de lui rendre doublement chère cette ville qui porte déjà son nom, car Marinette n'est qu'une corruption de Marie et, par suite, d'attirer sur cette place ses bénédictions particulières.

Puisse-t-il être agréable à cette bonne mère de favoriser mon intention et de bénir l'œuvre que j'ai en vue !

Tout est pour son honneur et le salut des âmes.

CHAPITRE I

Avant la Catastrophe

Coup-d'œil du pays

[11] Représentez-vous un pays couvert de forêts épaisses, au milieu desquelles vous rencontrez çà et là, le long des quelques chemins ouverts, une éclaircie plus ou moins étendue, quelquefois d'une demi-lieue de large pour donner place à une ville naissante ; d'autres fois de trois ou quatre arpents pour commencer une ferme. A l'exception de ces petites places où les arbres ont été coupés, puis brûlés, tout le reste n'est qu'un désert sauvage, mais majestueux. Du bois, partout du bois, rien que du bois aussi loin que vous allez de la Baie au nord et à l'ouest. Ces immenses forêts sont bordées à l'est par la *Baie Verte* du Lac Michigan, et par le lac lui-même.

La configuration du pays est généralement ondulée ; des vallées où croissent le cèdre et l'épinette, des collines sablonneuses couvertes de sapins, puis de grandes [12] espaces de terrain d'un sol riche et généreux où l'on trouve toutes les variétés de bois francs, le chêne, l'érable, le hêtre, le frêne, l'orme et le merisier.

La température de cette région est généralement assez régulière et propice aux récoltes qui commencent à y être essayées, et qui réussissent ordinairement. Les pluies y sont fréquentes et manquent rarement de tomber au temps désiré.

Causes naturelles du feu

L'année 1871 cependant fut exceptionnellement une année de sécheresse.

Les fermiers en avaient profité pour agrandir leur champ, coupant et brûlant le bois qui les embarrassait. Des centaines d'ouvriers, occupés à ouvrir un chemin de fer, en avaient fait de même, se servant de la hache et du feu pour avancer leur ouvrage. Les chasseurs et les indiens parcourent continuellement ces forêts, surtout en automne, époque où ils remontent les cours d'eaux pour pêcher la truite, et se répandent dans les bois pour chasser le chevreuil. Le soir venu, ils allument un grand feu à la place où ils se trouvent, préparent leur souper, et étendant leur couverture dont ils s'enveloppent, [13] ils dorment tranquilles, sachant que le feu éloignera les animaux sauvages qui pourraient passer près d'eux pendant la nuit. Le matin suivant, ils partent plus loin en laissant derrière eux le braisier qui les a protégés et réchauffés, sans s'occuper de l'éteindre. Les fermiers et autres en font de même. En sorte que ces bois, surtout en automne, sont remplis partout de feux allumés par la main des hommes, qui, trouvant facilement une grande quantité de feuilles et de branches sèches, se nourrissent et se propagent plus ou moins loin. Vienne un souffle de vent pour les exciter, ces feux prennent quelquefois un grand développement.

Deux ou trois fois avant le huit d'octobre, le vent, favorisé par la sécheresse, avait fait concevoir de grandes craintes et jeté l'alarme parmi les populations des environs. Quelques détails à ce sujet ne seront pas sans intérêts, et serviront à mieux faire comprendre les préparatifs du grand événement du huit octobre.

La catastrophe semble s'être plu à s'essayer d'avance et à multiplier ses avertissements.

Le 22 septembre, j'étais allé au *Sugar Bush*, ou Pays au sucre, place où se trouve [14] une grande quantité de fermes, aux environs de Peshtigo. J'y avais été appelé par mon ministère. Pendant que j'étais là, dans une ferme isolée, je cédai au désir d'une partie de chasse. Je pars donc, mon fusil sur l'épaule, et accompagné d'un enfant d'une douzaine d'années qui prétendait savoir se diriger dans le bois ; je m'avance plus ou moins loin en faisant la chasse aux faisans qui abondent en ces lieux. Au bout de quelques heures, m'apercevant que le soleil baissait, je dis à l'enfant qu'il fallait retourner du côté de la ferme. Il essaya de le faire, mais il ne sut plus s'orienter et perdit sa direction. Nous marchâmes, marchâmes encore, tantôt à droite, tantôt à gauche, et la ferme ne s'apercevait toujours pas. En moins d'une demie heure de recherches inutiles, nous fûmes complètement égarés, l'enfant et moi. C'était à la tombée de la nuit, au moment où la nature se prépare au repos ; pas un bruit ne se faisait entendre, si ce n'est çà et là le bruit d'un petit feu qui courait aux pieds des arbres sans les toucher et qui faisait craquer les

feuilles en les dévorant ; puis, le frôlement des branches au faîte des
[15] arbres; ce qui nous annonçait que le vent soufflait.

Nous criâmes longtemps sans être entendus. Je tirai nombre
de coups de fusil comme signe de détresse. Enfin une voix lointaine
nous arriva, puis une autre, puis plusieurs autres venant de différents
côtés. Inquiets de notre retard prolongé, les parents de l'enfant et les
serviteurs de la ferme avaient soupçonné notre détresse et s'étaient
mis à notre recherche, en prenant différentes directions pour nous
trouver plus sûrement. Attirés bientôt par nos cris et par les coups de
fusils, ils arrivent près de nous, mais un nouvel obstacle s'oppose à
notre rencontre. Excités par le souffle du vent, ces petits feux s'étaient
réunis et éparpillés au loin. Nous nous trouvâmes bientôt placés au
centre d'une circonférence de feu qui s'étendait plus ou moins loin
autour de nous. Les hommes ne pouvaient arriver jusqu'à nous, et
nous ne pouvions aller jusqu'à eux sans nous exposer à avoir les pieds
brûlés et à être étouffés par la fumée. Ils furent obligés de nous frayer
un passage en battant le feu avec des branches d'arbre pour arrêter
[16] sa marche sur un point par lequel nous nous échappâmes.

Le danger avait été beaucoup plus grand dans les places
ouvertes au vent. Le lendemain, en rentrant à Peshtigo, j'appris que
la ville avait couru un grand danger pendant que je m'étais égaré dans
le bois. Le vent s'était élevé, et son souffle, en excitant les feux,
poussait les flammes dans la direction des maisons. J'aperçus tout
autour de la ville des tonneaux dispersés de distance en distance et
qu'on avait remplis d'eau en cas du retour d'un nouveau danger.

Un autre incident qui m'arriva quelques jours avant la grande
catastrophe :

Je revenais en voiture de ma deuxième paroisse située sur la
rivière de Ménominie, distance de deux lieues environ. Je suivais
tranquillement le chemin public percé dans le bois, en remarquant çà
et là de petits feux qui brûlaient le long de la route tantôt sur un de
ses côtés et tantôt sur l'autre. Tout à coup, j'arrive à une place où le
feu brûlait des deux côtés à la fois et semblait avoir une plus grande
force qu'ailleurs. La fumée, poussée en avant, remplissait le chemin
et l'obscurcissait [17] tellement que je ne pouvais ni voir l'intensité de
l'incendie, ni juger de la grandeur du danger. Je crus qu'il n'était pas
sérieux parce que je suivais la direction du vent. J'entre donc, d'abord

avec hésitation, dans l'obscurité de ce nuage de fumée, que laissait sur ses derrières, le feu que le vent poussait en avant. Je presse vivement mon cheval qui refusait d'avancer. En cinq ou six minutes je sors enfin de ce labyrinthe de feu et de fumée. Là, je trouve une dizaine de voitures, arrêtées en tête de l'incendie qu'elles n'osaient affrontée.

"Peut-on passer ?" me crie l'une d'elles.

"Oui, puisque je viens de passer moi-même, mais lâchez la bride et fouettez votre cheval, si vous ne voulez pas être suffoqués."

Quelques-unes s'élancèrent en avant, d'autres ne l'osèrent pas et revinrent à Peshtigo.

Les avertissements ne manquèrent donc pas. En voici un autre exemple encore plus frappant que je transcris d'un article inséré dans un journal de Green-Bay. C'est le récit d'une bataille livrée au feu, à Peshtigo, dimanche, 24 septembre, [18] justement deux semaines avant la grande catastrophe.

Dimanche dernier, 24 septembre, un grand émoi, et je pourrais dire, une grande terreur, parcourut la ville de Peshtigo. Depuis plusieurs jours des incendies s'étaient montrés menaçants tout autour, au sud, au nord, à l'est et à l'ouest. Samedi, les flammes se répandirent en haut de la rivière, à une petite distance de la ville ; et vers le soir, on re-doutait un grand danger de la part des étincelles et des charbons embrasés que le vent charriait et soufflait sur la partie supérieure de la ville, du côté de la fabrique. Des gardes furent placés le long de la rivière. Le feu prit plusieurs fois aux brins de scie, aux bois secs, mais il fut promptement éteint.

C'était un grand spectacle de contempler l'incendie pendant cette même nuit. Il s'élançait jusqu'au sommet des plus grands arbres, les enveloppait d'un manteau de flammes, ou, s'enroulant autour d'eux comme un immense serpent, grimpait jusqu'au faîte, de là sautait aux branches et aux rameaux qu'il illuminait et courbait en les faisant [19] siffler, puis jetait tout autour ses mille langues de feu tandis que de son souffle impétueux il balayait les feuilles vertes et mugissait à travers la forêt comme une immense tempête.

À tous moments, quelques vieux et énormes sapins, dont l'immense tronc était devenu une colonne de flammes, s'écroulait avec un fracas semblable à celui du tonnerre, remplissant l'air dans sa chute, d'un nuage d'étincelles et de tisons embrasés, tandis qu'au-dessus de ce nuage de feu, s'étendait un autre nuage épais et noirâtre, composé de fumée résineuse. Le contraste lugubre, entre cette noirceur en haut et cette lumière éclatante en bas, semblait annoncer la mort et la destruction à tout ce qui était au-dessous.

Des milliers d'oiseaux, chassés de leurs juchoirs, voltigeaient tout autour ne sachant quelle route prendre, et jetaient dans les airs des cris épouvantés, ce qui rendait la nuit plus lugubre encore. On les voyait fuir de côté et d'autre en poussant des cris d'alarme, comme pour appeler leurs camarades, puis tournoyer un moment dans les airs et tout [20] à coup tomber et disparaître dans l'immense fournaise qui bouillait au-dessous d'eux.

Ainsi s'écoula cette nuit. Tous désiraient la pluie et plus d'un cœur pria pour l'obtenir.

Le dimanche matin, le vent était calme, les feux semblaient morts, et nous commençâmes à espérer que tout danger était passée.

Environ vers les 11 heures, pendant qu'un grand nombre était à l'église, le sifflet de la fabrique jette soudain un cri strident ; les églises se vident rapidement et chacun se précipite pour voir ce dont il s'agissait. Le feu avait pris de nouveau à la sciure de bois. Le vent s'était élevé et soufflait avec force du nord-ouest ; les feux dans le bois brûlaient avec plus de rage que jamais et approchaient de la rivière juste en face de la fabrique. L'air était littéralement rempli de charbons, d'étincelles de feu, qui tombaient de tous côtés, incendiaient le plus souvent et une grande activité était nécessaire pour empêcher les flammes de s'étendre. La pompe fut sortie, des centaines de seaux [21] furent apportés du magasin, et l'on fit tout ce qui pouvait être fait pour empêcher le feu d'entrer en ville.

Mais voici qu'un nouveau danger se présente sur un autre point. Le vent avait changé de direction. Les feux de l'ouest approchaient rapidement à leur tour, et il semblait que rien au monde, si ce n'est un miracle, ne pouvait sauver la ville d'une complète destruction. Un nuage de fumée étouffante soufflait sur nos visages et nous empêchait presque de faire quoi que ce fût. Des moyens énergiques cependant furent pris pour arrêter l'approche des flammes. Les chevaux de la Compagnie furent attelés pour charrier de l'eau, et, outre plusieurs habitants de la ville, plus de 300 ouvriers de la fabrique et du moulin à scie travaillèrent sans relâche. Les effets des maisons exposées à un danger plus immédiat furent emballés et transportés ailleurs. On s'attendait à une conflagration inévitable.

J'ai vu des feux courir dans les prairies avec la rapidité de la locomotive. Le feu dans les prairies est terrible et [22] grand sans doute, mais il est insignifiant comparé au feu des forêts. Autant les bois sont plus touffus, plus élevés et plus gros que les herbes des prairies, d'autant plus intense, plus brûlant et plus grandiose est l'incendie qu'ils produisent. Le feu dans les prairies, poussé par un vent violent, se précipite, glisse sur les herbes sèches et meurt faute d'aliment. Dans les bois il marche presque aussi rapidement, mais il ne s'éteint pas en jetant ses vagues en avant pour balayer le faîte des arbres et s'attaquer aux petites branches et aux feuilles. Il n'est pas aussi facile non plus de repousser l'approche du feu des bois. C'est comme si vous vouliez essayer d'arrêter la marche d'une avalanche de flammes déchaînées contre vous.

Au coucher du soleil, le vent diminuant, le feu s'apaisa. On en profita pour enlever les bois secs, jeter de l'eau partout et pour envelopper les maisons de couvertures mouillées. Tout cela se fit sous le poids d'une chaleur brûlante et au milieu d'une fumée horrible qui nous aveuglait et nous suffoquait. [23] Et ainsi se passa la nuit de ce dimanche. Le lundi, le vent avait tourné au sud et dissipé la fumée. Etrange chose ! La ville avait été épargnée. La fabrique resta fermée pour donner aux hommes le temps de se reposer, et aujourd'hui, 27 septembre, tout est tranquille, et a repris son train ordinaire.

Que voulaient dire ces alertes répétées qui jetèrent le trouble dans les populations pendant les trois ou quatre semaines qui précédèrent le grand événement ?

Sans doute elles pouvaient être considérées comme des effets naturellement amenés par la sécheresse, par les feux allumés de la main des hommes et par le vent qui venait de temps en temps souffler ces feux et les étendre, ainsi que je viens de le montrer, mais qui oserait dire qu'elles n'étaient pas voulues par celui qui est le maître des causes et de leurs conséquences ? Ne se sert-il pas le plus souvent de causes naturelles pour exécuter ses volontés et produire des effets surprenants ? Il serait difficile à quiconque qui aurait assisté comme moi au spectacle de ces effets surprenants qui suivirent, de [24] n'y pas voir la main de Dieu, et dès lors, toutes ces alertes qui précédèrent apparaissent comme des avertissements d'une grande catastrophe à laquelle il voulait qu'on se préparât.

Je ne sais si quelques-uns les considérèrent sous ce point de vue, mais plusieurs conçurent des craintes et prirent des précautions en cas d'un incendie général. Ils creusèrent la terre pour y enfouir les objets qu'ils voulaient conserver. La Compagnie fit enlever les matières sèches qui pouvaient être un aliment au feu, s'il venait à se ranimer, puis disposa tout autour de la ville une plus grande quantité de tonneaux qu'elle fit aussi remplir d'eau. Précautions sages sans doute, et qui eussent été bonnes dans un cas d'incendie ordinaire, mais dans l'événement qui survint, tous ces plans des hommes furent déconcertés et nulle de leurs précautions ne devait être trouvée suffisante. Elles servirent néanmoins à montrer plus clairement le *doigt de Dieu* dans le phénomène qui survint bientôt.

Pour moi, je restais indifférent à ces excitations diverses, et laissais les évènements [25] suivre leur cours sans chercher à me prémunir contre eux, et sans m'en préoccuper beaucoup. Disposition bien différente de celle que je devais ressentir plus tard dans la soirée du huit octobre.

Un mot sur l'une et l'autre de mes paroisses.

Peshtigo

Peshtigo est située sur la rivière de ce nom, à deux lieues environ de la Baie, avec laquelle elle était reliée par un petit chemin de fer. La Compagnie de Peshtigo, avec son esprit d'entreprise, ses ressources pécuniaires et ses établissements, dont le plus remarquable était une fabrique de cuves et de seaux qui occupait à elle seule plus de 300 ouvriers, la Compagnie, dis-je, répandait l'aisance dans tout le pays. Sa population, en y comprenant les fermiers des environs, était à peu près de 2,000 âmes. J'achevais vers cette époque une église qui était généralement regardée comme devant être un ornement de la place.

Ma résidence était près de l'église, à l'ouest de la rivière, qui en était éloignée de cinq ou six minutes de marche. Je note cette distance pour mieux faire comprendre ma fuite au milieu du feu.

Marinette

[26] Outre Peshtigo, j'avais une autre paroisse bien plus importante située sur la Rivière Ménominie, à son embouchure dans la Baie Verte. Elle s'appelle Marinette, du nom d'une métisse, regardée comme la reine des sauvages qui habitaient en cet endroit. Cette métisse avait reçu à son Baptême le nom de Marie, que, par corruption, on avait changé en celui de Marinette, ou petite Marie. De là le nom de Marinette donné à la place. C'est là que je bâtis aujourd'hui une église en l'honneur de Notre Dame de Lourdes.

A l'époque du feu, j'avais à Marinette une église, un superbe presbytère qui venait d'être achevé et où j'étais sur le point de venir résider, puis une maison en construction qui devait me servir pour une école paroissiale.

La population était à peu près le double de celle de Peshtigo.

Curieuse coïncidence

Avant d'entrer dans aucun détail, je dois encore noter une circonstance qui paraîtra providentielle aux yeux de plusieurs, bien qu'elle fût amenée par des causes naturelles.

A l'époque de la catastrophe, mon [27] église de Peshtigo en était arrivée au moment d'être plâtrée. L'ouvrage devait commencer le lundi. La chaux, la poussière de marbre, tout était préparé à la porte de l'église. Les bancs avaient été enlevés, ainsi que l'autel et les ornements du culte. Ne pouvant pas officier ce dimanche dans l'église, j'avais annoncé qu'il n'y aurait point de messe et j'avais fait prévenir les catholiques de la *Rivière aux cèdres* que j'irais passer ce dimanche au milieu d'eux. C'était une de mes missions, située sur la Baie Verte, quatre ou cinq lieus au nord de Marinette.

Le samedi donc sept octobre, pour accomplir ma promesse, je pars de Peshtigo, et me rends sur le dock de Ménominie pour m'embarquer sur le bateau à vapeur le *Dunlap*. J'attends là des heures entières, sans rien voir venir. C'était la seule fois de l'année que le bateau désappointait les voyageurs. Nous sûmes plus tard que le *Dunlap* passa comme à l'ordinaire, mais garda le large et ne crut pas prudent d'aborder. La température était basse, le ciel obscurci par une épaisse fumée, qu'aucun souffle de vent ne dissipait, ce qui rendait la navigation très [28] dangereuse, surtout à l'entour des côtes. Vers le soir, quand tout espoir de pouvoir m'embarquer fut perdu, j'attelle de nouveau mon cheval et reprends le chemin de Peshtigo. Après avoir averti le peuple que la messe se dirait dans ma maison le lendemain matin, j'organise, dans une de mes chambres, un autel provisoire, en me servant du tabernacle même que j'avais ôté de l'église, et après la messe, je refermai le Saint Sacrement dans le tabernacle avec l'intention de dire encore la messe le lundi matin.

Dans l'après-midi, je voulais partir pour Marinette où j'avais l'habitude d'aller chanter vêpres et donner une instruction chaque fois que la grand-messe était à Peshtigo, c'est à dire tous les quinze jours. Les personnes qui connurent mon projet s'y opposèrent fortement. Il y avait dans beaucoup d'esprits comme une vague frayeur de quelqu'évènement inconnu. J'éprouvais aussi cette crainte vague qui s'imposait à mon esprit malgré moi. C'était plutôt une impression qu'une conviction, car, en considérant que tout était comme à l'ordinaire, j'arrivais par le raisonnement à la conclusion [29] que le danger n'était qu'imaginaire, sans toutefois me sentir rassuré. Et si ce n'eût été la réflexion que les catholiques de Marinette me croyaient à la Rivière aux cèdres et par conséquent ne viendraient pas à vêpres, je serais sans doute parti. Cependant je n'en fis rien et j'eus l'air de céder aux obsessions qui me furent faites de ne pas m'éloigner.

Dieu me voulait au milieu du péril.

Le bateau qui n'aborda pas le samedi sept octobre, pour m'emporter loin de Peshtigo, obéit sans doute aux éléments qui ne lui permirent pas d'arriver à bord, mais Dieu n'est-il pas le maître des éléments et n'est-ce pas à lui qu'ils obéissent ? Je me trouvais donc à cette place de Peshtigo le dimanche soir huit octobre, où, d'après mes calculs, mes projets, et mes arrangements je ne devais pas me trouver.

Mon après-midi se passa, je ne sais trop comment ; toutefois dans une complète inactivité. Mes sens étaient en proie à cette inquiétude vague de quelqu'évènement sinistre que je ne savais définir, et d'un autre côté la raison me disait qu'il n'y avait rien à craindre, pas plus que huit ou quinze jours auparavant, moins encore, à [30] cause des précautions prises et des gardes nombreux qui veillaient à la sûreté publique. Ces deux sentiments opposés, dont l'un s'imposait malgré moi et sur lequel l'autre, bien qu'il fût le produit du raisonnement, n'avait aucune influence, me jetaient dans une espèce de torpeur morale et paralysaient toute mon énergie.

Au dehors tout servait à entretenir ces deux impressions si différentes. D'un côté, la fumée épaisse et obscurcissant le ciel, une atmosphère étouffante et lourde, une espèce de silence mystérieux dans l'air, présage ordinaire de la tempête, faisaient craindre en cas d'un vent soudain. D'un autre côté, le va-et-vient dans la rue de cent jeunes gens qui ne pensaient qu'à s'amuser, leurs chants, leurs rires et leur indifférence à l'état de l'atmosphère, me faisaient croire qu'il n'y avait que moi qui fut inquiet, et j'avais honte de manifester l'impression de terreur qui me poursuivait.

Pendant cet après-midi, un vieux garçon canadien, très intéressé à tout ce qui touchait à l'église, vint me demander la permission de creuser un puits près de [31] l'église, pour avoir de l'eau sous la main en cas d'accident, et pour en procurer au plâtrier qui devait venir le lendemain ; comme il n'avait aucun moment pour s'occuper de cet ouvrage pendant la semaine, je le lui permis. Quand il eut terminé son travail, il vint me dire qu'il y avait de l'eau en abondance, et ajouta avec un sentiment de grande satisfaction, "Père, ce n'est pas pour bien de l'argent que je donnerais ce puits, maintenant il sera facile de sauver l'église si le feu revient." Comme il était très fatigué, je le fis souper et l'envoyai se coucher. Une heure après il dormait profondément, mais Dieu veillait sur lui et sans doute en récompense de son amour pour l'église, il lui fournit le moyen de sauver sa vie ; tandis que dans cette même maison où il dormait plus de 50 personnes périrent tout éveillées qu'elles fussent.

Ce qu'on fait pour Dieu n'est jamais perdu, souvent même dans ce monde.

Vers les sept heures du soir, toujours agité et poursuivi par cette appréhension indéfinie, je sors de chez moi pour voir quelles sont les impressions des voisins. Je me [32] rends chez une bonne vieille veuve, Mme. Drees. Nous sortîmes ensemble dans son champ, le vent alors s'élevait par moments comme pour essayer ses forces, puis retombait bientôt. Elle n'était guère plus rassurée que moi, elle pressait ses enfants de prendre quelques précautions, mais ils s'y refusaient et riaient de ses frayeurs. A un moment donné, pendant que nous étions dans le champ, le vent s'était élevé plus fort qu'auparavant, j'aperçus çà et là les vieilles souches des arbres prendre en feu, sans aucun indice d'aucun charbon ou étincelle apporté sur eux, comme si ce vent eût été un souffle embrasé, capable de les enflammer lui-même par son seul contact. Nous éteignîmes ces feux ; le vent s'apaisa de nouveau, et la nature reprit son silence morne et mystérieux. Nous entrâmes à la maison. Je m'assieds, puis me relève bientôt. Je n'avais aucune énergie et cependant je ne pouvais rester en place nulle part ; je m'en retournai bientôt chez moi comme pour être seul et cacher cette crainte vague qui m'obsédait toujours de plus en plus.

En m'en retournant, je levai les yeux du côté de l'ouest d'où le vent était venu toutes les fois qu'il avait soufflé. [33] J'aperçus par-dessus la couche épaisse de fumée qui enveloppait la terre, comme un reflet au firmament, rouge, embrasé et immense, puis au milieu du silence qui régnait autour de moi, il arrivait à mon oreille comme un bruit sourdement mugissant et lointain qui annonçait que les éléments étaient troublés quelque part. Une résolution soudaine s'empara de mon esprit ; rentrer chez moi au plus vite et me préparer aux événements quel qu'ils dussent être sans hésiter davantage. D'inactif et d'indécis que j'étais auparavant, je devins tout à coup actif et déterminé. Cette résolution soulagea beaucoup mon esprit accablé auparavant. Je cessai de ressentir cette frayeur vague qui me poursuivait ; à partir de ce moment je n'eus plus peur, mais une autre impression s'imposa d'elle-même à mon esprit sans être amenée par aucun raisonnement de ma part ; *ne pas trop m'attarder à sauvegarder mes affaires et m'enfuir de bonne heure du côté de la rivière.* C'est la seule pensée qui m'occupa l'esprit désormais, qui fut le mobile de toutes mes actions, et cette pensée n'était accompagnée d'aucun sentiment de frayeur, ni de perplexité. Je me sentais à l'aise.

CHAPITRE II

Pendant la Catastrophe

[34] Il était à peu près huit heures et demie. Je pense d'abord à mon cheval, je cours le prendre dans mon étable et le mets en liberté dans la rue, en pensant que quoiqu'il arrivât, il avait plus de chance de se sauver étant libre qu'attaché dans son écurie. Je me mets ensuite à creuser dans le sable de mon jardin une fosse, environ de six pieds carrés de largeur sur six à sept pieds de profondeur ; bien que le sol fût aisé à remuer je mis longtemps pour la creuser. L'air était pesant, l'atmosphère énervante, et par conséquence les forces me manquaient. J'avais la respiration courte et gênée. La seule chose qui pouvait m'exciter à travailler presque contre la possibilité de remuer mes membres, était la certitude de plus en plus visible d'un grand cataclysme qui approchait et grandissait de moment en moment.

Cette rougeur au firmament du côté de [35] l'ouest, grandissait à vue d'œil, s'étendait et s'enflammait de plus en plus ; puis à chaque coup de bêche dans le sable de mon jardin j'entendais, au milieu du calme et du silence qui nous écrasaient encore, ce bruit sourd, mugissant et terriblement grandiose qui s'accentuait de minute en minute, et rapprochait de plus en plus de nous le fracas de son tonnerre retentissant. Ce bruit ressemblait comme au bruit confus de plusieurs chars et de plusieurs locomotives s'approchant d'une station de chemin de fer, ou au bruit de mille tonnerres roulant ensemble dans l'espace, avec la différence qu'il ne cessait jamais, mais s'enflait et grossissait sans cesse en se rapprochant.

La vue de ce feu sinistre au firmament, le bruit de ces tonnerres qui s'approchaient toujours en grandissant avec une majesté terrible, me donnaient une force surhumaine.

Pendant que je travaillais ainsi, j'entendais deux autres bruits de voix humaines que le silence et la stupeur générale laissaient facilement et distinctement arriver à mes oreilles, sans toutefois me distraire de mon travail. Je dois les raconter ici [36] pour montrer la légèreté des uns et la folie des autres.

Légèreté des uns

Une famille américaine, voisine de chez moi, avait une société réunie chez elle en partie de plaisir pour prendre le thé et s'amuser ensemble. La chambre où les personnes étaient réunies, ouvrait sur mon jardin, ils me voyaient et je pouvais facilement les entendre. Plus d'une fois, j'entendis les rires de quelques-uns des invités et spécialement des jeunes filles. Sans doute on se moquait de la peine que je prenais.

Vers les neuf heures, la société se sépara et Mme. Tyler, la maîtresse de la maison, vint près de moi. Les actions du prêtre font toujours impression même sur les Protestants.

"Père," me dit Mme. Tyler, "pensez-vous qu'il y ait du danger ?"

"Je n'en sais rien," lui dis-je, "mais j'ai de mauvais pressentiments, et je me sens poussé irrésistiblement à me préparer à quelque chose d'extraordinaire."

"Mais si le feu venait, père," ajouta-t-elle, "que faudrait-il faire ?"

"Dans ce cas, Madame, sauvez-vous à la rivière."

[37] Je ne lui donnai aucune raison pour en agir ainsi, je n'en avais point moi-même ; mais c'était mon idée fixe.

Peu de temps après, Mme. Tyler prenait le chemin de la rivière, où elle réussit à se sauver elle et toute sa famille. Je sus plus tard que des huit invités qu'elle avait eus cette soirée, tous périrent à l'exception de deux.

La folie des autres

A une très faible distance de chez moi, de l'autre côté de la rue, se trouvait un cabaret. Cette maison de boisson enivrante avait été remplie d'ivrognes toute la journée. Deux cents jeunes gens, dit-on, étaient arrivés à Peshtigo, le dimanche matin, par le bateau à vapeur, pour y travailler au chemin de fer qui était en voie de construction. Ils s'étaient répandus dans la ville où plusieurs avaient retrouvé des camarades ; un grand nombre d'eux avaient pris logement dans le cabaret voisin de chez moi. Peut-être y avaient-ils passé à boire le temps de la messe. Ces jeunes gens, la plupart ivres le soir, n'étaient guère en état de prendre part à la stupeur des honnêtes gens, ni de faire aucune attention à l'étrangeté de l'état de la nature.

[38] Pendant que je travaillais dans mon jardin, plusieurs d'eux étaient sortis du cabaret et se tenaient sur le perron ou dans la cour de la maison. Il était facile de voir qu'ils étaient ivres, rien qu'à les entendre se battre, se rouler à terre, puis fatiguer l'air à l'envi de cris sauvages, de hurlements, et de blasphèmes horribles...

Dès mes premiers pas dans la rue, pour aller à la rivière quand la tourmente éclata, le vent me jeta du côté de ce cabaret... un silence de mort s'opéra soudainement parmi eux, comme si la raison leur eût été rendue, ou comme si la terreur les eut soudainement frappés. Je n'entendis plus un cri. Ils rentrent dans la maison, en ferment les portes, comme pour laisser la mort au dehors, deux minutes plus tard la maison n'était plus...

Que sont-ils devenus ?

Je n'en sais rien.

Reprenons maintenant notre récit.

Après avoir achevé de creuser la fosse dont j'ai parlé, je m'empresse d'y enfouir mes malles, mes caisses remplies d'effets, mes livres, mes ornements d'église, les plus précieux de mes objets qui me tombent sous la main, et je recouvre le tout de sable à peu près à un pied d'épaisseur.

[39] Pendant que j'enfouissais mes malles, ma domestique avait elle-même recueilli dans un panier plusieurs petits objets précieux en argent que j'avais en dépôt, croix, médaillons, chapelets, etc., et ne sachant ce qu'elle faisait, elle sortit, courut jusqu'au †2e magasin†, et y déposant son panier sur le seuil de la porte, elle revint chercher sa cage de canaris que la tempête lui enleva bientôt des mains ; éperdue et hors d'haleine, elle me criait de laisser le jardin et de partir.

Le vent avant-coureur de l'orage soufflait de plus en plus fort. La rougeur au firmament s'empourprait de plus en plus ; et le fracas de ces mille tonnerres semblait s'être jeté déjà sur nous, tant il s'était rapproché ; je ne pense plus qu'à sauver mon Saint Sacrement. Je ne l'avais pas perdu de vue, mon projet était de l'emporter avec moi. Je cours donc à la chambre où était mon tabernacle, je présente la clef sur la serrure, pour l'ouvrir et en retirer le Saint Sacrement : cet objet des objets, le plus précieux de tous, surtout aux yeux d'un prêtre, mais, sans doute à cause de ma précipitation, la clef au lieu d'entrer dans la serrure, m'échappe et [40] tombe à terre… Courir après une chandelle pour la chercher était perdre du temps et je n'en avais point à perdre. J'enlève le tabernacle lui-même avec tout ce qu'il contenait et l'emporte au dehors. Ma voiture se trouvait là, je le dépose dessus avec l'intention de remmener en voiture puisque je ne pouvais pas le porter. Je me disais en moi-même, "je rencontrerai quelqu'un en route qui m'aidera à traîner ma voiture." Mon tabernacle chargé, je rentre dans ma maison pour prendre mon calice qui n'avait pas été placé dans le tabernacle.

C'est alors que j'aperçus un phénomène qui me frappa beaucoup, des étincelles qui s'enflammaient subitement avec le pétillement de quelques grains de poudre touchés par le feu, voltigeaient de chambre en chambre. Je compris que l'air était saturé d'un certain gaz et si ce gaz, pensais-je, s'enflamme, rien qu'au contact du souffle d'un vent chaud, qu'en sera-t-il quand le feu lui-même en touchera la masse, amoncelée peut-être ? Le phénomène était menaçant mais je n'avais pas peur, j'étais prêt à partir, et il me semblait que j'étais sauvé.

J'avais au dehors de ma porte, dans [41] une cage attachée au mur, un geai que je gardais depuis longtemps. Tout le monde connaît l'instinct des oiseaux à prévoir l'orage. Ce pauvre geai sautait, s'agitait comme un être perdu, il poussait des cris aigus et se jetait contre les bandeaux de sa cage comme pour les briser et s'échapper. Je le plaignis de ne pouvoir rien faire pour lui. Mes deux lampes brûlaient sur la table, je leur fis mes adieux : "bientôt," leur dis-je, "vous verrez une lumière qui éclipsera la vôtre."

Je regarde comme très providentielle cette disposition d'esprit, voisine de l'enfantillage. Elle maintint mon courage dans la traverse que j'allais subir, en m'en voilant l'horreur et le danger. Toute autre disposition d'esprit, plus en rapport avec la situation, eût paralysé mes forces et j'eusse été perdu.

J'appelle mon chien qui, refusant de me suivre, va se cacher sous mon lit où il rôtit ; je cours à ma clôture pour en ouvrir la barrière et sortir avec ma voiture. Je touchais à peine la première planche, quand le vent de violent qu'il était depuis quelque temps, tombe tout à coup en tourbillon ; ce tourbillon arriva avec la soudaineté [42] d'un coup de foudre et m'ouvrit le chemin pour sortir de ma cour ; planches, barrière, clôture, tout est enlevé à la fois et vole dans l'espace. "Le chemin est ouvert," me disais-je en moi-même, "partons."

Sauve qui peut

Nous partîmes en effet mais un peu tard. Impossible de dire le trouble que j'eus soit pour me tenir debout, soit pour respirer, soit pour retenir ma voiture que l'ouragan m'arrachait des mains, soit pour garder mon tabernacle en place. Arriver à la rivière toute seule sans avoir rien à surveiller était plus qu'une personne pouvait faire, plusieurs n'y réussirent pas et périrent en route. Comment se fait-il que j'aie réussi ? C'est encore aujourd'hui un problème pour moi.

L'air n'était plus de l'air respirable, mais une immonde assemblage de poussière, de sable, de cendres, de charbons, de fumée et de feu. On ne pouvait ni ouvrir les yeux, ni voir son chemin, ni reconnaître personne, quoique la rue fût pleine de monde, de voitures qui se croisaient et quelquefois se heurtaient comme dans un *sauve qui peut*. Les uns se dirigeaient vers la rivière, d'autres luttaient contre [43] l'ouragan et fuyaient la rivière. On entendait un immense vacarme, ou plutôt, comme mille vacarmes discordants et assourdissants mêlés ensemble. Des piaffements de chevaux, des chutes de cheminées, des craquements d'arbres déracinés, des sifflements stridents de mille vents déchaînés, des pétillements de feu qui courait comme la foudre de maison en maison, mais pas un bruit de voix humaine, comme si chacun eût été muet de stupeur. On se heurtait sans se regarder, sans se parler et sans se consulter. Un silence de mort régnait parmi les vivants, la nature muette seule se faisait entendre. En rencontrant les voitures chargées de monde et fuyant dans une direction opposée à la mienne, il ne me vint pas même à la pensée qu'il vaudrait peut-être mieux pour moi de les suivre. Probablement il en fut de même de leur côté. Chacun courait fatalement à sa destinée.

Dès mes premiers pas dans la rue, la bourrasque me jette à terre et m'emporte avec la voiture près de l'auberge dont j'ai parlé. Plus loin, je suis renversé sur quelque chose d'immobile à terre ; ce quelque [44] chose était une femme et une petite fille, toutes les deux mortes. Je soulevai une tête qui retomba comme un plomb. Je prends ma respiration et sans dire un mot, je me relève pour être renversé encore.

A une place de cette route à la rivière je rencontre mon cheval que j'avais lâché dans la rue. Me reconnut il, ou reconnut-il sa voiture, ou se trouva-t-il là par hasard ? Je n'en sais rien, mais à un moment où je me relevais de parterre je sentis sa tête appuyée contre mon épaule. Tous ses membres tremblaient. Je balbutie son nom, et lui fais signe de me suivre, mais il ne bougea pas. Il fut trouvé rôti à cette même place.

Arrivé vers la rivière, les maisons qui l'avoisinaient étaient en feu, le vent soufflait ce feu et ses débris sur l'eau. Le lieu n'était pas sûr. Je continue donc ma route sur le pont pour traverser de l'autre bord. Le feu avait déjà pris au pont. Là se voyait un pêle-mêle effroyable et impossible à décrire, chacun pensait trouver le salut de l'autre côté de la rivière. Ceux qui demeuraient à l'est se jetaient à l'ouest, et ceux qui résidaient à l'ouest se jetaient à l'est. En sorte que le [45] pont était encombré de bétail, de voitures, de femmes, d'enfants et d'hommes qui se croisaient et se poussaient pour trouver une issue.

Arrivé parmi cette cohue de l'autre bord, mon intention était de descendre le cours de la rivière, à une portée de fusil au-dessous de la Digue, ou je savais que le terrain s'affaissait et que l'eau était peu profonde, mais cela me fut impossible. Le moulin à scie qui se trouvait de ce côté, à l'angle du pont, était en feu ; le grand magasin de la Compagnie qui lui faisait vis-à-vis de l'autre côté du chemin, était aussi en feu. Le feu de ces deux édifices, se joignait à travers la rue, et nul ne pouvait traverser cet enfer sans mourir à l'instant ; force me fut donc de remonter la rivière à gauche, au-dessus de la Digue où l'eau atteignait graduellement une grande profondeur. Arrivé à une certaine distance du pont, dont je redoutais l'écroulement, mon premier soin est d'envoyer ma voiture dans l'eau, aussi loin que possible, en laissant mon tabernacle par-dessus. C'est tout ce que je pouvais faire pour lui.

Désormais je n'avais plus à penser qu'à ma vie. Le tourbillonnement des vents dans son ascension continuelle avait pour [46] ainsi dire pompé la fumée, la poussière et les cendres. On y voyait clair. Le bord de la rivière, aussi loin qu'on pouvait regarder, était couvert de personnes debout, immobiles au bord de l'eau. Les uns avaient les yeux ouverts et levés au ciel, la langue tendue. La plupart n'avaient aucune idée et ne savaient que faire, plusieurs pensaient instinctivement qu'il n'y avait rien à faire et se croyaient à la fin du monde, ainsi qu'ils me le dirent plus tard.

Sans rien dire, (les efforts que j'avais fait pour arriver jusquelà avec ma voiture m'avaient mis hors d'haleine et la violence de la tourmente empêchait toute articulation de la voix), je pousse dans la rivière ceux qui m'avoisinent. Une personne surprise par l'eau en ressort de suite et lâche un cri à moitié étouffé : "je me mouille" ; mais il valait mieux se mouiller que de brûler. Je la reprends et l'entraîne avec moi aussi loin que possible. A l'instant même j'entends sur toute la longueur du rivage un claquement des eaux ; chacun avait suivi mon exemple. Il en était temps ; l'air manquait pour la respiration, l'intensité de la chaleur croissait. [47] Quelques minutes plus tard nul n'aurait pu résister.

Dans l'eau

Il était à peu près dix heures quand nous entrâmes dans la rivière. Je ne savais ni le temps que nous y resterions, ni ce qui nous arriverait, et cependant, chose étonnante, ma destinée ne me préoccupait nullement depuis le moment que, cédant à l'impulsion qui me pressait intérieurement de me préparer au danger, j'avais résolu d'aller à la rivière, j'étais et demeurais sous cette même impression de légèreté d'esprit qui me permettait de lutter contre les plus grands obstacles et de traverser les dangers les plus émouvants, sans même penser qu'il y allait de ma vie. Une fois dans l'eau jusqu'aux oreilles, je croyais être à l'abri du feu, mais il n'en fut pas ainsi ; il courait sur l'eau comme sur terre, l'air en était rempli, ou plutôt l'air était du feu. Le feu prenait à nos têtes.

Il fallait frapper l'eau avec nos mains et la faire ruisseler sans cesse sur nos cheveux et sur la partie de la figure que le besoin de respirer nous empêchait de plonger. C'est ce que je fis continuellement. Des vêtements, des couvertures [48] avaient été jetés dans la rivière, sans doute pour les soustraire au feu. On les voyait flotter de tous côtés. Je m'empare de ceux qui se présentent sous ma main pour en couvrir la tête des personnes qui se serraient contre moi et se pendaient à mes épaules. Ces vêtements séchaient vite dans cette chaleur de four et prenaient feu dès qu'on cessait de les arroser.

L'horrible tourbillon qui avait commencé quand je sortais de ma cour, avec son tournoiement continuel de vents opposés, avait, comme je l'ai déjà dit, clarifié l'atmosphère; la rivière était claire, plus claire que le jour, et en regardant en amont et en aval, toutes ces têtes perçant au-dessus du niveau de l'eau, les unes nues, les autres couvertes, toutes ces mains clapotant dans l'eau, et la jetant à poignée sur leurs têtes, on avait une vue d'un effet impossible à décrire, d'une beauté lugubre et grandiose, et tant était loin de moi la peur et l'anxiété auraient dû dominer dans mon esprit, que quelquefois je prenais cet étrange spectacle sous son côté comique et en riais en moi-même.

Lorsque, détournant mes regards de la rivière, je les portais au dehors, à droite, à [49] gauche, au firmament, je ne voyais que du feu ; tout brûlait, les maisons, les arbres et l'air. Au-dessus de ma tête, aussi loin que ma vue pouvait s'étendre dans l'espace, hélas ! trop bien éclairée, je ne voyais que des flammes, d'immenses volumes de flammes, couvrant le ciel et roulant les uns sur les autres en s'agitant avec violence : comme on voit, dans un temps d'orage, une mer de nuage rouler ses vagues, qu'une horrible tempête tourmente dans les airs.

Près de moi, sur le bord de la rivière, s'élevait le magasin de la fabrique, immense bâtiment à trois étages, rempli de cuves, de seaux et autres produits. Quelquefois je pensais que si le vent venait à tourner, nous pourrions être couverts des débris embrasés de ce magasin, mais je m'en préoccupais peu. Au moment où j'entrais dans l'eau, je vis le feu prendre à cet établissement ; il ne mit pas longtemps à le détruire, en moins d'un quart d'heure les grosses poutres étaient à terre et le reste brûlé ou enlevé dans l'espace.

Quelques incidents

Près de moi se trouvait une femme qui s'appuyait sur un billot pour se tenir à l'eau, une vache survint. [50] Il y eut une dizaine de ces animaux que l'instinct poussa dans la rivière, et qui, de cette manière, sauvèrent leur vie. Cette vache, en nageant, remua le billot, et la femme s'enfonça dans l'eau. Je la crus perdue ; mais bientôt je la vis suspendue d'une main à une des cornes de la vache, et de l'autre s'arrosant la tête avec l'eau de la rivière. J'ignore combien de temps elle fut dans cette position critique, mais j'ai su plus tard que la vache nagea vers le rivage, emportant son fardeau avec elle ; et ainsi, ce qui devait perdre cette femme, fut précisément la cause de sa préservation.

Une autre femme, au moment où j'entrais dans la rivière, arrive essoufflée et terrifiée, elle traînait un enfant à sa main, et croyait en avoir un autre enveloppé dans un tas de linges en désordre, qu'elle avait sans doute ramassés à la hâte et qu'elle serrait dans ses bras. O terreur ! en ouvrant ces linges pour chercher son enfant, elle ne le trouve plus... sans doute, elle l'avait laissé glisser sur le chemin. Rien ne peut peindre la stupéfaction de cette mère. Un cri moitié articulé et moitié étouffé s'échappe de ses entrailles ; "ah ! mon enfant !", puis elle fait des efforts pour percer [51] la foule et se jeter au courant. Le tourbillon du vent était moins fort sur l'eau que sur terre et permettait de parler. J'essayais en quelques mots de tromper cette mère, en lui disant que son enfant avait été recueilli, puis sauvé, mais elle ne tourna pas même son regard vers moi, il restait, fixé, immobile et tendu du côté de l'autre bord de la rivière. Je la perdis de vue, je sus plus tard qu'elle réussit à se précipiter dans le courant où elle trouva la mort.

Tout alla assez bien pour moi pendant les trois ou quatre premières heures de ce bain trop prolongé, grâce, je pense, au mouvement que je me donnais en jetant continuellement de l'eau sur ma tête et sur celle de mes voisins pour en tenir les flammes éloignées.

Il n'en était pas de même de quelques-unes des personnes qui étaient auprès de moi. Je sentais dans l'eau les jambes de l'une trembler, ses dents claquer. La réaction commençait à se produire, et le froid à pénétrer dans les membres. Je craignais qu'un trop long séjour dans l'eau amenât les crampes, et par suite, la mort. J'essayais donc de sonder l'état de la température, [52] en remontant un peu vers le rivage ; mais à peine mes épaules furent-elle hors de l'eau, que j'entends une voix me crier, "Père, le feu sur vous."

Le temps n'était pas encore venu de sortir de cette prison d'eau et de feu. Il fallait lutter encore. Une dame qui ne m'avait pas quitté depuis notre entrée dans la rivière et qui, comme tout le monde, était restée muette jusque-là, me dit alors : "Père, ne pensez-vous pas que c'est la fin du monde ?"

"Je ne le crois pas," lui répondis-je, "mais si tous les pays sont brûlés comme le nôtre semble l'être, la fin du monde ne tardera pas à venir pour nous." Elle se tut et moi aussi.

Enfin tout finit ici-bas, même le malheur. Le moment approchait où il allait être possible de retourner sur terre. Déjà on pouvait se passer d'arrosage. Je me retirai vers le rivage et m'assis sur un billot, n'étant de cette manière qu'à moitié dans l'eau. Je commençai alors à trembler de tous mes membres. Un jeune homme s'en aperçut et me jeta une couverture sur les épaules. Je me sentis un peu plus à l'aise, et bientôt après je pus sortir enfin de ce bain forcé qui avait duré à peu près cinq heures et demie.

Chapitre III

Après la Catastrophe

Prostration

[53] Je sortis de la rivière vers les trois heures et demie du matin. Dès lors, ma disposition d'esprit fut bien différente, mais surtout celle de mon corps. Et aujourd'hui en me rappelant ces souvenirs, je vois que le moment où j'ai couru le plus grand danger pour ma vie, fut précisément celui où il semble que je devais en être quitte. L'atmosphère, qui avait été brûlante comme celle d'un four, devenait graduellement de plus en plus froide. Après avoir été si longtemps dans l'eau, il ne fallait pas une grande intensité de froid pour que j'en fusse affecté. Je l'étais beaucoup. Mes vêtements étaient imbibés d'eau. Le feu ne manquait pas, et je pouvais sécher ceux de dessus, mais ceux de dessous restaient humides et me glaçaient. L'humidité avait pénétré dans mes os et surtout dans mes poumons. Je tremblais de tous [54] mes membres à côte des braisiers les plus chauds laissés par les débris des maisons. En un mot, j'éprouvais une prostration complète du corps et de l'esprit. Je pouvais difficilement me remuer. Je pensais que j'allais mourir et n'en avais aucun souci. Je sentais mes poumons serrés comme dans un étau, et ma gorge s'enfler. Je ne pouvais pas parler ; et c'est à peine si j'avais la force de faire quoique ce fût pour me ranimer.

Exténué et à moitié privé de vie, je m'étends sur le sable de la grève. Ce sable était encore chaud, sa chaleur me ranime un peu. J'ôte mes souliers et mes bas pour mettre mes pieds plus en contact avec la chaleur du sol, ce qui me soulagea beaucoup.

J'étais à côté de ce grand magasin de la fabrique dont les solives brûlaient à terre. Les cercles des cuves et des seaux étaient restés entassés au milieu des débris qui brûlaient encore. Il y en avait beaucoup, amoncelés les uns sur les autres. Je les touchai avec mes mains dans l'intention d'y poser mes bas pour les sécher, mais je les trouvai trop brûlants, et je n'osai pas leur confier, ni mes souliers ni mes [55] bas, car c'était tout ce qu'il me restait. Et cependant, ce qui est encore aujourd'hui un problème pour moi, il y avait un grand nombre d'hommes, couchés sur leur ventre, et étendus immobiles sur ces cercles de fer. Etaient-ils morts ? ou, transpercés par l'humidité, cherchaient-ils là la chaleur que je demandais au sable ? je n'en sais rien ; j'étais trop anéanti moi-même pour m'occuper d'eux.

C'est alors aussi que mes yeux commencèrent à me faire souffrir horriblement, et il en était de même, plus ou moins, pour tous ceux qui ne les avaient pas tenus couverts pendant cette longue tempête de feu. Bien que l'eau n'eût pas cessé de ruisseler sur ma figure, la chaleur les avait considérablement atteints, sans que je m'en fusse aperçu d'abord. Cette cruelle cuisson que j'éprouvais dans mes yeux, jointe à cette paralysie de toutes mes forces, me fit rester longtemps couché sur le sable dont la chaleur me ranimait.

Quand je m'en sentis la force, j'ôtai les uns après les autres mes habits mouillés, les fit sécher au braisier du magasin, et les replaçai sur moi secs et chauds, sans que la modestie de personne [56] en fut offensée. Chacun s'en tirait comme il pouvait, et nul ne faisait attention à ce que faisait son voisin. Cette opération me produisit un grand soulagement, je pouvais respirer plus à l'aise, ma poitrine fut moins serrée.

Enfin le jour vint à poindre sur cette scène d'horreur et de destruction que nul ne connaissait encore. On vint m'appeler pour changer de place et me rendre à un autre endroit du rivage où tout le monde était réuni. J'essayai de suivre les autres, mais je ne le pus pas ; l'inflammation de mes yeux avait augmentée, je ne pouvais pas les ouvrir, et j'étais complètement aveugle. Quelqu'un me donna la main et me conduisit à cette place où étaient déjà les autres. C'était une petite vallée au bord de l'eau, abritée de tous les côtés par des collines de sable. C'était justement la place où j'avais l'intention de me réfugier pendant le tourbillon de la nuit précédente. Quelques personnes avaient réussi à s'y retirer et furent comparativement beaucoup moins maltraitées. La tourmente de flammes avait passé trop haut dans les airs pour atteindre cette place ; les arbustes et les herbes [57] qui y croissaient n'avaient pas été touchés.

Nous voilà donc tous réunis dans cette vallée comme les débris survivants d'une bataille ; les uns sains et saufs, les autres plus ou moins blessés. Quelques-uns l'étaient beaucoup, et surtout une bonne vieille femme qui, n'ayant pas eu assez de force pour entrer dans la rivière, s'était tenue couchée sur le bord, une partie de son corps dans l'eau et l'autre hors de l'eau, et par conséquent exposée au feu. Elle était là étendue sur l'herbe, horriblement brûlée ; elle souffrait d'atroces douleurs à en juger par ses cris. Comme elle allait mourir et qu'elle me demandait, on me conduisit auprès d'elle. Mais je fus un pauvre consolateur. Je ne pouvais ouvrir les yeux pour la voir, je ne pouvais presque pas parler et me sentais trop abattu moi-même pour lui donner du courage. Elle mourut quelque temps après.

Ceux d'entre nous qui en avaient la force se répandaient autour pour s'informer de leurs parents qu'ils n'avaient pas encore revus, et revenaient en nous apportant d'affreuses nouvelles sur les ruines de la place et les personnes brûlées qu'ils prétendaient [58] avoir vues. L'un de ces explorateurs vint me trouver. Il me dit qu'il avait traversé de l'autre bord de la rivière, que toutes les maisons étaient brûlées, ainsi que l'église, et qu'il avait vu plusieurs personnes mortes le long des chemins et tellement défigurées par le feu qu'il n'avait pas pu les reconnaître. "Hé bien !" lui dis-je, "s'il en est ainsi, nous irons tous à Marinette, j'ai là une grande église, une belle maison qui vient justement d'être finie, et une école, je puis loger beaucoup de monde."

Vers les huit heures, on étendit à la place où nous étions une grande tente en toile, que la Compagnie avait fait venir d'en dehors, pour abriter les infirmes, les enfants et les dames. Elle était à peine tendue que quelqu'un vint m'engager à m'y retirer. J'y allai de suite, je m'étends dans un coin, je me fais aussi petit que possible pour laisser de la place aux autres. Mais l'employé de la Compagnie, qui avait reçu la charge d'organiser cette tente, n'avait pas eu les yeux brûlés pendant la nuit ; il m'aperçut bien vite. C'était un de ces hommes durs et grossiers qui semblent n'avoir jamais vécu qu'avec [59] les loups. Cependant il avait une tendre compassion pour les dames, et il ne voulait personne autre que des dames sous sa tente. A peine étais-je étendu dans le coin où je m'étais blotti qu'il se met à vomir un torrent d'injures et de blasphèmes contre moi en m'ordonnant de sortir. Je ne répondis pas un mot, je fis un demi-tour sur mon côté et me trouvai au dehors de sa tente. Une des dames présentes répondit pour moi à ce jureur brutal, et chercha vainement, je pense, à lui apprendre la politesse. Je n'ai jamais su le nom de cet homme, et j'en suis bien aise.

Déjeûner sur l'herbe

Les neuf et dix heures arrivèrent. Après les épreuves d'une telle nuit, bien des estomacs soupiraient pour un peu de thé ou de café chaud. Mais comment se procurer un pareil luxe au milieu de ce désert en ruine ? Quelques jeunes gens parcoururent les alentours de la place et rapportèrent plusieurs choux d'un champ voisin. On ôta les premières feuilles qui étaient brûlées, la partie saine fut coupée en tranches minces et distribuée à ceux qui se sentaient capables d'en manger. Un morceau de chou [60] cru et froid, n'était guère restaurant pour des êtres exténués comme nous l'étions, mais que faire puisqu'il n'y avait rien de mieux ?

Enfin, les gens de Marinette apprirent notre sort et nous envoyèrent vers une heure, des voitures chargées de pain, de café et de thé. Ces voitures devaient en même temps remmener tous ceux qu'elles pourraient charger. J'avais hâte d'avoir des nouvelles de Marinette. Je m'adressai à l'un de ceux qu'on avait envoyé à notre secours. "Y a-t-il eu du feu aussi à Marinette ?"

"Oh ! nous avons eu bien peur, mais Dieu merci, personne n'a péri. Nous n'avons perdu que des maisons."

"Des maisons ?"

"Oui, père, presque toutes les maisons et moulins à partir de votre église jusqu'à la Baie."

"Et mon église ?"

"Elle est brûlée."

"Et mon joli presbytère ?"

"Il est brûlé."

"Et mon école ?"

"Brûlée aussi."

"Est-ce possible ? moi qui avais promis aux pauvres malheureux de Peshtigo de les emmener à Marinette !"

Ainsi tout m'avait été enlevé dans la même heure. Mes deux églises, mes deux presbytères, mon école... tout ce que possédaient mes églises [61] et tout ce que je possédais en propre.

Repos

Entre une et deux heures je partis sur une des voitures de Marinette. Les bous soins, dont je fus l'objet de la part de mes paroissiens, me remirent sur pied assez vite. Dès le mardi soir, je pus visiter quelques personnes plus ou moins brûlées et les préparer à la mort du mieux qu'il me fut possible, dans le dénuement où j'étais de tout ce qui est nécessaire dans ces cas. Comme je me sentais assez fort, je voulus retourner à Peshtigo, dans la nuit du mardi au mercredi. Le soir je fis donc mes préparatifs : les vêtements que je portais avaient été considérablement endommagés dans la rivière et j'aurais voulu renouveler ma toilette, mais je n'y réussis pas. Les magasins, craignant le sort de Peshtigo, avaient emballé et enterré tout ce qu'ils avaient de bon. Je ne pus trouver qu'un pantalon grossier d'une couleur jaunâtre que les manœuvres portent pour travailler dans les moulins à scie. Je le pris, faute de mieux, et m'embarquai, à dix heures du soir sur un bateau à vapeur qui devait cette nuit-là même partir pour Green Bay en s'arrêtant au port de Peshtigo. La nuit fut très [62] tempêteuse, et ce ne fut que vers le point du jour, que le bâtiment osa démarrer. Nous arrivâmes par une très grosse mer, au havre de Peshtigo, vers les neuf ou dix heures du matin. Je ne m'y arrêtai que quelques heures pendant lesquelles je visitais, là aussi, plusieurs personnes malades, débris plus eu moins détruits par le feu.

Retour à Peshtigo

A une heure de l'après-midi un wagon devait emmener les hommes qui, depuis le feu, s'en allaient chaque jour, matin et soir, chercher et enterrer les morts de la ville de Peshtigo. Je pris place avec eux. Les locomotives de la Compagnie, ayant été brûlées, des chevaux les remplaçaient. Nous avançâmes ainsi jusqu'à la rencontre du passage du feu. Nous fîmes le reste du chemin à pied, espace d'environ une demie lieue. Ce qui me permit de contempler de loin et de près les ravages et les ruines de la tempête.

Hélas ! quoique prévenu, par tout ce que j'avais entendu dire, je n'étais pas préparé à voir l'horrible spectacle, qui se présenta devant mes yeux.

Vue du champ de bataille

Il est triste d'avoir à parler, de ce que personne ne [63] peut exprimer et aucune expression dépeindre. C'était le mercredi après-midi, 11 octobre, que je revoyais la place où avait été Peshtigo. Je ne retrouvais plus rien de ce qui, trois jours auparavant, avait existé, ni les arbres, ni les clôtures, ni les maisons. Tout avait été consumé. Quelques débris charbonnés restaient debout, pour montrer la furie de la dévastation qui avait passé en cet endroit. De quelque côté qu'on allât, on marchait sur des cendres. Les rails du chemin de fer avaient été courbés et tordus, les bois qui leur servaient d'appui, n'existaient plus. Les souches des arbres avaient été réduites, le cœur qui restait debout était comme pétrifié. Tout autour de ces souches, je remarquai une multitude de trous qui descendaient dans la terre. C'était la place des racines. Je plongeai ma canne dans ces trous profonds, en me demandant ce que c'était que ce feu qui, non content de dévorer ce qui était à la surface, avait porté ses ravages jusqu'au sein de la terre. Puis, à mes yeux étonnés rien ne montrait où avait été la ville, si ce n'est les chaudières des deux locomotives, [64] les roues des wagons et les travaux en briques ou en pierre de la fabrique. C'est tout ce qui restait debout. Le reste n'était plus qu'un désert, mais un désert qui pleurait et faisait pleurer, comme un champ de bataille après une mêlée meurtrière. Çà et là des cadavres carbonisés, de bœufs, de vaches, de chevaux, de porcs. Ceux des hommes, femmes, et enfants avaient déjà été relevés et enterrés — on pouvait les compter en comptant les petits monticules de terre fraîchement remuée.

Retrouver les rues était un problème difficile, j'eus grande peine à me diriger au milieu de cette désolation et de retrouver la place où avait été ma maison. Arrivé là, je cherche l'endroit où j'avais enfoui mes malles ; j'aperçois à terre, sur le sable, la bêche qui m'avait servi à creuser, et que j'avais jetée à quelque distance ; la moitié du manche était brûlée, le reste était resté intacte ; je me servis de cette ruine pour découvrir mes effets. Au premier soulèvement du sable, une odeur suffocante, comme celle du souffre, s'exhale au dehors. Mon linge au premier abord me sembla conservé. Le seul endroit où étaient les plis se trouvait [65] noirci, le reste n'avait pas changé de couleur, mais au toucher, il s'en allait en pièce, il n'avait plus de consistance ; comme si la chaleur l'eut consumé *à l'étouffée* ou si quelque courant électrique l'eut traversé.

Là encore tout était perdu.

Quelques briques calcinées, des verres fondus, des croix, des crucifix plus ou moins détruits, indiquaient seuls la place où avait été ma maison, et la carcasse carbonisée de mon chien, celle où avait été ma chambre. Je descends ensuite ce chemin qui allait de ma maison à la rivière, et que j'avais suivi la nuit de la tourmente. Là, les carcasses d'animaux étaient plus nombreuses que partout ailleurs, surtout aux approches du pont. Je revis mon pauvre cheval à la même place où je l'avais rencontré, mais tellement défiguré que ce ne fut qu'avec grande peine que je pus m'assurer que c'était bien lui. Son corps était enflé sous l'effet de la chaleur ; son flanc éclaté laissait sortir une partie de ses entrailles qui étaient rôties.

[66] Ceux qui possèdent un cheval dont les services leur sont agréables, ne s'étonneront pas de ce que je parle deux fois du mien. Il y a, entre le maître et son cheval, une sympathie comme celle qui existe entre deux amis, et qui survit même à la mort.

En parcourant ces ruines, je fis bientôt la rencontre de quelques êtres vivants dont quelques-uns s'approchèrent et entrèrent en conversation avec moi. Là, c'était un père qui cherchait un ou deux de ses enfants, et qui n'avait encore rien découvert. "Si au moins je pouvais retrouver leurs os," me dit l'un d'eux, "mais le vent aura enlevé ce que le feu n'aura pas dévoré." Ici, des enfants cherchaient leur père…, des frères cherchaient leurs frère…, des époux cherchaient leurs épouses… Mais je ne vis pas de femmes. Il n'y en avait plus sur cette scène d'horreur qu'elles n'auraient pas pu contempler.

Et tous ces hommes, ces chercheurs de morts, avaient plus ou moins souffert eux-mêmes dans cette bataille contre le vent et le feu. Les uns avaient une main brûlée, d'autres le bras ou le côté ; tous étaient [67] à moitié couverts de morceaux d'habits noircis et déchirés. Apparaissant eux-mêmes par leur tristesse et leur accoutrement, comme une ruine au milieu de toutes ces ruines…

Ils me montrèrent les places où ils avaient retrouvé des tels et des tels. "Là, une mère trouvée couchée sur la figure avec son enfant caché dans son sein, qu'elle avait vainement essayé de soustraire au feu."

"Ici, toute une famille, père, mère et enfants tous calcinés et raccourcis par la chaleur."

"Dans les ruines de la pension de la Compagnie, il y avait près de 70 personnes tellement détruites qu'on ne pouvait reconnaitre ni sexe, ni âge."

"Là-bas, dans ce puits, nous avons retiré 16 cadavres."

"Un des ouvriers de notre église avait son couteau à la main, son cou était coupé, deux de ses enfants avaient aussi le cou coupé ; mais non sa femme, morte et rôtie près d'eux."

Cet homme s'appelait Towsley. Il avait en effet travaillé à mon église de Peshtigo pendant toute la saison d'été ; sans doute en voyant sa femme tomber à ses côtés, et toute impossibilité d'échapper au feu, sa raison se troubla, et, pour éviter les horreurs d'une mort par le feu, il [68] prit son couteau et trancha la tête à ses enfants, puis à lui-même. Cette horrible folie du suicide se répéta dans plusieurs autres endroits, et fut produite par les mêmes causes.

Ces récits, joignant leur horreur à ce que je voyais d'affreux sous mes yeux, me glacèrent l'âme de terreur !

Manque de cordes pour pendre un coquin

Hélas ! faut-il avoir à noter un incident qui n'aurait jamais dû se produire au milieu d'une pareille scène ? Pendant que j'étais sous les impressions pénibles dont je viens de parler, mon attention fut appelée d'un autre côté par un bruit de voix humaines, qui annonçait quelqu'évènement nouveau. Voici ce qui arrivait. Au milieu de la consternation générale, il se rencontra un homme assez vil pour oser insulter la mort et les grandes douleurs qu'elle inspirait à tous. Cet homme, pour satisfaire sa cupidité, profanait les cadavres, en les dépouillant des objets que le feu avait épargnés. On venait de le prendre en flagrant délit. On forme une espèce de jury, son châtiment est mis aux voix, et à l'unanimité on le condamne à être pendu sur place. Mais [69] comment faire ? où trouver une corde ? le feu n'avait rien laissé. Quelqu'un imagine de remplacer la corde par une chaîne en fer dont on se servait pour traîner les billots. La chaîne est apportée et mise à son cou ; mais l'opération traîne en longueur à cause de sa difficulté. Le coupable demande grâce. La pitié, que ce champ désolé inspirait à tous, descend dans l'âme des juges, qui le laissèrent aller en liberté, après lui avoir fait demander pardon à genoux de ses sacrilèges profanations. Peut-être ne se proposaient-ils que de l'effrayer.

Dès que je connus ce dont il s'agissait, je me retirai à l'écart, loin du bruit et de l'agitation. J'avais besoin d'être seul. Je me dirige donc un peu en dehors de la ville sur ce chemin d'Oconto où j'avais vu tant de voitures se précipiter, en tournant le dos à la rivière, au moment où je m'y dirigeais moi-même, en traînant mon tabernacle. Je n'allai pas bien loin pour en voir plus que je n'aurais voulu. Tout avait péri de ce côté, et péri en tas, car les voitures étaient chargées de monde qui, fuyant la mort, la rencontrèrent vite et horrible. On ne retrouvait dans les [70] places où le feu les avait saisies, que les cercles des roues. Le reste n'était qu'un amas de chairs brûlées, d'ossements calcinés. On avait de la peine à distinguer les restes des chevaux d'avec les restes humains. Les ouvriers de la Compagnie étaient occupés à démêler ces restes qu'ils enterraient sur le bord du chemin en attendant que leurs parents, s'il leur en restait, pussent les reconnaître et leur donner une sépulture plus convenable.

Je les laissai continuer leur triste besogne et revins vers la place où avait été mon église. Là tout était cendre aussi, excepté ma cloche. Chose étonnante ! ma cloche avait été jetée à 50 pieds au large, une partie était restée intacte et l'autre moitié avait été fondue et s'étendait sur le sable en feuilles argentées. Le son de cette cloche avait été le dernier son entendu au milieu de la bourrasque. Ce son lugubre résonne encore à mon oreille et me rappelle l'horreur qu'il présageait. Mon cimetière touchait à l'église ; j'attendais un enterrement qui vint bientôt. C'était un jeune homme, mort la veille, des suites d'atroces brûlures qu'il avait eues. Quelle [71] pauvre cérémonie ! Jamais prêtre plus destitué de tout ce qui sert en pareille occasion, n'a procédé aux cérémonies, d'enterrement. Ni église pour aller prier, pas même une maison, ni surplis, ni étole, ni rituel. Rien que la prière et la bénédiction du cœur ! J'avais trouvé cette destitution plus triste encore auparavant, dans les trois ou quatre circonstances où les mourants me demandaient l'onction dernière, que je ne pouvais pas leur donner.

Je quittai le cimetière le cœur bien gros, et me dirigeai vers la rivière pour traverser de l'autre bord, et chercher mon tabernacle dont je ne savais rien encore. Une grande consolation m'attendait. Jamais il n'en vint de plus à propos.

Mon tabernacle

Je traversai la rivière sur les débris des solives du pont qu'on avait rejointées, de manière à offrir un passage à ceux qui osaient s'y aventurer. Le passage était très périlleux. A peine étais-je de l'autre côté qu'un de mes paroissiens, accourant à ma rencontre, me dit avec enthousiasme : "Père, vous savez ce qui est arrivé à votre tabernacle ?"

[72] "Je ne sais rien du tout, que lui est-il arrivé ?"

"Venez voir, père, oh ! c'est un grand miracle !"

Je me rendis donc à la place de la rivière où j'avais lâché ma voiture, chargée de mon tabernacle, en la poussant aussi loin que possible dans la profondeur des eaux. Cette voiture avait été soulevée par la tourmente et renversée sur son côté ; le tabernacle, enlevé par le vent avait été jeté sur les billots qui couvraient une partie des eaux. Tout avait été plus ou moins touché par le feu, charbonné et noirci, billots, caisses, malles, tout ce qui surnageait sur l'eau, et mon tabernacle se dressait là, au milieu de ces noirceurs plus ou moins enfumées, dans tout l'éclat de la blancheur de sa peinture, tel qu'il était auparavant. Je le laissai là, dans cette place où la bourrasque l'avait jeté, pendant deux jours, pour laisser à chacun le temps de l'observer. Il le fut beaucoup, mais pas autant qu'il l'aurait été à une autre époque. Chacun de ceux qui restaient sur cette scène d'horreur, avait trop à penser pour lui-même, et avait l'esprit trop troublé par les pertes de ceux qu'il pleurait. Les catholiques généralement regardèrent [73] ce fait comme un miracle. Le bruit s'en répandit vite et créa une grande sensation.

Hélas ! tout s'efface chez l'homme, surtout les bonnes impressions qu'amènent ou l'épreuve ou les bénédictions divines. Le temps et les préoccupations de cette vie en éteignent jusqu'au souvenir. Combien il y en a-t-il aujourd'hui parmi les rares survivants de Peshtigo qui voient encore Dieu et dans le châtiment qu'ils ont éprouvé et dans la préservation de mon tabernacle qui les a tant frappés cependant ?

Quand j'eus fini l'ouvrage qui me retint trois jours sur ces tristes bords, je retirai mon tabernacle du milieu de la rivière et l'envoyai à Marinette, où je devais bientôt aller célébrer la messe. Quand ce moment fut venu, je forçai la porte et l'ouvrit. Chose aussi étonnante que sa conservation pendant le feu ! Je retrouvai l'hostie consacrée intacte dans l'ostensoir, les secousses violentes qu'il avait essuyées n'avaient pas même fait ouvrir le saint ciboire ; l'eau n'avait pas pénétré l'intérieur, et le feu avait respecté le dedans comme le dehors ; jusqu'à l'étoffe [74] légère de soie qui en garnissait les côtés intérieurs, tout fut trouvé en parfait état de conservation.

Ce tabernacle, cet ostensoir et ce saint ciboire, qui n'ont aucune valeur intrinsèque, ont un prix inestimable à mes yeux. Je les tiens pour des reliques précieuses et jamais je ne les regarde ou les touche sans me sentir pénétré d'un sentiment de vénération et d'amour que je n'éprouve jamais, en touchant d'autres objets de la même nature sous une forme plus belle et plus riche. Dans ma petite chapelle de Marinette, qui remplace mon église brûlée, depuis deux ans, c'est le même tabernacle, qui est sur mon autel, renfermant encore ce saint ciboire, et cet ostensoir sauvés du feu. Je m'en sers tous les jours avec orgueil et les regarde comme des trophées donnés par Dieu et arrachés à l'ennemi.

Revenons sur la rivière de Peshtigo que j'ai quittée pour parler de mon tabernacle. Je n'ai plus à m'en occuper que pour un peu de temps.

Avant de retirer mon tabernacle de dessus les billots je restai là trois jours et deux nuits, occupé tantôt à aider à la recherche des morts, [75] tantôt à pêcher dans la rivière plusieurs objets que j'avais jetés à brassée dans ma voiture au moment de quitter ma maison et qui avaient été renversés avec elle dans la rivière. Le plus précieux de tous était mon calice que je fus assez heureux de retrouver ainsi que la patène. Je fus beaucoup aidé en cela par la baisse du niveau de l'eau ; on avait ouvert la Digue et lâché les eaux qu'elle relie à une profondeur de 15 à 20 pieds. Cette opération fut nécessaire pour retrouver les cadavres des personnes qui, prises par des crampes ou entraînées par le courant, s'étaient noyées pendant la nuit de l'ouragan.

Pendant ces trois jours, nous n'eûmes pour habitation que cette tente en toile dont le bénéfice m'avait été refusé le lundi précédent. Elle nous servait d'abri pendant nos repas que nous prenions debout et sur le bout du doigt, et la nuit, elle nous abritait pendant notre sommeil ; je parle de ceux qui, habitués à dormir partout, étaient capables de trouver le repos en cet endroit ; pour moi, je ne le pouvais pas. Nos lits étaient très économiques. Le sable du rivage nous [76] servait de matelas et une couverture nous abritait du froid.

Ce fut pendant une de ces journées que j'eus connaissance du sort de Chicago. Un docteur venu de *Fond du Lac* pour soigner les brûlés, avait apporté la gazette avec lui, et nous lut les terribles ravages des feux survenus, chose étrange, la même nuit, presque à la même heure, non seulement à Peshtigo mais dans plusieurs localités différentes et surtout à Chicago. Cet incendie de Chicago, proclamé par les milles voix des journaux et des télégraphes, fut vite porté au loin où il créa un grand émoi de compassion en faveur de la ville infortunée. Ce qui détourna beaucoup l'attention du monde des ravages bien autrement grandioses et destructeurs dont nous étions les victimes.

Le vendredi 13, dans l'après-midi, j'avais à peu près fini mon ouvrage sur cette triste rivière de Peshtigo. La plupart des victimes retrouvées avaient été enterrées et tous les infirmes emmenés dans différentes directions. Epuisé de fatigue et de privations, je ne pouvais guère tenir plus longtemps en cet état de dénuement et de manque de repos ; une voiture, qui était [77] venu apporter des secours, allait repartir pour Oconto ; j'en profitai pour me rendre dans cette ville où j'avais des amis qui m'attendaient avec impatience. Je restai deux jours à me reposer chez l'excellent père Vermare, curé de l'église française. Le lundi suivant, je partis pour Green Bay afin de rendre visite à mon évêque Mgr. Melcher, hélas mort aujourd'hui où j'écris ces lignes.

Les bruits les plus contradictoires avaient circulé à mon sujet, comme il arrive en pareil cas. Les uns m'avaient dit brûlé dans mon église où je m'étais rendu pour prier au moment de la tempête. D'autres m'avaient fait brûler dans ma maison, et d'autres enfin m'avaient fait noyer dans la rivière. Naturellement excité par tous ces rapports que ma présence lui rappelait, Monseigneur, en me voyant, s'écrie avec sa vivacité ordinaire. "Oh ! vous voilà donc enfin, j'ai été bien inquiet sur votre compte ! Pourquoi ne m'avez-vous pas écrit ?"

"Monseigneur, je ne le pouvais pas," lui répondis je, "je n'avais ni papier, ni plume, ni encre, rien que l'eau de la rivière."

Puis, il m'offrit généreusement ce qui pouvait [78] m'être nécessaire, à prendre soit dans sa bibliothèque soit dans son garde-robe. Ce que je refusai en lui disant qu'il me restait encore assez de paroissiens sur la rivière de Ménominie et que c'était à eux à me secourir et non pas à lui. Ensuite il me nomma à une autre paroisse en me disant que j'avais bien assez souffert pour mériter le repos et qu'en restant avec ma population, à moitié détruite, il me faudrait trop souffrir encore. Mais considérant le malheur de mon peuple laissé sans prêtre à un moment où il leur était si nécessaire et le besoin qu'il avait de garder celui qui, habitué à les aimer, partagerait plus volontiers leur pauvreté, j'obtins la permission de rester.

Cependant, les souffrances que j'avais endurées commençaient à montrer le ravage qu'elles avaient produit dans ma constitution ; cela à un tel point que Monseigneur dit à l'abbé Crud, curé de Green Bay qui m'avait invité à prêcher pour la Toussaint, qu'il ne fallait pas compter sur moi, que le feu avait désorganisé mon cerveau. Je ne sais s'il en était ainsi, seulement je sais très bien que j'étais terriblement faible, mais, espérant me [79] remettre après quelques mois de repos, je résolus de voyager pour remettre ma santé et de profiter de mon voyage dans l'intérêt de mes paroisses détruites. Mon intention était d'aller jusqu'en Louisiane et de revenir par l'est, mais je dus bientôt m'apercevoir que mes forces trahissaient mon courage.

Arrivé à St. Louis, je fus attaqué par une fièvre quotidienne qui me mettait à terre chaque jour pendant trois ou quatre heures, et qui ne contribuait pas peu à m'enlever mes forces. Je n'allai donc pas plus loin. Le bon peuple de St. Louis me montra une grande sympathie. Je me suis fait dans cette ville des amis que je n'oublierai plus, et qu'il me sera toujours agréable de revoir. Je ne mentionnerai pas ici leur nom, mais il est écrit dans mon cœur en lettres ineffaçables. Je ne puis rien par moi-même pour leur montrer ma reconnaissance, mais je dirai leur nom à la très bonne et très puissante Notre Dame de Lourdes, dans son église de Marinette. Elle saura suppléer à mon incapacité.

Je viens de mentionner les habitants de St. Louis comme ayant droit à ma reconnaissance, je serais injuste de passer [80] sous silence ceux de mes paroissiens et de mes amis du Wisconsin, qui spontanément m'offrirent les premiers secours que réclamait ma détresse. Je ne les oublie pas non plus. Il m'est doux de me rappeler ces élans du cœur, comme celui d'un de mes amis d'Oconto qui, voulant me faire accepter des habits plus décents que ceux que je rapportais du feu, et que je refusais de prendre, "je le veux," dit-il, "car je sais que si j'étais à votre place vous voudriez me rendre le même service."

Quelques détails en dehors de mon récit

Il me semble bon de noter ici quelques-uns des phénomènes extraordinaires et des caractère particuliers de ce feu étrange, quoique je n'aie pas vu moi-même de mes yeux plusieurs de ces faits. J'étais trop au centre du ravage pour voir ce qui se passait au loin. Ce n'est pas celui qui est au milieu de la bataille qui en voit le mieux l'ensemble et les détails, c'est celui qui la contemple de quelque point qui domine sur la plaine.

Force de la bourrasque

Des forêts d'arbres énormes d'érables, fortement et profondément cramponnés au sol, furent déracinée, brisées et tordues comme on tord [81] une baguette de noisetier. Un arbre laissé debout çà et là est une exception. On les voyait entassés et couchés les uns sur les antres en tous sens ; leurs branches réduites en cendres, et leur tronc charbonné et noirci. Quelques-uns assurent avoir vu de grosses maisons en bois soulevées de leur place par deux courants contraires et enlevées comme une paille dans les airs où se trouvait le courant de feu, et alors seulement s'embraser et être mises en pièces et en cendre en un instant.

Cependant la vitesse du tourbillon qui était vent et feu à la fois, n'était nullement proportionnée à sa force terrible. On peut s'assurer par le temps où la tourmente commença au sud-ouest, comparé au temps où elle finit au nord-est, que la vitesse n'excédait pas deux lieues à l'heure. Le tourbillon se mouvait en cercle, s'avançant lentement comme pour avertir de son passage prochain.

Intensité de la chaleur

Plusieurs effets étranges démontrent que l'intensité de la chaleur produite par le feu fut extrême et inouïe par place. J'ai déjà mentionné les racines des souches poursuivies par le [82] feu et consumées jusqu'à leur extrémité dans les profondeurs de la terre. J'ai plongé ma canne dans ces excavations et me suis assuré que nulle profondeur n'avait arrêté la combustion.

Des tonneaux de clous ont été trouvés fondus quoique placés en dehors de tout foyer de flammes.

D'immenses quantités de poissons de toute grosseur moururent ; ils couvraient la rivière et flottaient au courant le matin qui suivit l'orage. Quelle fut la cause de leur mort ? l'intensité de la chaleur, ou le manque de la quantité d'air nécessaire à leur respiration, cet air étant violemment pompé par le courant qui se précipitait vers le foyer incandescent se mouvant dans l'espace ? Ou bien, périrent-ils par l'effet de quelque gaz empoisonné.

Gaz

On peut difficilement douter que l'air fut un moment saturé d'un gaz inflammable et destructeur de la vie humaine. J'ai mentionné ces bulles d'air voltigeant dans mes chambres au moment où j'ai quitté ma maison. En allant à la rivière j'ai rencontré des couches d'air, des places, où je ne pouvais pas respirer et je devais me coucher à terre pour [83] prendre mon souffle, quand le torrent du vent ne m'y jetait pas malgré moi. Pendant que j'étais dans la rivière en levant les yeux en haut, j'apercevais, ainsi que je l'ai dit, comme une mer de feu s'agiter violemment et rouler d'immenses vagues de flammes les unes sur les autres ; ceci se passait à une hauteur prodigieuse dans le ciel, et par conséquent loin de toute matière combustible. Comment expliquer ce phénomène sans admettre que d'énormes couches d'un gaz quelconque étaient amoncelées dans l'air ?

Chose étrange ! Beaucoup de cadavres n'avaient aucune marque de brûlure sur leur corps et cependant dans leur poche trouvée intacte, leur montre, des sous de cuivre, ou autres objets en métal, étaient fondus. Comment y eut-il alors des vies humaines qui échappèrent par-ci par-là dans les fermes et dans les bois ? Il est difficile de répondre à cette question. La tempête n'eut pas partout une rage égale. Ce ne fut pour les survivants qu'une affaire de chance, nul ne peut se vanter d'avoir eu plus de présence d'esprit qu'un autre. Généralement ceux qui se trouvaient dans quelque partie basse du terrain, [84] surtout s'ils trouvaient à leur disposition, quelque excavation, ou comme les sauvages, quelque terre fraîchement labourée pour s'en couvrir, purent sauver leur vie. Le plus souvent le torrent du feu passait à une certaine hauteur et ne touchait la terre que dans ses parties élevées. Aussi nul ne pouvait se tenir debout sans être presque instantanément frappé de mort.

Chose plus étrange encore

Certaines personnes, au moment où le tourbillon fondit tout à coup, effrayées et surprises, sortirent dehors pour voir ce qui arrivait et consulter les éléments ; plusieurs assurent avoir été témoins d'un phénomène qui tient du merveilleux. Ils virent un grand objet noir, semblable à un ballon ; cet objet tourbillonnait avec grande violence dans l'air, au sommet des arbres et s'avançait menaçant vers la maison qu'il semblait choisir à son gré. A peine touchait-il la maison que ce ballon éclatait avec grand bruit, comme une bombe remplie de poudre et, à l'instant même, des ruisseaux de feu jaillissaient dans toutes les directions. Avec la rapidité de l'éclair, la maison choisie était enveloppée [85] de flammes au dedans et au dehors de telle sorte que les personnes qui étaient à l'intérieur, le plus souvent n'avaient pas le temps de s'enfuir.

Ravages

Il est assez difficile de mesurer l'étendue du terrain détruit par le fléau, à cause de l'irrégularité de sa marche. Cependant, on peut dire sans exagération que le pays ravagé du sud-ouest au nord-est de Peshtigo ne s'étend pas loin de quinze à vingt lieues en longueur sur cinq ou six en largeur.

Le nombre des morts de Peshtigo, y compris les fermiers des environs, n'a pas été moindre que 1,000, c'est-à-dire à peu près la moitié de sa population. On en a compté au-delà de 800 disparus parmi les personnes connues ; mais que d'étrangers, dont quelques-uns étaient arrivés le matin même, qui n'avaient pas encore été enregistrés nulle part, et dont le nombre restera à jamais inconnu.

Et parmi ceux qui échappèrent à cet enfer de feu, beaucoup sont morts depuis, des suites de l'épreuve, et beaucoup d'autres en meurent encore chaque jour ! Un médecin de Green Bay a prédit qu'avant dix ans, tous ces pauvres échappés, seront [86] morts à cause du ravage que la fumée, l'air, l'eau et le feu ont opéré dans leur constitution. Si la prophétie continue à se réaliser mon tour viendra aussi.

Puissé-je alors avoir fini mon église de Notre-Dame de Lourdes, à Marinette, où il se trouvera quelques âmes reconnais-santes qui prieront pour le repos de mon âme !

Conclusion

[87] Pendant que je passais à Terre Haute (Indiana) en allant à St. Louis, deux mois à peine après la catastrophe que je viens de raconter, je vis dans un journal de cette localité, qu'un orateur Protestant devait le soir même, donner une conférence publique sur ce grand événement. Le sujet de sa conférence était : *Les feux de nos jours, image du feu qui doit dévorer la terre à la fin des temps.* Le sujet m'intéressait trop pour ne pas m'arrêter. J'assistai donc à cette conférence qui n'attira qu'un très petit nombre d'auditeurs, tant il est vrai, que les hommes d'aujourd'hui sont comme au temps de Noé, et comme ils seront aux derniers jours, indifférents à tous les avertissements du ciel.

Le savant conférencier avait groupé, après des recherches laborieuses, tous les grands feux du passé, et s'appuyant deux fois sur mon propre témoignage qu'il avait recueilli dans les journaux, il s'appliqua à montrer la supériorité du feu de [88] nos jours, qui, par l'étrangeté de son caractère, était une image et un précurseur de celui qui doit consumer la terre à la fin du monde.

Et en effet, ce déchaînement des éléments, ce mugissement de la tempête, ce tremblement du sol, ce ciel et cette terre en feu, ces peuples stupéfiés et séchant de peur, n'est-ce pas là la description que les saintes Écritures nous donnent sur les derniers temps ?

Mais pourquoi ces avertissements précurseurs ? et pourquoi tombent-ils inégalement sur des peuples également coupables ?

Qui peut sonder les desseins de Dieu ? Peut-être est-ce parce que Dieu est beaucoup oublié aujourd'hui, surtout par ceux qui le connaissent et devraient le servir. N'est-il pas vrai qu'aujourd'hui beaucoup de chrétiens, marchent, agissent et vivent en un mot, comme s'ils n'avaient ni créateur à obéir, ni sauveur à remercier, ni âme à sauver ? Et s'il est vrai que Dieu a créé l'homme, s'il est vrai qu'il est descendu sur la terre pour le racheter, il a sur lui des droits rigoureux. Ces droits étant méconnus et foulés aux [89] pieds, notre faible raison elle-même nous dit qu'il doit de temps en temps les rappeler et les proclamer par ces grands cataclysmes qui montrent à ceux qui veulent voir qu'il est, quoique nous fassions, notre seigneur et maître et que nous devrions le traiter comme tel. N'est-ce pas ainsi qu'il en agissait autrefois envers son peuple choisi quand il devenait ingrat et prévaricateur ? Les droits de Dieu sur l'homme et les obligations de l'homme envers Dieu sont les mêmes aujourd'hui que sous l'ancienne loi.

Sans doute l'oubli de ces obligations est général, mais aussi quels sont les peuples aujourd'hui vraiment exempts de châtiments ? Le fléau de Dieu se diversifie mais se promène partout. Et si sa justice semble plus pesante sur les uns que sur les autres, si sa voix est plus tonnante et plus terrible ici qu'ailleurs, c'est peut-être parce qu'il désire que dans le châtiment d'un petit nombre, des milliers d'autres entendent l'éclat de sa colère et en profitent pour revenir à lui. Quand il fit pleuvoir le feu et le souffre sur Sodome, l'Ecriture ne dit pas que Sodome était la seule ville criminelle. Dans le châtiment égale à [90] celui de Sodome, dont je viens de faire le récit, Peshtigo, qui n'était peut-être pas plus criminelle que d'autres villes, épargnées cependant, est la Sodome moderne pour servir d'exemple à tous…

Et nunc reges intelligite,
erudimini qui judicatis terram. (Psaume 2)

"Et maintenant, ô peuples, ouvrez les yeux ;
instruisez-vous, ô nations de la terre.

"Commencez à craindre le Seigneur et à le servir, ou tremblez si vous ne vous réformez pas, de peur que le Seigneur vous punisse de mort à cause de vos ingratitudes, car sa vengeance s'enflamme et éclate comme la foudre ; heureux, heureux tous ceux qui mettent leur confiance en lui seul !"

Appendice

[91] Je viens, non pas de faire la description d'un terrible fléau, mais de raconter ce que j'en ai vu et souffert moi-même. Si je me suis exprimé clairement, le lecteur aura pu voir aussi bien que moi le doigt de Dieu dans cet événement. Je sais que je ferai plaisir à plusieurs personnes, en ajoutant au récit qui précède un fait qui montre aussi le doigt de la Sainte Vierge, c'est-à-dire son intervention en faveur de ceux qui mettent leur confiance en elle. Ce fait s'est passé pendant une autre tempête de vent et le feu, qui survint, dans la même nuit, à la même heure que celle dont je fus victime à Peshtigo, mais à neuf ou dix lieues loin de moi ; et cette distance qui nous sépare est formée par les eaux de la Baie Verte.

Je dois nécessairement raccourcir les détails et être prudent dans mes expressions pour ménager la modestie des uns et la délicatesse des autres, parmi les [92] personnes vivantes dont il faut que je parle et qui pourraient lire ces lignes.

Près de Green Bay, dans une langue de terre qui s'avance au nord-est, entre le lac Michigan et la Baie Verte, habite une colonie belge. On pense généralement que leur nombre s'élève de 8,000 à 10,000 âmes. C'est un peuple religieux, simple et industrieux mais la plupart sont très insouciants pour faire donner à leurs enfants l'instruction qu'ils n'ont pas reçue eux-mêmes. Au milieu de cette colonie, se trouve une fille, âgée aujourd'hui de quarante ans environ, dépourvue des dons de la fortune et de la nature, mais riche en dons de la grâce et de la vertu. Elle s'appelle Adèle Brice. Ceux qui l'ont connue enfant en Belgique m'ont dit qu'elle s'était toujours distinguée, dès son bas âge, par une grande piété pour Dieu, une parfaite charité pour le prochain et une entière confiance dans la Sainte Vierge. Et aujourd'hui tout le monde qui l'approche s'aperçoit bien vite, que ces vertus n'ont fait que grandir et se fortifier dans son âme. Il y a dix ou douze ans, cette colonie belge n'avait point de prêtre résidant au milieu d'elle, et cette [93] pieuse fille ne craignait pas de faire chaque semaine, à pieds, et de grand matin, deux lieues et demie pour aller, dans la paroisse voisine, se confesser, entendre la sainte messe et communier, pour revenir en toute hâte reprendre son travail de chaque jour au sein de sa famille pauvre.

Elle revenait un matin après avoir communié. Tout à coup, le long du petit sentier qu'elle sauvait dans le bois, elle aperçoit une Dame majestueuse et toute brillante. Cette Dame se tenait devant elle comme suspendue entre deux arbres, qui bordaient le chemin. La pieuse fille, surprise et émue, mais non effrayée, tombe à genoux, prie, et se relève bientôt. Elle ne dit rien à ses compagnes de ce qu'elle avait vu, mais elles avaient été témoins de son émotion, et cette apparition mystérieuse commença dès lors à se répandre de proche en proche. La semaine suivante, Adèle Brice retourne, comme de coutume, à la paroisse voisine pour satisfaire sa dévotion. En revenant, à la même place, la même apparition se présente à elle, en présence d'un plus grand nombre de compagnes qui revenaient de [94] la messe avec elle. Cette seconde apparition contribua beaucoup à en répandre la nouvelle par tout le bois. On en parlait beaucoup mais d'une manière bien différente. Les uns s'étonnaient, les autres se moquaient ; mais personne encore ne croyait que la Sainte Vierge pût avoir quelque chose à faire avec une fille, qu'ils étaient habitués à regarder en tout semblable à une autre. Cependant plusieurs se promirent de l'accompagner à son prochain voyage et de juger par eux-mêmes. C'est ce qui eut lieu bientôt.

Après avoir fait sa confession, entendu la sainte messe, et communié, Adèle Brice reprend son chemin ordinaire, pour revenir travailler à la ferme de ses parents. Mais cette fois, elle était accompagnée par un beaucoup plus grand nombre de personnes, parmi lesquelles se trouvaient quelques hommes. Chacun s'entretenait en route de l'événement qui faisait grand bruit à travers le bois, chacun se promettait de l'examiner avec soin, s'il se renouvelait, et donnait son opinion à ce sujet. Cette opinion était très variée naturellement. La pieuse fille était calme et confiante, elle avait prié beaucoup pendant [95] la messe, et s'était abandonnée à la divine Providence. Soit qu'on lui en eut donné la pensée, soit que cette pensée lui eut été inspirée d'en haut, elle avait résolu d'interroger cette belle Dame, si elle se représentait devant elle. On arrive à l'endroit du chemin, où la Dame s'était montrée deux fois déjà auparavant...

Tout à coup, elle apparaît de nouveau, mais plus belle, plus brillante et plus souriante que les autres fois. La pieuse fille tombe à genoux, et commence avec cette majestueuse Dame qui, loin de lui inspirer aucune frayeur, lui inspirait, au contraire, une grande confiance, une longue conversation, dont je ne rapporterai que ce qui est nécessaire à mon sujet. Elle lui dit :

"Bonne mère, que voulez-vous de moi."

"Je veux," lui répondit la Dame, "que tu instruises mes enfants. Tu viens de recevoir mon fils, et tu as bien fait, mais ces pauvres enfants le reçoivent sans savoir ce qu'ils font, et grandissent dans l'ignorance de la Religion. Je veux que tu les instruises et surtout, que tu les prépares à leur première communion."

"Comment ferai-je cela, bonne mère, je [96] ne suis qu'une pauvre ignorante moi-même ?"

"Va et ne crains rien. Je t'aiderai."

A partir de ce moment, fidèle à sa mission, on vit cette fille aller de village en village, à travers le bois, en temps de neige, de pluie et de chaleur. Ni les fatigues, ni les moqueries de plusieurs ne purent l'arrêter. Elle réunissait autant d'enfants qu'elle pouvait, et quand elle avait fini sa leçon dans un endroit, elle allait dans un autre. Travail pénible et ingrat, qu'elle a continué plusieurs années. Un bon prêtre enfin fut trouvé pour cette colonie. Ce prêtre conseilla à cette pieuse fille de collecter au dehors une somme d'argent, capable de l'aider à bâtir une école, qui lui permit de réunir les enfants autour d'elle, au lieu d'épuiser sa santé à marcher elle-même à leur poursuite dans le bois. Ce sage conseil fut suivi.

Aujourd'hui, elle possède deux choses qui lui sont bien précieuses : une école, capable de contenir plus de cent enfants qui, chaque année, sont préparés à la première communion ; et une petite chapelle bâtie à la place même où la Sainte Vierge lui apparut, et dans laquelle elle [97] garde, comme une relique, l'arbre sur lequel s'est faite l'apparition. Ces deux maisons sont en bois, simples, mais propres et confortables. Tout autour de ces deux édifices, s'étendent six arpents de terrain qui ont été cédés à cette pieuse fille, et qu'elle-même a cédés à Mgr. l'Evêque de Green Bay. Ces six arpents sont entourés d'une clôture en planches, autour de laquelle serpente un petit chemin par lequel passe la procession solennelle qui a lieu, chaque année, à deux époques fixes ; procession, qui attire plus de quatre mille pèlerins des environs.

L'ouvrage, auquel Adèle Brice pouvait suffire seule au commencement, a considérablement progressé et serait maintenant au-dessus de ses forces. La Providence lui a envoyé du secours. Cinq ou six jeunes filles, aussi pieuses qu'elle, sont venues se joindre à elle, et partagent son œuvre de dévouement.

Voilà le lieu et les circonstances qui l'ont fait ce qu'il est aujourd'hui. Voici maintenant le fait dont je voulais parler et qui va montrer la protection de la Sainte Vierge, sur ceux qui ont confiance en elle :

[98] Le huit d'octobre, 1871, le tourbillon de vent et de feu tomba aussi sur cette colonie belge où il fit aussi, sur plusieurs lieues d'étendue, une grande destruction de fermes et de bois, sans toutefois enlever autant de vies humaines qu'à Peshtigo. Or, quand la bourrasque éclata, les pieuses filles se dirent à elles-mêmes, "Si la Sainte Vierge a besoin encore de nous, elle saura nous protéger, si non, elle nous laissera brûler avec les autres." Animées de ces sentiments de confiance, elles courent dans leur chapelle, prennent la statue de la Sainte Vierge, et, à genoux, elles la portent en procession tout autour du Sanctuaire bien-aimé, en récitant leur chapelet. Quand le vent et le feu soufflaient trop fort sur un côté de la chapelle, et qu'elles ne pouvaient pas avancer, sans s'exposer à être asphyxiées, elles attendaient que la bourrasque diminuât, ou changeât de direction, en continuant à prier et à espérer.

Ainsi se passèrent pour elles de longues heures de cette nuit terrible. Je ne saurais pas dire si, humainement parlant, et avec les seules forces de la nature, elles furent capables de rester vivantes [99] au milieu de cet ouragan, mais je sais bien que, sans miracle, elles ne l'auraient pas pu à Peshtigo.

Le matin venu, on constata les effets déplorables de l'incendie. Les maisons et les clôtures du voisinage, tout avait été brûlé, tout, excepté l'école, la chapelle et la clôture qui entoure ces six arpents de terre consacrés à la Sainte Vierge. Cette clôture avait été touchée et entamée en plusieurs endroits, mais, comme si le feu eût eu l'intelligence de ce qu'il faisait, il s'était arrêté là, pour abattre ou consumer, tout ce qui la touchait, pour ainsi dire, car le chemin qui tourne tout autour n'a pas plus de huit ou dix pieds de largeur. Cette place comme sanctifiée par l'attouchement de la Mère de Dieu, apparaissait semblable à une île verdoyante au milieu d'une mer de cendres... Depuis ce temps-là, ces pieuses filles de Marie continuent leur œuvre de dévouement au milieu de ce pauvre peuple belge, avec plus de courage et de confiance encore, parce qu'elles ont une preuve de plus, que telle est la volonté de la Sainte Vierge.

Réflexion importante

En racontant le [100] fait qui précède, je n'ai nullement l'intention de rappeler un miracle, pas plus que je n'appelle miracle, la préservation de mon tabernacle au milieu du feu de Peshtigo. L'un et l'autre de ces faits m'ont édifié et en les redisant ici je n'ai pas d'autre but que d'édifier les autres.

Je n'ai pas non plus la prétention de rien décider par rapport à cette apparition de la Sainte Vierge et du pieux pèlerinage qui en est résulté. L'Autorité Ecclésiastique n'a rien dit encore ; elle laisse faire le bien sans se prononcer, en attendant quelque preuve plus irrécusable et plus éclatante pour porter son jugement. Evidemment il ne m'appartiendrait pas à moi, de devancer ce jugement épiscopal.

Je n'ajoute qu'un mot : si qu'un de mes lecteurs en a la facilité, je l'engage à se transporter sur les lieux et à aller visiter cet humble pèlerinage, qui est le seul encore, je crois, aux Etats-Unis, et qui ne fait que commencer. Là, il verra, et pourra questionner la pieuse fille, Mlle. Adèle Brice, qui est, sans l'avoir voulu, l'âme et l'héroïne d'une bonne œuvre qui progresse de jour en jour, et je suis sûr, que comme moi, et comme toutes les [101] personnes qui y vont avec une intention droite, il s'en retournera édifié et le cœur content, si non convaincu de la réalité de l'apparition.

FIN

ENGLISH VERSION

The Finger of God Is There!
or A Moving Episode of a Strange Event
Told by An Eyewitness

Reverend Pernin

Missionary to the United States

With the Approbation of His Excellency the Bishop of Montreal

To benefit the Church of Our Lady of Lourdes

Marinette, Wisconsin

Transivimus per ignem et aquam

Et eduxisti nos in refrigerium (Psalm 65)

We passed through fire and through water

But you brought us out from there to give us rest

Montréal Eusèbe Senécal Publisher

Nos. 6, 8, & 10, Rue St. Vincent

1874

Table of Contents

Approbation

[5] We the undersigned, Bishop of Montreal, have read the booklet entitled *The Finger of God Is There*, etc., by the Reverend Pernin, and we have been deeply moved.

As we feel strongly that this work cannot but interest the faithful of our diocese, whose hearts are open to all the afflicted, we earnestly recommend that they read it. We also think it our duty to advise them to keep a copy of this booklet in their homes, so as to read and reread it frequently in the family circle, to have constantly before their eyes striking examples that show how good God is to those whom he wishes to save and at the same time how terrible he is when compelled to visit his avenging arm on those he must punish.

Moreover, sales of this book benefit the church of Our Lady of Lourdes, now being built in Marinette. All will doubtless feel obliged by purchasing it to encourage this excellent work, which will redound to the glory of God and the good of souls.

Montreal, May 24, 1874

Feast of Our Lady of Good Help

+Ignace Bourget, Bishop of Montreal

Preface

[7] Why did it take these two and a half years after the great catastrophe to publish this account? For two main reasons: first, my health, weakened by the ordeal, has been quite uncertain since that miserable time and has not allowed me to involve myself in this work. Second, the many activities to which I have had to devote myself to attend to the spiritual needs of my people, who had lost everything, and the troubles through which I myself have passed took up all my time while leaving me no leisure.

Why write this account today, which, although it concerns an episode of one of the most striking phenomena of our time, is beginning to pass into history, more and more forgotten each day? Two reasons as well: several eminent persons, among them two distinguished bishops, one in the United States and one in England, have urged me to write this account, which in their judgment could benefit many souls. It is my duty to accept their advice, as I hold them in greatest affection and esteem. [8] Second, in publishing these lines I also hope to interest many charitable persons in my work and to win from them the financial assistance I need to bring to a successful conclusion my work of rebuilding in Marinette.

The following two passages, which I translate from two articles published in the New York *Freeman's Journal*, will make sufficiently clear the nature and the difficulties of my enterprise.

New York, June 28, 1873

A desert blooms again

Sunday, June 8th, was a day long to be remembered by the Catholics of Marinette, Wisconsin. It was the occasion of a visit from their Bishop, Rt. Rev. Melcher, of Green Bay, for the purpose of laying the corner-stone of the new Church that is to supply the place of the one destroyed by the devastating and memorable fire of 1871.

There were four Masses celebrated by the Fathers present...

The document placed in the foundation-stone was as follows:

Pius the Ninth being Pope,

Joseph Melcher, Bishop of the Diocese,

U. S. Grant, President of the United States,

C. C. Washburn, Governor of the State of Wisconsin,

A. Druiding, St. Louis, Mo., Architect,

P. Pernin, Pastor of the Catholic Church of Marinette,

and Very Rev. W. Corby, SS. C., Preacher,

many priests being present, besides a vast concourse of people,

this corner-stone was blessed by the Ordinary of the Diocese of Green Bay for this Church, which is a building in honor of the Blessed Virgin Mary of Lourdes, and for the salvation of many.

[9] All this is the index of the endeavors of our esteemed Pastor, Rev. Pernin, to promote the welfare of his people. The parish, although laboring under disadvantages from the loss of their Church and property in the late fire, promises, under his energetic direction, to be one of the most flourishing in this part of the country. With his zeal and labor he cannot fail to win the love and esteem of his parishioners, and advance the cause of holy religion in this place.

The second passage is from the same source, January 18, 1874, sent to the editor of the *Freeman's Journal* on the occasion of my silver wedding, that is, the twenty-fifth anniversary of my priesthood. I will mention only the part of the article that relates to my rebuilding program.

The Catholics of Marinette suffered severely during the fearful fires that about two years ago devastated Upper Michigan and Wisconsin. Their church was destroyed, and they have been struggling ever since to replace it. Their good Pastor, Rev. P. Pernin, has been working very hard, and, with the limited means at his command, has until now only succeeded in getting the new church about half finished.

Father Pernin, although laboring under many disadvantages, did not forget the wants of the children under his charge, and after the most strenuous efforts has succeeded in erecting a parochial school. The zeal of the Pastor has been generously assisted, not only by the Catholic, but by the Protestant portion of the inhabitants; but they have been able to accomplish very little in consequence of the heavy losses they sustained by the fire. The school is not yet open for want of means, but it is hoped that assistance will soon come from some unexpected quarter.

[10] I have dedicated my church to Our Lady of Lourdes, today celebrated throughout the world for the miracles of love and mercy that she spreads everywhere.

It is, I believe, the first church in the United States consecrated to the Blessed Virgin under this new title. By choosing her as an appropriate patron, I have intended to make doubly dear to her the town that already bears her name — for Marinette is just a diminutive of the name Marie — and so to call down on this place her special blessings.

May this loving mother kindly favor my intention and bless the work I have in view!

All of it is in her honor and for the salvation of souls.

Our Lady of Lourdes Church, Marinette (seen in a postcard ~1905), first so named in the United States, commissioned by Pernin of architect Adolphus Druiding (1838–1899) and dedicated in 1876.

Chapter I

Before the Catastrophe

A brief look at the land

[11] Imagine a country covered with dense forests, in the middle of which here and there you suddenly meet, along a few opened roads, a more or less extended clearing, sometimes half a league wide, giving space for a nascent town, or perhaps three or four acres, for starting a farm. With the exception of these little spots where the trees have been cut down, then burned, everything else is forest, wild but majestic. Trees, trees everywhere, nothing but trees as far as you go from the Bay either north or west. These immense forests are bordered to the east by the Green Bay of Lake Michigan and by the lake itself.

The terrain is generally of rolling hills, with valleys where grow cedar and spruce, sandy hills covered with pine, and wide open [12] spaces of soil rich and fertile where are found all varieties of hardwood, oak, maple, beech, ash, elm, and wild cherry.

The climate of the region is generally pretty regular and suitable for the crops that they are beginning to try to grow there and that usually succeed. Rains are frequent and rarely fail to fall at the right time.

The fire's natural causes

Even so, 1871 was an exceptionally dry year. Farmers had taken advantage of that to expand their clearings, cutting down and burning the woods that stood in their way. Hundreds of workers opening a railroad did the same, availing themselves of axe and fire to advance their work. Hunters and Indians range continually over these forests, especially in the fall, when they go upstream to fish for trout and spread through the woods stalking deer. Come evening, they light a big fire wherever they happen to be, prepare their supper, and, laying out the covering that wraps them, [13] sleep peacefully, knowing that the fire will keep away wild animals that might pass near them during the night.

Wisconsin loggers. City of Merrill, Wisconsin *(top)*. *Loading a railroad car.* Manitowish Waters Historical Society *(bottom)*.

The next morning, they go farther on leaving behind them the smoldering campfire that protected and kept them warm without bothering to extinguish it. Farmers and others do the same. The result is that these woods, especially in the fall, are everywhere full of fires lit by human hand that find fuel easily enough with all the leaves and dry branches and spread a good deal. Come a breath of wind to stir them, these fires sometimes grow quite large.

Two or three times before October 8th, wind, encouraged by the dry conditions, had frightened the people of the area and sounded an alarm. A few details on this subject will not be without interest and will serve a better understanding of the buildup to the great happening of October 8th. The catastrophe seems to have enjoyed practicing before the main event and multiplying its warnings.

On Friday September 22, I had gone to Sugar Bush, an area near Peshtigo with [14] quite a number of farms. I had been called for my ministry. While I was there, at an isolated farm, I gave in to the desire for a hunting expedition. So off I go, shotgun on my shoulder, accompanied by a 12-year-old boy who claimed he knew how to guide us through the woods. I go on a fair distance pleasantly hunting pheasant, which abounds in those parts. After a few hours I saw that the sun was setting and I tell the boy we should be heading back to the farm. That's what he tried to do, but he no longer knew where he was and had lost his sense of direction. We hiked, we hiked some more, now right, now left, but the farm was not getting any closer. In less than half an hour of useless exploration we were completely lost, the boy and I. It was nightfall, the moment when nature prepares itself for rest. Not a sound was making itself heard, except that here and there was the sound of a little fire running along the base of the trees without touching them and making the leaves crackle while consuming them and the rustling of the [15] treetop branches, which told us the wind was rising.

We shouted for a long time without being heard. I fired a number of rifle shots as a distress signal. Finally, a faraway voice reached us, then another, then several others coming from different directions. Anxious because we were long overdue, the boy's parents and their farmhands suspected we were in distress and decided to search for us, spreading out to make sure to find us. Before long they heard our cries and rifle shots and got close to us, but a new obstacle stood in the way of our meeting. Fanned by the blowing of the wind, those little fires had joined together and spread a good distance. We found ourselves positioned at the center of a circumference of fire that stretched pretty much all the way around us. The men could not get to us and we could not make it to them without running the risk of burning our feet and being suffocated by the smoke. They were obliged to fight their way through by beating the fire with tree branches to stop [16] its progress long enough for us to escape.

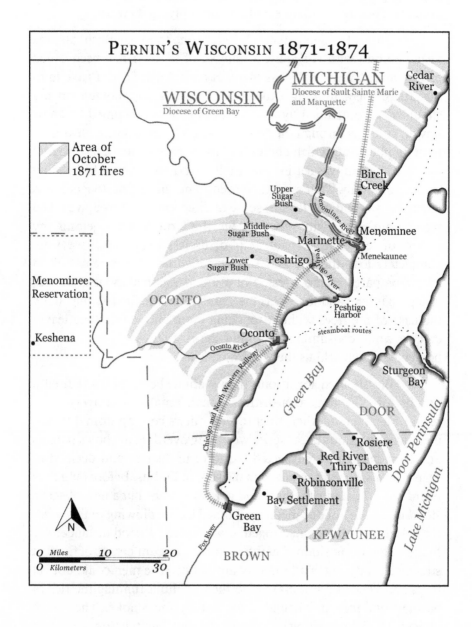

Pernin's Wisconsin 1871-1874

The danger had been much greater in places open to the wind. Returning to Peshtigo the next day I learned that the town had been in great danger during the time I had been lost in the woods. The wind had risen and its force, fanning the flames, pushed the fire toward buildings. I noticed hogsheads filled with water had been placed at intervals all over town in case of new danger.

Something else that happened to me a few days before the great catastrophe:

I was returning by buggy from my second parish, located on the Menominee River about two leagues away. I was peacefully traveling the public road cut through the woods while noticing every so often small fires burning along the way on one side or the other. Abruptly I come to a spot where fire was burning on both sides at once and seemed to have a greater intensity than elsewhere. The smoke that was pushed forward filled the road and obscured it [17] so that I could neither see how hot the fire was nor judge the extent of the danger. I believed that it was not serious because I was traveling in the direction of the wind. So, hesitant at first, I enter the darkness of this cloud of smoke that the fire left behind as the wind pushed it forward. I vigorously urge my horse onward. He balked at moving ahead. Five or six minutes later I emerge at last from this labyrinth of fire and smoke. At that point I find some ten carriages, stopped at the head of the fire that they did not dare challenge.

"Can we get through?" one carriage called out to me.

"Yes, since I just got though myself, but loosen your reins and whip your horse if you don't want to be suffocated."

Some ventured forward, others did not dare and returned to Peshtigo.

Warnings, then, were not wanting. Here is another still more striking example that I translate from an article published in a Green Bay newspaper. It is the account of a battle fought with fire, in Peshtigo, Sunday, September 24 [18] just two weeks before the great catastrophe.

Sabbath, the 24th inst., was an exciting, I might say, a fearful, time in Peshtigo. For several days the fires had been raging in the timber near here between this and Oconto, and to the north and east of us... Saturday the fire burned through to the river about a mile above town, and Saturday night much danger was apprehended from the sparks and cinders that blew across the river, into the upper part of town near the factory. A force was stationed along the river, and although the fire caught in the saw dust, and dry slabs, several times, was promptly extinguished. It was a grand sight, the fire, that night. It burned to the tops of the tallest trees, enveloped them in a mantle of flame, or winding itself about them like a huge serpent crept to their tops, out upon the branches and wound its huge folds about them and [19] hissing and glaring lapped out its myriad fiery tongues while its fierce breath swept off the green leaves and roared through the forest like a tempest.

Ever and anon some tall old pine, whose huge trunk had become a column of fire, fell with a thundering crash, filling the air with an ascending cloud of sparks and cinders, while above being a dense, black cloud of resinous smoke, that, in its strong contrast to the light beneath, seemed to threaten death and destruction to all below.

Thousands of birds, driven from their roost, flew about as if uncertain which way to go, and made night hideous by their startled cries. Frequently they would fly hither and thither, calling loudly for their mates, then hovering for a moment in the air [20] suddenly dart downward, and disappear in the fiery furnace beneath. Thus the night wore away while we earnestly hoped, and many hearts fervently prayed, for rain.

Sunday morning the fires had died down so that we began to hope that the danger had passed. About eleven a.m., while we were sitting in the church... the steam whistle of the factory blew a wild blast... We incontinently left the minister there and rushed out to see what was the matter. Fire had caught in the saw dust near the factory again, but before we reached the spot it was extinguished. The wind had suddenly risen and was blowing a gale from the northwest. The fires in the timbers were burning more fiercely than ever, and were approaching the river directly opposite the factory. The air was literally filled with the burning coals and cinders, which fell and caught frequently, and the utmost diligence was necessary to prevent them from spreading. The engine was brought out and hundreds of pails [21] from the factory were manned, and everything that was possible done to prevent the fire from entering the town.

But now a new danger arose. The fires to the west of the town and south of the Oconto was approaching the town rapidly, and it seemed nothing short of a miracle could save the village from utter destruction. A cloud of hot blinding smoke blew in our faces and made it extremely difficult to see or do anything; but prompt and energetic means were taken to check the approaching flames...

The Company's teams were set to hauling water, and the whole force of over three hundred of the laborers in the factory and mills were on the ground, besides other citizens. Goods were packed up, and moved from buildings supposed to be in most danger and a general conflagration seemed inevitable.

I have seen fires sweep over the prairies with the speed of a locomotive, and the prairie-fire is grand and [22] terrific; but beside a timber fire it sinks into insignificance. In proportion as the timber is denser and heavier and loftier than the prairie grass, is the timber fire intenser, hotter, grander than the prairie fire. The fire on the prairie before a high wind will rush on and lap up the light dead grass and it is gone in a breath. In the timber it may move almost as rapidly but the fire does not go out with the advance waves which sweep over the tops of the trees and catches the light limbs and foliage. Nor is there the same chance to resist the approach of fire in the timber. It is as though you attempted to resist the approach of an avalanche of fire hurled against you.

With the going down of the sun the wind abated and with it the fire. Timber was felled and wet with water thrown over it —buildings were covered with wet blankets and all under the scorching heat, and in a blinding, suffocating smoke that was enough to strangle one, [23] and thus passed the night of Sunday.

Monday the wind veered to the south, and cleared away the smoke. Strange to say not a building was burned— the town was saved. Monday the factory was shut down to give the men rest... At the present writing all is quiet and moving forward as usual...

What did they mean, these repeated alarms that caused such anxiety in people during the three or four weeks that preceded the great event? Doubtless they could be considered the natural consequence of the dryness, of the fires set by human hands, and of the wind that came from time to time to blow and spread these fires, as I just explained. But who will dare say that they were not willed by him who is the master of causes and their effects? Does he not more often use causes in nature to accomplish his will and produce amazing results? It will be difficult for anyone who attended as I did the spectacle of the amazing effects that followed [24] not to see the hand of God in them. If that is true, all the alarms that preceded appeared as warnings of a great catastrophe for which he wanted us to be prepared.

I do not know if anyone thought of them from that perspective, but many were frightened and took precautions against a general conflagration. They dug holes in the earth to bury what they wished to save. The Peshtigo Company saw to the removal of all combustible material that might fuel fire if it started up again and positioned all around town more hogsheads filled with water. Wise precautions, surely, and they would have been effective against an ordinary fire, but in the ensuing event all these human plans were confounded and none of the precautions were to be found sufficient. They served nonetheless to show more clearly *the finger of God* in the phenomenon that soon followed.

As for me I remained indifferent to all the excitement and let events [25] take their course without much effort to fortify myself against them and without very much worrying, a mood far different from that which I would have to live through later on the evening of October 8th.

A word about my two parishes.

Peshtigo

Peshtigo is located on the river of that name, about two leagues from the Bay, to which it had been linked by a small railroad. The Peshtigo Company, with its enterpreneurial spirit, financial resources, and commercial establishments, of which the most noteworthy was a tub and bucket factory that alone employed 300 workers, the Company, I say, spread prosperity to the whole area. The population, including nearby farmers, was about 2,000 souls. Around that time I was finishing construction of a church that people generally thought would be an adornment to the community. My residence was near the church, west of the river, a five or six minute walk. I mention this distance as background to my escape in the midst of the fire.

Peshtigo Company Mill Dam and Sash Factory, 1867.
New York Public Library.

Marinette

[26] Besides Peshtigo I had another much more important parish, located on the Menominee River where it empties into Green Bay. The town is called Marinette, named for a métisse regarded as queen of the savages who lived there. The baptismal name of this métisse was Marie, which changed through use to Marinette, or little Marie, whence the name of the town, Marinette. That is where I am today

building a church in honor of Our Lady of Lourdes. At the time of the fire in Marinette I had a church, a fine rectory just completed that I was about to move into, and also a house under construction meant to serve me as a parish school. The population was almost double that of Peshtigo.

A curious coincidence

Before going into any detail, I must mention a circumstance that will appear providential in the eyes of many, though one brought about by natural causes.

At the time of the catastrophe my [27] church at Peshtigo was just about to be plastered. The work was to have begun on Monday. The lime, the marble dust, everything was ready at the door of the church. The pews had been removed as well as the altar and liturgical furnishings. As I was unable to officiate in church that Sunday, I had announced that there would be no Mass and informed the Catholics of Cedar River that I would spend that Sunday with them. It was one of my missions, located on Green Bay four or five leagues north of Marinette.

The Catholics of Cedar River, Michigan, whom Pernin attended in people's houses, built their first mission church in 1886.

On Saturday then, October 7th, as promised, I leave Peshtigo and proceed to the Menominee wharf to board the steamboat *Dunlap*. I waited there for hours without seeing anything coming, the only time all year that the boat disappointed its customers. We learned later that the *Dunlap* had come as usual but kept offshore and thought it imprudent to land. The weather was lowering, the sky obscured by thick smoke that no gust of wind was blowing away, which made navigation very [28] dangerous, especially near shore. Towards evening, when I despaired of catching my boat, I hitch up my horse again and take the road back to Peshtigo. After I notified the people that Mass would be said in my house the next morning, I arrange in one of my rooms a temporary altar, using for it the tabernacle that I had removed from the church, and after Mass I reserved the Blessed Sacrament in the tabernacle, intending to say Mass again on Monday morning.

In the afternoon, I wanted to leave for Marinette, where I would usually go to sing Vespers and give instruction in the faith whenever High Mass was in Peshtigo, that is, every other week. Those who learned of my intention were strongly opposed. In many minds there was a vague dread of an unknown something that was going to happen. I too in spite of myself felt this vague fear weighing on me. It was more an inkling than a firm belief. As I considered that there was nothing out of the ordinary, I came to the rational conclusion [29] that the danger was only in our minds, without, even so, having reassured myself. And had I not reflected that the Catholics of Marinette thought that I would be at Cedar River and so would not be coming for Vespers, I would surely have gone. As it happened, I stayed where I was and pretended to give in to the vehemence urging me not to go away.

God wished me in the midst of the danger.

The boat that never landed on Saturday, October 7th to take me far from Peshtigo had of course obeyed the conditions that prevented its docking, but is God not the master of all circumstances and is it not he whom they obey? In this way I found myself in Peshtigo Sunday evening, October 8th, a place where by my calculations, my plans, and my arrangements I ought not to have been.

My afternoon went by, I really don't know how, but in any event, in complete inactivity. My mind was prey to that vague uneasiness about ominous developments that I did not know how to define exactly, but on the other hand reason was telling me that there was nothing to fear any more than there had been a week or two before and indeed less [30] because of the precautions taken and the many watchmen who were ensuring public safety. These two conflicted feelings, of which one intruded on me in spite of myself and over which the other had no influence, even though it was the product of rational argument, threw me into a kind of moral lethargy and paralyzed all my energy.

In the wider world, everything served to reinforce those two so different feelings. The thick smoke obscuring the sky, a heavy, stultifying atmosphere, a kind of mysterious silence in the air, the ordinary sign of a storm, made me afraid whenever the wind picked up suddenly. On the other hand, the comings and goings in the street of a hundred young people thinking only of having a good time, their songs, their laughter, their disregard for the weird atmosphere, made me think that it was only me who was worried, and I was ashamed to admit to a feeling of terror that I could not get rid of.

During that afternoon, an older man, unmarried, a Canadian who took great interest in the affairs of the church, came to me to ask permission to dig a well near [31] the church so that we would have water at hand in case of emergency and the plasterer would have it available when he came the next morning. He had not had time to do this work during the week, so I allowed it. When he finished, he came to me to say that now there was water in abundance and added proudly, "Father, I wouldn't trade that well for any amount of money. Now we can easily save the church if there's another fire." He was very tired, so I made him supper and sent him off to get some rest. An hour later he was sound asleep, but God watched over him and, surely in recompense for his love for the church, furnished him the means of saving his life, even though in that same house where he slept more than 50 people perished, awake though they were.

What we do for God is never lost, often even in this world.

Towards seven in the evening, still upset and haunted by that shapeless apprehension, I go out my door to see how my neighbors felt about things. I [32] visit a nice old widow, Mrs. Drees. We walked out together on her field. The wind stirred at times as if testing its strength, then soon abated. She was hardly less worried than I. She urged her children to make preparations, but they refused and laughed at her fears. At one point while we were out on the field, the wind rose stronger than before. I saw here and there old tree stumps catching fire, with no sign of a hot coal or spark that had kindled it, as if that wind had itself been a burning breath, capable on its own of setting them on fire by mere contact. We put out those fires, the wind fell again, and nature resumed her silence, gloomy and mysterious. We went back to the house. I sit down, then stand up again. I had no energy, but I couldn't sit still anywhere. I soon went back home to be alone and try to hide that vague fear that was more and more obsessing me ceaselessly.

While returning home, I looked west, the direction from which the wind had come every time it rose. [33] I discerned above the thick layer of smoke that enveloped the earth something like a reflection in the heavens, red, glowing and immense. Then in the midst of the silence that reigned around me there reached my ears something like a sound of howling, muffled and far away, that announced that somewhere the elements were disturbed. A sudden resolution seized my spirit to get back home immediately and prepare without further hesitation for whatever it was that was certainly about to happen. However listless and indecisive I had been before, I suddenly became active and determined. This decision came as a relief to a spirit previously overwhelmed. I stopped feeling that vague fear that had haunted me. From that moment I was afraid no more, but another feeling intruded itself on my mood all on its own without my having caused it by reasoning: *do not waste too much time safeguarding my things and escape immediately the river.* This was my only thought thereafter, the motivation for all my actions, and that thought was entirely without a feeling of fear or uncertainty. I felt at peace.

Chapter II

During the Catastrophe

[34] It was about half past eight. I think first of my horse. I run to my stable to lead him out and give him freedom in the street, thinking that, whatever happened, he had a better chance of survival being free than tied up in his stall. I then set myself to digging a pit in the sand of my garden, about six square feet wide and seven feet deep. Though the earth was easy to move, it took me a long time to dig it. The air was heavy, the atmosphere unnerving, and that weakened me. I had shortness of breath and difficulty breathing. The only thing that could rouse me to work although I could hardly move my limbs was the certainty, increasingly visible, of a great cataclysm approaching and growing moment by moment.

The redness of the western sky [35] grew visibly, widened, and was more and more enflamed. Between each spadeful of sand from my garden I heard, in the midst of the calm and the silence that crushed us still, this muffled sound, howling and frightfully enormous, that sharpened from minute to minute and brought closer and closer to us the crash of its resounding thunder. The sound was like the jumbled sound of many railroad cars and locomotives approaching a railway station, or the sound of a thousand thunders rolling together in the open sky, the difference being that it never stopped, but swelled and grew ceaselessly as it got closer.

The sight of this sinister fire in the heavens, the noise of those thunderings that ever approached, growing with a horrifying majesty, gave me a superhuman strength.

As I worked like this, I heard two other sounds, human voices that the complete, stunned silence allowed easily and distinctly to reach my ears, without even so distracting me from my work. I must mention them here [36] to show how some did not take the situation seriously enough and how some were fools.

Some were insufficiently serious

An American family, my neighbors, had some people over that evening for tea and conversation. The room where the friends were gathered opened onto my garden. They saw me and I could easily hear them. More than once, I heard the laughter of some of the guests, especially the girls. No doubt they were mocking the trouble I was taking.

Around nine o'clock, the party broke up and Mrs. Tyler, the mistress of the house, came up to me. Whatever a priest does always makes an impression, even on Protestants.

"Father," said Mrs. Tyler, "do you think we are in danger?"

"I have no idea," I tell her, "but I have a bad feeling and I feel the irresistible urge to prepare myself for something extraordinary."

"But if fire were to come, Father," she added, "what should we do?"

"In that case, Madame, escape to the river."

[37] I gave her no reason to do that, I had no reason myself, but it was my obsession.

A little after that, Mrs. Tyler took the road to the river, where she managed to save herself and her whole family. I learned later that of the eight guests she had had to her soirée all but two perished.

Others were foolish

A very short distance from my house, across the street, was a saloon. This house of intoxicating beverage had been filled all day with drunkards. Two hundred young men were said that Sunday morning to have arrived in Peshtigo by steamboat to work on the railroad that was under construction. They had spread throughout the city, where a number had found comrades. Many of them took a room in the saloon right near my house. Perhaps they had been drinking there during the time they might have attended Mass. These young men, most of them drunk at night, were hardly in a fit state to take part in the anxious silence of decent people or to pay any attention to the strange thing going on in the natural world.

Pernin's Peshtigo, October 1871

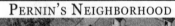

Pernin's Neighborhood

a - Assumption Church and cemetery
b - Area of Pernin's rectory, garden, and stable; of the Drees and Tyler family homes; and of the place where Pernin buried his valuables.
c - Area of the noisy saloon.

From a panoramic map of Peshtigo published a month before the fire in Madison, Wisconsin by Thaddeus Mortimer Fowler (1842-1922). Library of Congress, Geography and Map Division 93681235.

Places
A - Assumption Catholic Church
B - Church cemetery
C - Area of Pernin's house
D - Mill Dam
E - Congregational Church
F - Peshtigo Company Wooden Ware Factory and Warehouse
G - Peshtigo Company Sash Factory and Saw Mill
H - Peshtigo Company Store
I, J - Peshtigo Company boarding houses
K - Site of the house that survived the fire, now 150 S. Beebe Ave.
L - Railroad from Peshtigo Harbor
M - Peshtigo House Hotel

Pernin's Route
1 - Fire leaping between the Saw Mill (G) and the Store (H) prevents Pernin from going right after crossing the bridge.
2 - After crossing the bridge Pernin heads left.
3 - Area where Pernin and others enter the river.
4 - After the fire Pernin is guided to a small valley of sandy hills where he and others recover.
5 - Area of the Company's survivors' tent.
6 - Pernin's post-fire approach to the town.

[38] While I was working in my garden, several of them had come out of the saloon and were standing on the front steps or in the building's yard. It was easy to see that they were drunk, just to hear them fighting, rolling on the ground, and tiring the air repeatedly with savage screams, howls, and horrible profanity.

As I took my first steps into the street on my way to the river when the tempest broke, the wind threw me towards the saloon... a deathly silence was suddenly at work among them, as if their reason had been restored or as if terror had struck them suddenly. I heard outcry no longer. They go inside closing the doors, as if to shut death outside. Two minutes later the house was no more...

What became of them?

I have no idea.

Let me now continue my narrative.

After I finished digging the pit I mentioned, I hurry to bury in it my trunks, boxes filled with my property, my books, my church ornaments, the most precious things that fall to hand, and I cover it all over with sand about a foot deep.

[39] While I was burying my trunks, my housekeeper had herself collected in a basket a number of small, precious silver objects that I had in safekeeping, crosses, religious medals, rosaries, etc., and not knowing what she was doing, went out, ran as far as the †second store†, and dropped her basket off at the doorstep. She returned to collect her cage of canaries, which the blast soon tore away from her hands. Distraught and out of breath, she screamed that I should leave the garden and get out of there.

The wind, forerunner of the storm, was blowing stronger and stronger. The redness in the heavens was blushing a deeper red and the roar of those thousand thunderings seemed now to have been thrown right on top of us, so close had it come. I think only of saving my Blessed Sacrament. I hadn't lost sight of my plan to take it with me. So I run to the room where my tabernacle was. I try to put the key in the lock intending to open it and remove the Blessed Sacrament, that object of objects, most precious of all, especially in the eyes of a priest, but, no doubt because of my hurrying, the key instead of going in the lock gets away from me and [40] falls to the ground. To run around for candlelight to search for it was a waste of time and I had none to waste.

I pick up the tabernacle itself with all that it contained and take it outside. My buggy was there, I put the tabernacle down with the intention of moving it in the buggy since I could not carry it. I said to myself, "I will meet someone on the way who will help me pull my buggy." My tabernacle loaded, I go back into my house to get my chalice, which had not been placed in the tabernacle.

Just then I saw quite a striking phenomenon: sparks that were unexpectedly igniting with the sparkling of gun powder lit by fire fluttered from room to room. My understanding was that the air was saturated with some kind of gas, and if this gas, I thought, ignites on mere contact with a breath of a hot wind, what will happen when the real fire touches the bulk of it, maybe accumulated all in one place...? The phenomenon was menacing, but I was not afraid. I was ready to leave and it seemed to me that I was safe.

I had outside my door, in [41] a cage attached to the wall, a jay that I had kept as a pet for a long time. Everyone knows how birds by instinct can predict a storm. This poor jay jumped, flapped like a lost being, shrieked, and threw himself against the bars of his cage as if to break them and escape. I felt terrible that I could do nothing for him. My two lamps were burning on the table. I bid them my farewells. "Soon," I told them, "you will see a light that will overshadow your own."

I consider most providential a frame of mind that was close to being like a child. It sustained my courage in the hard passage I was about to undergo by hiding from me the horror and the danger. Any other frame of mind, more appropriate to the realities of the situation, would have paralyzed my strength and I would have been lost.

I call my dog, who refuses to come with me and goes to hide under my bed where he burns to death. I run to my fence to open the gate and go out with my buggy. I had scarcely touched the gate, when the wind, violent as it had been for some time, suddenly became a tornado. This tornado came with the abruptness [42] of a thunderbolt and opened the way for me to leave my yard: pickets, gate, fence, everything is instantly removed and flies into space. "The way is open," I said to myself, "let's go!"

Every man for himself

We did leave, but a little late. Impossible to describe the trouble I had standing upright, or breathing, or holding onto the buggy that the hurricane was tearing from my hands, or keeping my tabernacle on it. Getting to the river on one's own even without having anything to take care of was more than one person could do. Many failed and perished on the way. How did I make it? It is still something I wonder about today.

The air was no longer air fit to breath, but a foul assemblage of dust, sand, ash, coals, smoke, and fire. You could not open your eyes, or see your way, or recognize anyone, though the street was full of people and of vehicles that crossed and sometimes crashed into one another. It was every man for himself. Some were heading for the river, others were battling [43] the hurricane and fleeing the river. There was an immense, incredible noise or rather a thousand incredible noises, discordant and deafening, jumbled all together: the stomping of horses, the collapse of chimneys, the crashing of uprooted trees, the screeching hissing of a thousand winds unleashed, the crackling of fire as it ran like lightning from house to house, but no sound of a human voice, as everyone became mute with terror. People crashed into one another without looking, without speaking, without discussion. A deathly silence reigned among the living; nature alone unspeaking made itself heard. When I met vehicles packed with people and fleeing in the opposite direction, it did not even occur to me that it might be worthwhile to follow them. Probably it was the same on their side. Everyone ran inevitably to their destiny.

As I took my first steps into the street, the firestorm throws me to the ground and carries me and my buggy toward the rooming house I mentioned. Further along, I was knocked down onto something unmoving on the ground. That something [44] was a woman and a little girl, both dead. I lifted a head that fell like a lead weight. I take a breath and, without saying a word, I get up to be knocked down again.

At one place along my way to the river I meet my horse, whom I had let loose in the street. Did he recognize me or did he recognize his buggy or did he find himself there by chance? I have no idea, but at a moment I was getting back up from the ground I felt his head pressed against my shoulder. All his limbs were trembling. I stammered his name and signaled him to follow me, but he did not budge. He was found burned to death in that same place.

I got to the river. The buildings along it were on fire. The wind was blowing the fire and its debris over the water. The place was not safe. So, I continue my way over the bridge to cross to the other side. The bridge had already caught fire. There was a frightful pell-mell impossible to describe: everyone thought that there was safety on the opposite side of the river. Those who lived on the east side drove themselves to the west side and those who lived on the west side drove themselves to the east side. This insured that the [45] bridge was blocked by crowds of cattle, vehicles, women, children, and men who were pushing each other out of the way to find an escape.

I made it through this chaos to the other side. My intention was to go downriver, within rifle range below the Dam, where I knew that the ground was flatter and the water shallower, but it was impossible. The sawmill on that side, at the corner of the bridge, was on fire, and the Company's big store across the street was also on fire. The two burning structures combined over the road into one big fire. Crossing that hell would have meant instant death. So, I was forced to go upriver off the bridge to the left, above the Dam where the water gradually became very deep. When I got a certain distance from the bridge, which I feared would collapse, my first concern is to push my buggy in the water as far as possible leaving in it my tabernacle. That's as much as I could do for it.

From then on all I had to think about was my life. The swirling winds in their constant rising had been, [46] so to speak, pumping out the smoke, dust, and ash. We could see clearly. The riverbank, as far as one could see, was lined with people standing, unmoving on the bank. Some had their eyes open and raised to the sky, their tongues stretched out. Most had no idea what to do. Many thought instinctively that there was nothing to do and believed that we had come to the end of the world, as they told me later.

Without saying anything — my struggle to have gotten only that far with my buggy had put me out of breath and the violence of the turmoil prevented my voice from articulating anything distinctly — I push into the river those who were right next to me. One person unpleasantly surprised by the water got out immediately and lets loose a half muffled cry, "I'm getting all wet." But it was better to moisten than to burn. I got hold of that person and together we dragged ourselves in as far as we could. At that very moment I hear along the whole shore a clattering of the waters. Everyone had followed my example. It was time. There was no air to breathe, the heat was more intense. [47] A few minutes later no one could have withstood it.

In the water

It was about ten o'clock when we entered the river. I did not know how long we would stay there, or what would happen to us, and yet, surprisingly, my destiny had not worried me at all from the moment when, yielding to the impulse that urged me interiorly to prepare myself for danger, I had resolved to go to the river. I was and I remained under that same feeling of lightheartedness, which allowed me to struggle against the greatest obstacles and to pass through the most terrifying dangers without even realizing that my life depended on it. As soon as I was in water up to my ears, I thought I was protected from fire, but it was not so. The fire ran on water as on land, the air was full of it, or rather the air was fire. The fire set our heads on fire.

We had to hit the water with our hands and splash it again and again over our hair and the parts of the face that the need to breathe prevented us from putting under. This is what I did continuously. Clothes, blankets [48] had been thrown into the river, presumably to preserve them from the fire. We saw them floating on all sides. I grab some that come to hand to cover the heads of those who huddled on me and hung on my shoulders. These clothes dry quickly in the furnace of heat and catch fire as soon as you stop keeping them wet.

The horrible tornado that had started when I left my yard, with its ceaseless twisting of opposing winds, had, as I said, cleared the atmosphere. The river was bright, brighter than day, and as we looked upstream and downstream at all those heads peeping above the water line, some bare, some covered, all those hands splashing the water and throwing it copiously on their heads, we all saw a sight impossible to describe, a beauty bleak and awe-inspiring, and so far was I from the fear and anxiety that ought to have overcome my spirit, sometimes I could even see the comic side of this strange show and laughed at it to myself.

When, turning my sights away from the river, I looked beyond, to the right, to the [49] left, to the heavens, I saw nothing but fire. Everything was burning, the buildings, the trees, and the air. Above my head, as far as my sight could extend into space, alas! too well illuminated, I saw nothing but flames, huge volumes of flames, covering the sky and rolling on top of one other in their violent movement, like an ocean of storm clouds we see rolling its waves when a terrible tempest torments the air.

Near me, on the riverbank, stood the factory warehouse, a huge three-story facility, filled with tubs, buckets, and other products. Sometimes I thought if the wind decided to shift we could be covered with the burning debris from the warehouse, but I didn't care much. From the time I entered the water, I saw this establishment catching fire. Its destruction did not take long. In less than a quarter hour its large beams were on the ground and the rest was burned or carried off into space.

Some incidents

Near me was a woman supporting herself on a log to keep above water. A cow appeared. [50] There were some ten of these animals that instinct drove to the river and so saved their lives. This cow swam into the log, knocked the woman off it, and she sank into the water. I thought she was lost, but then I saw her with one hand hanging onto one of the horns of the cow and with the other splashing her head from the river. I do not know how long she was in this critical situation, but I learned later that the cow swam towards shore, taking its load with it, and so what might well have destroyed this woman was precisely what saved her.

Another woman, just as I entered the river, arrives breathless and terrified. She was leading a child by the hand and thought she had another rolled in a bundle of messy rags that she had probably picked up in a hurry and that she was holding tightly in her arms. Oh terror! As she opened the bundle to look for her child, she doesn't find him there anymore. She must have let him slip out along the way. Nothing can portray the disbelief of this mother. A cry half articulated and half muffled escapes from deep inside her, "Ah, my child!" Then she tries to get through [51] the crowd and throw herself into the deep water. The whirlwind was weaker over the water than on land and we could speak. I tried with a few words to mislead this mother by telling her that her child had been found and saved, but she did not even look at me. Her eyes were fixed, unmoving, and bent on reaching the river's other shore. I lost sight of her. I later learned that she managed to throw herself into the deep water where she found death.

Peshtigo riverbank and bridge today, across from where Pernin and friends entered.

Things went well enough for me during the first three or four hours of this overly prolonged bath, thanks, I think, to the movement I made as I continually threw water on my head and on that of my neighbors to keep the flames at bay. It was not the same for some of the people alongside me. I could feel in the water the legs of one woman shivering, her teeth chattering. People began to react as the cold penetrated their limbs. I feared that staying in the water too long would cause cramps and then death. So I tried to gauge what the temperature was by [52] going back a little towards shore. But hardly were my shoulders out of the water when I heard a voice cry out, "Father, you are on fire!"

The time had not yet come to emerge from this prison of water and fire. The struggle had to go on. A lady who hadn't left me since we entered the river and who, like everyone else, had said nothing until then said to me, "Father, don't you think that this is the end of the world?"

"I don't believe it is," I replied, "but if all countries have been burned like ours seems to have been, it won't be long before the end of the world comes for us." She fell silent and so did I.

Everything here below eventually ends, even misfortune. The time was coming for a possible return to land. Already we could do without splashing water on ourselves. I went back to shore and sat down on a log, that way being only half submerged in water. And then my every limb began to shiver. A young man noticed and threw me a blanket for over my shoulders. I felt a little more comfortable and soon after I was finally able to emerge from the obligatory bath that had lasted about five and a half hours.

Chapter III

After the Catastrophe

Prostration

[53] I emerged from the river around half past three in the morning. From then on, I was quite a different person, in my spirits and especially in my body. And today as I recall these memories I see that the moment when I ran the greatest danger to my life was precisely when you would have thought that I had already managed to escape. The atmosphere, which had been as hot as a furnace, was gradually cooling off. It didn't take much cold to affect someone who had been in the water so long. I was very affected. My clothes were soaked with water. There was no lack of fire and I could dry my outer garments, but my underwear stayed damp and froze me. Moisture had penetrated my bones and especially my lungs. My every limb shivered [54] even next to the hottest charcoal fires left behind by the collapse of buildings. In a word, I experienced a complete prostration of body and mind. I could hardly move. I thought I was going to die and I didn't care. I felt my lungs tightening as if in a vise and my throat was swollen. I couldn't speak. I scarcely had the energy to do anything to bring myself back to life.

Exhausted and half dead, I stretched out on the sand of the shore. This sand was still hot; its warmth revived me a little. I take off my shoes and socks to put my feet more in contact with the warmth of the ground, which felt good.

I was next to the big factory warehouse whose beams were burning on the ground. Tub and bucket hoops were stacked amid the debris, which was still burning. There were many piled one on top of another. I touched them with my hands intending to hang my socks on them to dry, but I found them too hot and dared not entrust them with my shoes or [55] socks because they were all I had left. However, something I still wonder about today, there was a large number of men lying on their stomachs stretched out motionless over these iron hoops. Were they dead? or waterlogged and looking for the heat that

I sought in the sand? I have no idea. I was too wiped out myself to deal with them.

Just then too my eyes started hurting terribly, the same thing, more or less, that happened to anyone who had not kept them covered during the long firestorm. Although there had always been water flowing over my face, the heat had affected them considerably, without my noticing it at first. The cruel baking that I experienced in my eyes, together with the paralysis of all my strength, kept me lying on the sand a long while. Its heat was reviving me.

When I felt the strength, I took off my wet clothes one at a time, dried them in a charcoal fire in the warehouse, and put them back on dry and hot. No one's modesty [56] had been offended. Everyone did the best they could and no one was paying attention to what their neighbor was doing. This procedure brought me great relief, I could breathe more easily, my chest was less constricted.

Finally day came to dawn on this landscape of horror and destruction that no one had yet seen. People came to invite me to move to another place on the shore where everyone was gathered. I tried to follow the others, but I couldn't. The inflammation in my eyes had increased, I couldn't open them, and I was completely blind. Someone gave me their hand and led me to that place where others were already. It was a small valley at the edge of the water, sheltered on all sides by hills of sand. It was just the place where I had intended to take refuge during the whirlwind of the previous night. Some people had successfully fled there and were comparatively much less ill-treated. The turmoil of flames had passed too high in the air to reach this place. The shrubs and grass [57] that grew there were not touched.

So there we all were, gathered in that valley like the surviving wreckage of a battle, some safe and sound, others injured to varying degrees. Some were badly injured, especially a good old woman who, without strength enough to enter the river, had been lying on the edge, part of her body in the water and the other out of the water and therefore exposed to fire. She was lying there on the grass, horribly burned. She suffered excruciating pain, to judge by her screams. As she was going to die and asked for me, someone took me to her. But I was a poor comforter. I couldn't open my eyes to see her. I could barely speak and felt too shattered myself to give her courage. She died some time later.

Pernin's small valley of refuge made by hills of sand seen today from across the Peshtigo River.

Those of us who had the strength dispersed around town for information about family members whom they had not yet seen and came back bringing us frightful news about the ruins of the place and of people burned whom they claimed [58] to have seen. One of these explorers came to find me. He told me that he had crossed to the other side of the river, that all the buildings had burned down including the church, and that he had seen many people dead along the roads and so disfigured by the fire that he couldn't recognize them. "Well," I tell him, "in that case, we will all go to Marinette. I have a big church there, a nice house that has just been finished, and a school. I have room for a lot of people."

Towards eight o'clock, they pitched a large canvas tent where we were, which the Company had arranged to bring in, to shelter the injured, the children, and the ladies. It was barely set up when someone came to urge me to rest there. I went right away, I lie down in a corner, I make myself as small as possible to leave room for others. But the Company employee who had been given responsibility for organizing the tent had not had his eyes burned during the night. He saw me right quick. He was one of those tough, coarse men who seem only ever to have lived with [59] wolves.

However, he had tender compassion for the ladies, and he wanted no one but ladies under his tent. No sooner was I lying scrunched up in the corner when he began to disgorge a torrent of insults and profanity against me ordering me to get out. I responded not a word. I did an about face, rolled on my side under the canvas, and found myself outside his tent. One of the ladies present answered this blasphemous brute for me and tried in vain, I think, to teach him some manners. I never knew the name of that man and of that I'm very glad.

Picnic on the grass

Nine o'clock arrived. Ten o'clock. After the ordeal of such a night, you can imagine how nice a little tea or hot coffee would have been. But where to find something so luxurious in the middle of a ruined desert? A few young people scoured the surroundings and came back with a bunch of cabbages from a nearby field. We removed the outer leaves, which were burned. The good parts we cut into thin slices and served to those who felt able to eat them. A piece of cabbage, [60] raw and cold, was hardly restorative for beings as exhausted as we were, but what was there to do when there was nothing better?

Finally, people in Marinette learned of our fate and around one o'clock sent us vehicles loaded with bread, coffee, and tea. These vehicles were also to return with as many as they could carry. I was eager for news of Marinette. I spoke to one of our rescuers. "Was there also a fire in Marinette?"

"Oh! we were scared, but thank God no one was killed. We lost only houses."

"Houses?"

"Yes, Father, almost all the houses and mills starting from your church to the Bay."

"And my church?"

"It burned."

"And my nice rectory?"

"It burned."

"And my school?"

"Burned too."

"Can it be? and I had promised to take the poor unfortunates of Peshtigo to Marinette!"

So was everything taken from me at the same hour, my two churches, my two rectories, my school, all that my churches possessed, [61] and all that I possessed personally.

General state of feeling in Marinette and Menominee

Between one and two o'clock I left in one of the wagons for Marinette and after arriving there stayed for some time at the residence of one of my parishioners, Mr. F. Garon, receiving under his hospitable roof all the care my condition required.

The two banks of the river, respectively named Marinette and Menominee and which united formed another parish, were strangely changed in appearance. These two sister towns, one situated on the south and the other on the north side of the river, were no longer recognizable. Life and activity had entirely given way to silence and a kind of woeful stupefaction. Only a few men were to be seen walking around, looking after their property or asking for details of the conflagration at Peshtigo from those who had just arrived from that ill-fated spot. No women were to be seen in the streets or even in the houses, which had been abandoned. The children too, with their joyous cries and noisy mirth, had disappeared from the scene. These shores, a short while since so animated, now resembled a desert and it was a movement of overwhelming and uncontrollable terror that had created this, as it were, solitude, the terror of the night before when the tempest of fire came surging on from Peshtigo, consuming all that part of Marinette that lay in its path.

Learning of the fate that had overtaken Peshtigo further increased this general feeling of alarm until it culminated in a perfect panic. Dreading a catastrophe similar to that of Peshtigo's, many families rushed to the Bay, embarking on the steamers *Union*, *Dunlap*, and *St. Joseph*, which had been kept near the shore so as to afford a refuge to the terrified inhabitants. The consternation was indescribable and one unfortunate man arriving at the boat panting and breathless fell dead from fear or exhaustion.

These boats afforded anything but a safe place of refuge, for if the conflagration had broken out as suddenly and raged as fiercely as it had at Peshtigo, nothing could have preserved them from the flames and the only alternative left to those on board would have been death by fire or water. Fear, however, is generally an untrustworthy counsellor and the expedients it suggests remarkably ill-chosen. The inhabitants of Marinette and Menominee passed the night of October 8th dispersed in the different boats and it is unnecessary to add that few slept during those hours of strange anxiety.

Terror effectively banished slumber, producing the result fear generally does on the Christian soul, turning it instinctively to prayer, even as the terror-stricken child casts itself into the arms of the mother it has summoned to its help. What are we, poor mortals exposed to the wild fury of the unchained elements, but helpless children?

The Catholics who were present fell to their knees with one accord and prayed aloud, imploring the ruler of the elements to stay his vengeful arm and spare his people. They prayed without shyness or human respect. Doubtless, there were present those who had perhaps never learned to pray or who had forgotten how to accomplish that all important duty and these latter might in other circumstances have felt annoyed at such public manifestations of devotion. But in this hour of common peril all hearts involuntarily turned toward heaven as their only resource. There were no expressions of incredulity, impiety, or bigotry evinced by anyone. The Protestants who were present, being unacquainted with the Catholic formula of prayer, could not unite their supplications with those of the Catholics, but they encouraged them to continue their devotions, and when they paused, begged them to start again.

Danger is a successful teacher, its influence immediate and irresistible. No reasoning succeeds so quickly in making men comprehend the greatness of God and their own insignificance, his almighty power, and their own helplessness. Nothing else detaches souls so completely from earth and raises them towards him on whom we all depend. The preceding details, furnished by individuals coming and going from the boats, were full of interest to me. During this time, I remained with my kind host Mr. Garon, being too ill to leave the house.

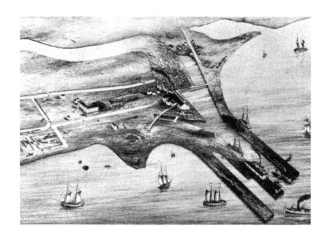

Peshtigo Harbor, 1871. Wikimedia Commons.

The intensive ministrations of which my parishioners made me the object got me back on my feet fairly quickly. From Tuesday evening I was able to visit a few people who were burned to varying degrees and prepare them for death as best as I could, utterly lacking where I was everything necessary in those circumstances. I felt strong enough, so I decided to return to Peshtigo during the night of Tuesday and Wednesday. So, in the evening I made my preparations. The clothes I was wearing had been badly damaged in the river and I wanted to clean up and change my clothes, but I did not succeed. The stores, fearing the fate of Peshtigo, had packed and buried all their goods. I could find only the coarse, khaki pants laborers wear to work in the sawmills. I took them faute de mieux and at ten o'clock in the evening embarked on a steamboat that was leaving that night for Green Bay, putting in at the port of Peshtigo. The night was quite [62] stormy and it was not until daybreak that the vessel dared set out. On a very heavy sea we arrived at Peshtigo Harbor around nine or ten in the morning. I stayed for a few hours attending there also a number of ailing people, wreckage destroyed to varying degrees by the fire.

Return to Peshtigo

At one o'clock in the afternoon a wagon was leaving to take the men who in the aftermath of the fire were going every day, morning and evening, to seek and bury the dead from the town of Peshtigo. I took a place with them. The Company locomotives had been burned, so horses substituted. In that way we proceeded until we came to where the fire had passed. We went the rest of the way on foot, a distance of about half a league. This allowed me to contemplate from a distance and from up close the ravages and ruins of the storm.

Alas! Though forewarned by all that I had heard people say, I was not prepared to see the horrible spectacle that presented itself before my eyes.

View of the battlefield

It is sad to have to speak of that which no one [63] can express and no expression can portray. It was Wednesday afternoon, October 11, when I saw again the place where Peshtigo had been. I no longer found anything of that which, three days before, had existed, not trees, not fences, not houses. All had been consumed. Some charred debris remained standing, to show the fury of the devastation that had passed by this place. Whichever way we went, we walked on ashes. The railroad tracks had been bent and twisted; their wooden supports had vanished. The lower tree trunks had been shrunk, the heart that remained upright was as if petrified. Surrounding the stumps, I noticed a multitude of holes going down into the earth. This was where the roots had been. I stuck my walking stick into these deep holes, wondering what it was with this fire that, not content to devour what was on the surface, had carried its devastation to the bosom of the earth. To my astonished eyes appeared nothing of where the town had been except the boilers of two locomotives, [64] wagon wheels, and the factory's stone and brick work. The rest was now only a desert, but a desert that was crying and making people cry, as a field of battle after a murderous melee. Here and there were charred bodies, of steer, of cows, of horses, of hogs. Those of men, women, and children had already been recovered and buried; you could count them by counting the small mounds of earth freshly disturbed.

Finding streets again was a difficult problem. I found it very hard to make my way in the middle of this desolation and find the place where my house had been. When I got there, I look for the place where I had buried my trunks. I see on the ground, on the sand, the spade I had dug with and that I had thrown some distance away. Half the handle was burned, the rest remained intact. I used this ruin to uncover my things. When first I stirred the sand, it breathed out a suffocating odor, like that of sulfur. At first glance I thought my linen had been preserved. The only places where it was [65] blackened were where it had been folded. The rest had not changed color, but when I touched it, it fell apart, it could no longer hold together, as if the heat had cooked it *à l'étouffée* or an electric current had crossed it.

Again, all was lost.

Some charred bricks, melted glass, crosses, crucifixes pretty much destroyed, alone indicated the place where my house had been, and the charred carcass of my dog where my bedroom had been. I then go down the road that went from my house to the river and that I had followed the night of the storm. There, the carcasses of animals were more numerous than anywhere else, especially on the approaches to the bridge. I saw again my poor horse in the same place where I had met him, but so disfigured that only with great difficulty was I was able to assure myself that it was in fact he. His body was swollen by the effect of the heat; his side had burst and was letting out some of his roasted entrails.

[66] Those who own a horse whose services are pleasant to them will not be surprised that I speak twice of mine. There is between the master and his horse a sympathy like that which exists between two friends and which survives even death.

Wandering these ruins I soon met some living beings, some of whom approached and began to converse with me. Over there, one of them was a father seeking one or two of his children and who had as yet found nothing. "If I could only find their bones," he said to me, "but the wind must have blown away whatever the fire left behind." Over here, children sought their father, brothers sought their brother, husbands sought their wives. But I saw no women. There were no longer any of them in this scene of horror that they would not have been able to contemplate.

And all these men, these seekers for the dead, had all in various ways suffered in the battle against the wind and the fire. Some had had a hand burned, others an arm or side. All were [67] half covered in bits of clothing blackened and ragged, looking themselves, in their sadness and in the way they dressed, like a ruin amidst these ruins.

They pointed out to me the places where they had found so and so. "There a mother was found lying face down, hiding in her bosom the child she had vainly tried to protect from the fire."

"Here a whole family, father, mother, and children, all burnt to ash and shrunken by the heat."

"In the ruins of the Company boardinghouse there were nearly 70 people so disfigured that no one could tell their sex or age."

"Down there, in this well, we recovered 16 bodies."

"One of the workers on our church had his knife in his hand, his throat was cut, two of his children had their throat cut as well, but not his wife, dead and roasted near them."

This man was named Towsley. He had indeed worked on my church in Peshtigo during the whole summer. Doubtless seeing his wife fall near them and the utter impossibility of escaping the fire, he lost his mind, and, to escape the horrors of a death by fire, he [68] took his knife and sliced off his children's heads and then his own. This horrible madness of suicide repeated itself in many other places and was brought about by the same causes.

These stories, combining their horror with the frightfulness I saw before my eyes, froze my soul with terror.

No rope to hang a villain

Alas! must we take note of an incident that should never have happened in the middle of such a scene as that? While I was facing the painful emotions I have just spoken of, my attention was drawn elsewhere by the sound of human voices announcing some new happening. This is what it turned out to be: in the midst of the general consternation was encountered a man vile enough to dare insult death and the great sorrow it inspired in all. This man, to satisfy his greed, was desecrating dead bodies, stripping them of property that the fire had spared. He had just been caught in the act. A sort of jury is formed, his punishment is put to the vote, and unanimously he is condemned to be hanged on the spot. But [69] how to do it? where to find a rope? the fire had left nothing. Instead of rope someone has the idea of using an iron chain, one of the ones used to transport logs. The chain is brought and put around his neck; but this difficult procedure is taking too long. The culprit begs for mercy. Pity, which the desolate field did inspire in everyone, descends on the soul of the judges, who let him go free, after having made him beg forgiveness on his knees for his sacrilegious acts of desecration. Maybe they just wanted to scare him.

As soon as I knew the outcome, I went off by myself, away from the noise and the commotion. I needed to be alone. So I make my way out of town a little on Oconto Avenue, where I had seen so many vehicles rushing along, turning their back to the river at the moment I was actually on my way there pulling my tabernacle. I didn't go far before seeing more than I would have liked. Everything had perished on this side, and perished in piles, for the cars were loaded with people who, while trying to flee death, encountered one quick and horrible. In the [70] places where the fire had gotten them there were only wheel rims to find. The rest was but a heap of burnt flesh, charred bones. It was difficult to distinguish the remains of horses from human remains. Company workers were busy untangling these remains, which they buried by the side of the road while waiting for their relatives, if they had any left, to have the chance to identify them and give them a more suitable burial.

I let them continue their sad labor and returned to the place where my church had been. There too everything was ash, all except my bell. Amazingly, my bell had been thrown 50 feet away. One part had stayed intact and the other half had melted and lay on the sand in silvery leaves. The sound of this bell had been the last sound I heard in the midst of the firestorm. That gloomy sound still rings in my ear and reminds me of the horror it presaged. My cemetery was adjacent to the church. I was waiting for a burial, which soon came. He was a young man who died the day before from the horrific burns he had suffered. What [71] a poor ceremony! Never has a priest more destitute of what such an occasion requires tried to conduct a burial service. No church to attend for prayer, not even a house, no surplice, no stole, no sacramentary. Nothing but prayer and a blessing from the heart. I had found the lack of what I needed even sadder before this, on the three or four occasions when the dying asked me for extreme unction, which I could not give them.

I left the cemetery with a heavy heart and headed out to cross the river and look for my tabernacle, of which I knew nothing yet. A great consolation awaited me. It could never have come at a better time.

My tabernacle

I crossed the river over the wreckage of the bridge's joists, which had been rearranged so as to offer passage to those who dared tread. The passage was very dangerous. No sooner was I on the other side than one of my parishioners enthusiastically ran up to meet me: "Father, do you know what happened to your tabernacle?"

[72] "I know nothing at all, what happened to it?"

"Come and see, Father. Oh, it is a great miracle!"

So, I went to the place on the river where I had let go of the buggy carrying my tabernacle, pushing it as deeply into the water as possible. The buggy had been lifted in the turmoil and flipped over on its side; the tabernacle had been taken up by the wind and thrown on the logs that covered part of the water. Everything had been more or less touched by the fire, charred, and blackened, logs, crates, trunks, everything that floated on the water. My tabernacle stood up straight there in the middle of that rather smoky blackness in all the brilliance of the whiteness of its paint, just as it was before. I left it there where the firestorm had thrown it for two days to give everyone a chance to see it. It did a lot of good, but not as much as it would have at another time. All those who spent time at this scene of horror had too much of their own situation to think about and in spirit were too troubled by the loss of those they were mourning. Catholics generally regarded [73] the event as a miracle. Talk spread quickly and it made a great sensation.

Alas! everything fades in human life, especially the good intentions prompted either by a time of trial or by divine blessings. They die away amid the events and concerns of this life and are forgotten. How many are there today among the rare survivors of Peshtigo who still see God both in the punishment they experienced and in the preservation of my tabernacle, which struck them so strongly at the time?

When I had finished the work that kept me three days on these sad shores, I took my tabernacle from the middle of the river and sent it on to Marinette, where I was soon to go to celebrate Mass. When the time came, I forced the door and opened it. Something as stunning as its preservation during the fire! I found the consecrated host intact in the ostensorium. The violent jarring it had weathered had not even made the holy ciborium open. The water had not penetrated inside and the fire had respected inside as well as out, including even the [74] light silk fabric that lined the sides. All was found in a perfect state of preservation.

This tabernacle, this ostensorium, and this holy ciborium, which have no intrinsic value, have an inestimable value in my eyes. I hold them as precious relics and never look at them or touch them without feeling penetrated with sentiments of veneration and love as I have never experienced even while touching objects of the same nature under a form more beautiful or rich. In my small chapel in Marinette, which temporarily takes the place of my church burned two years ago, it is the same tabernacle that is on my altar, still containing the holy ciborium and ostensorium saved from the fire. I use them every day with pride and regard them as trophies given by God and snatched from the enemy.

Let us return to the Peshtigo River that I left to talk about my tabernacle. I will not have to take much more time over it.

Before recovering my tabernacle from its position on the logs I spent three days and two nights, sometimes busy assisting in the search for the dead, [75] sometimes fishing out from the river objects that I had thrown by the armful into the buggy when I left my house and that had spilled over with it into the river. The most precious of all was my chalice, which I was quite happy to find, as well as the paten. A drop in the water level helped me greatly. The Dam had been opened and released the waters of a reservoir normally 15 to 20 feet deep. This procedure was necessary to finding the bodies of people who had been seized by cramps or swept away by the current and drowned during the night of the hurricane.

During those three days, our only accommodation was a canvas tent, the benefit of which I had been denied the previous Monday. It was our shelter for meals, which we ate standing up and with our fingers, and at night it sheltered our sleep. By "our" I mean those who were used to sleeping in the open and were capable of falling asleep in such a place. I was not. Our beds were very economical. River sand [76] served us for a mattress and one blanket was shelter from the cold.

During one of those days I learned of Chicago's fate. A doctor who had come from Fond du Lac to treat burn victims brought the newspaper with him and read to us the terrible devastation of fires that occurred, strangely enough, on the same night, almost at the same time, not only in Peshtigo, but in many different localities, and especially Chicago. This Chicago fire, proclaimed by the thousand voices of journals and telegraphs, was quickly reported all over and stirred great feelings of compassion for the unfortunate city. This turned the world's attention very much away from the far greater and more destructive devastation of which we were the victims.

On the afternoon of Friday the 13th, I had almost finished my work along the sad Peshtigo River. Most of the victims found had been buried and all the injured taken in different directions. Exhausted from fatigue and hardship, I could hardly take any more in this state of destitution and sleep deprivation. A wagon that [77] had come to bring supplies was about to return to Oconto. I took the opportunity to leave: I had friends there who were impatiently waiting for me. I stayed two days resting with the excellent Father Vermare, pastor of the French church. The following Monday, I left for Green Bay finally to visit my bishop, His Excellency Joseph Melcher, alas!, dead today as I write these lines.

The most contradictory rumors had circulated about me, as happens. Some said that I was burned in my church where I had gone to pray during the storm. Others had me burned in my house and others had me drowned in the river. Upset, naturally, by all the reports that my presence reminded him of, His Excellency looked at me and cried out, brisk as usual, "Oh! So there you are, finally, I was very worried about you! Why didn't you write me?"

"Excellency, I couldn't," I replied. "I had no paper, no pen, no ink, nothing but river water."

He then generously invited me to take whatever I might [78] need either from his library or from his closet. I declined, telling him that I still had plenty of parishioners on the Menominee River and that it was up to them to help me and not him. Then he appointed me to another parish saying that I had suffered enough

Joseph Melcher (1806-1873), first Catholic bishop of Green Bay (1868-1873), supported Pernin's establishing Our Lady of Lourdes parish. Diocese of Green Bay.

to deserve a rest and that by staying with my half destroyed congregation I would have to suffer too much more. But as I considered the misfortune of my people left without a priest at a time when they needed him the most and how important it was that they keep the one who was already accustomed to loving them and would more willingly share their poverty, I won his permission to stay.

The sufferings I had endured, however, began to reveal the damage they had done to my constitution, so much so that His Excellency told Father Crud, a pastor in Green Bay who had invited me to preach on All Saints' Day, that he should not count on me, that the fire had scrambled my brain. I do not know if it was so, but I did know very well that I was terribly weak. But in the hope [79] of recovery after a few months' rest, I decided to travel to restore my health and to profit by my trip in the interest of my ruined parishes. My intention was to go all the way to Louisiana and return from the east, but soon I had to recognize that my strength betrayed my determination.

When I got to St. Louis, I was attacked by a prolonged fever that laid me low every day for three or four hours, which contributed little to my regaining my strength. So I didn't go any farther. The good people of St. Louis showed me great kindness. I made friends there that I will never forget and whom it will always be a pleasure to see again. I will not mention their names here, but they are written in my heart in indelible letters. I can do nothing by myself to show them my gratitude, but I will mention their names to the very good and very powerful Our Lady of Lourdes in the church dedicated to her in Marinette. She will make up for my incapacity.

I have just said that the people of St. Louis have a right to my thanks. It would be unjust to pass over [80] in silence those of my parishioners and my friends in Wisconsin who spontaneously offered me the immediate help my emergency called for. I do not forget them either. It is a pleasure for me to recall those heartfelt impulses, like that of one of my friends from Oconto who wanted me to accept his offer of clothes more decent than those that I was wearing after the fire and that I declined to take. "I want you to," he said, "because I know that if I were in your place you would want to do me the same service."

Some details beyond my story

I would like at this point to take note of some of the extraordinary phenomena and peculiarities of this strange fire even if I was not an eyewitness to many of them. I was too much at the center of the devastation to see what was happening at a distance. It is not the soldier in the midst of battle who best can see the whole and the details, but the one who contemplates the plain from the perspective of higher ground.

The force of the firestorm

Forests of enormous maple trees, clamped securely and deeply to the ground, were uprooted, broken, and twisted as easily as one twists [81] a hazel switch. A tree left standing here or there was an exception. They could be seen piled up and lying on top of one another every which way, their branches reduced to ashes and their trunks charred and blackened. Some claim to have seen in the flow of the fire large wooden houses lifted from their spot by two opposing currents and blown away like a straw in the wind and only then catch fire and instantly disintegrate to ash.

The speed of the whirlwind, however, which was wind and fire at the same time, was in no way proportionate to its terrible force. We have evidence, from the time when the storm started in the southwest as compared to the time when it ended in the northeast, that its speed was not more than two leagues an hour. The whirlwind moved in a circle, advancing slowly as if to give warning of its next direction.

Intensity of the heat

Several strange effects show that the intensity of the heat produced by the fire was in places extreme and unheard of. I have already mentioned the roots pursued by [82] fire from their stumps and consumed to their very end in the depths of the earth. I stuck my walking stick down these tunnels and checked that no depth had stopped the combustion.

Hogsheads of nails were found melted, although located at a distance from any concentration of flame.

Huge quantities of fish of all sizes died. They covered the river and floated with the current on the morning that followed the storm. What caused their death? the intensity of the heat? or the lack of air enough for them to breathe, because it was being forcibly pumped out by the current rushing towards the fire's glowing center as it moved through space? or did they perish from the effect of some poisonous gas?

Gas

One can hardly doubt that the air was for a moment saturated with a gas flammable and destructive of human life. I mentioned those tiny globules of air flying about my rooms at the moment I left my house. On my way to the river, I encountered layers of air, places where I could not breathe and had to lie down on the ground to [83] catch my breath, the times I was on the ground when the torrent of wind had not put me there against my will. While I was in the river casting my eyes upward I perceived, as I said, something like a sea of fire, in violent commotion, rolling immense waves of flames one over the other, and all this happened at a prodigious height in the sky, and, consequently, far from any combustible material. How to explain this phenomenon without positing that immense quantities of some sort of gas had accumulated in the air?

Strangely, many of the bodies had no burn marks, yet, in pockets of clothing found still intact, their watches, copper coins, and other metal objects had melted. How were there people who escaped with their lives here and there both on farms and in the woods? A question difficult to answer. The tempest did not rage equally everywhere. For survivors it was only a matter of chance. No one could boast of having had more presence of mind than anyone else. Generally, those who happened to be in low lying land, [84] especially those with some place dug out available to them, or like the savages some freshly plowed earth to cover themselves with, were able to save their lives. Most often the torrent of fire passed at a certain height and only touched ground slightly elevated. No one could stand upright without being almost instantly struck dead.

Something stranger still

Some people, at moments when the whirlwind might suddenly die down, frightened and surprised, would go outside to see what was happening and check on conditions. Many claim to have been witness to a phenomenon that seemed miraculous. They saw a large black object resembling a balloon. This object was whirling with great violence in the air at the tops of trees and advanced menacingly towards a house that it seemed to choose deliberately. Barely had it touched the house when the balloon burst with a loud explosion, like a bomb filled with gunpowder, and instantly after that streams of fire gushed forth in all directions. With the quickness of a lightning bolt, the chosen house was enveloped [85] in flames inside and out, such that the persons inside for the most part had no time for escape.

Destruction

It is rather difficult to calculate the extent of the area destroyed by the scourge because of the irregularity of its progress. It can, however, be said without exaggeration that the country destroyed from the southwest to the northeast of Peshtigo is not far from fifteen to twenty leagues in length by five or six in width.

The death toll from Peshtigo, including local farmers, was not less than 1,000, that is to say, about half its population. More than 800 known missing have been counted, but the number of anonymous victims, some of whom had arrived that very morning and had not yet been registered anywhere, will forever remain unknown.

And among those who escaped this fiery hell many have since died as a result of the ordeal and many others are still dying from it every day. A doctor from Green Bay predicted that within ten years all these poor survivors will be [86] dead from the damage that smoke, air, water, and fire have done to their constitution. If the prophecy continues to be fulfilled, my turn will also come.

May I by then have finished my church of Our Lady of Lourdes in Marinette, where it will find grateful souls who will pray for the repose of my soul!

Conclusion

[87] As I was passing through Terre Haute, Indiana on my way to St. Louis a little more than two months after the catastrophe I have just related, I saw in a local newspaper that a Protestant speaker that same evening was giving a public lecture on the great event. The subject of his lecture was: "The fires of our days as image of the fire that must devour the earth at the end of time." The subject interested me too much not to stop, so I attended the lecture. It drew only a very small audience, so true it is that people today are as they were in the days of Noah and as they will be in the last days, indifferent to all the warnings of heaven.

The learned lecturer after extensive research had grouped all the great fires of the past and relying twice on my own testimony, which he had gathered from the newspapers, undertook to demonstrate the greater severity of the fires of [88] our time, which in their strange character are an image and a precursor of the one that must consume the earth at the end of the world.

And indeed, this unleashing of the elements, this roar of the storm, this trembling of the earth, this sky and this earth on fire, these people amazed and withering in fear, is this not the description that Sacred Scripture gives us of the last days?

But why these precursory warnings? and why do they fall unequally on peoples equally guilty?

Who can fathom the designs of God? Perhaps it is because God is much forgotten today, especially by those who know him and ought to serve him. Is it not true that today many Christians walk, work, and, in a word, live as if they had no creator to obey, no savior to thank, no soul to save? And if it is true that God created man, if it is true that he came down to earth to redeem him, he has strict rights over him. When these rights are ignored and trampled [89] underfoot, our weak reason itself tells us that he must from time to time remind us of them and proclaim them by the great cataclysms that show to those who want to see that he is, however we act, our lord and master and that we should treat him as such. Isn't that how he once would act towards his chosen people when they became ungrateful and corrupt? The rights of God over man and the obligations of man to God are the same today as under the old law.

The forgetting of these obligations is widespread, no doubt, but at the same time what peoples today are truly exempt from chastisement? God's scourges are varied, but they show themselves everywhere. If his justice seems heavier on some than on others, if his voice sounds more thunderous and terrible here than elsewhere, it is perhaps because he wishes that in the chastisement of a small number thousands of others hear of the brilliance of his wrath and profit by it and return to him. When he made fire and brimstone rain down on Sodom, the Scripture does not say that Sodom was the only offending city. In the chastisement [90] that I have just written an account of, equal to that of Sodom, Peshtigo, perhaps no more offending than other towns that were nevertheless spared, is the modern Sodom meant to serve as an example to all.

> *Et nunc reges intelligite,*
> *erudimini qui judicatis terram.* (Psalm 2)

> "And now, O peoples, open your eyes,
> be instructed, O nations of the earth.

"Begin to fear the Lord and serve him, or tremble if you do not reform, lest the Lord punish you with death for your ingratitudes, because his vengeance flames and bursts bright as lightning. Happy, happy those who put their trust in him alone!"

Appendix

[91] What I have just done is not to have described the whole of the terrible disaster, but only to have told what of it I saw and suffered myself. If I have expressed myself clearly, the reader will have been able to see as well as I do the finger of God in what happened. I know many will be pleased if I add to the preceding account an event that shows also the finger of the Blessed Virgin, that is to say, her intervention to grant favor to those who put their confidence in her. It happened during another storm of wind and fire, on the same night, at the same hour as the one of which I was a victim at Peshtigo, but nine or ten leagues away, the distance between us over the waters of Green Bay.

I must of necessity abridge details and be prudent in what I say so as to preserve the modesty of some and the sensitivities of others among the [92] living of whom I must speak and who might read these lines.

Near the city of Green Bay, on a peninsula that extends northeast into Lake Michigan and forms Green Bay, lives a colony of Belgians. The population is generally thought to be eight to ten thousand souls. They are a religious people, simple and hard-working, but for the most part quite remiss in giving their children the religious instruction that they never received themselves. Found in this settlement is an unmarried woman, today about 40, lacking in the gifts of fortune and of nature, but rich in the gifts of grace and of virtue. Her name is Adèle Brice. Those who knew her as a child in Belgium have told me that she had always been distinguished, from early age, by a great piety for God, perfect love of neighbor, and complete confidence in the Blessed Virgin. And today, everyone who gets to know her sees at once that these virtues have only grown and become stronger in her soul. Ten or twelve years ago her Belgian settlement had no resident priest of its own and this [93] devout woman had no fear to travel each week, on foot, early Sunday morning, two and a half leagues to the neighboring parish, to confess, hear holy Mass, and receive communion, then to return in all haste to take up her everyday work in the bosom of her poor household.

She was returning one morning after receiving communion. Suddenly, along the little trail she would follow through the woods, she saw a Lady, majestic and intensely bright. The Lady stood before her as if suspended between two trees that bordered the path. The devout woman, amazed and deeply moved, but not frightened, falls to her knees, prays, and then gets up. She said nothing to her companions of what she had seen, but they had witnessed her reaction and talk of this mysterious apparition began thereafter to spread by word of mouth.

The next week, Adèle Brice returns as she always did to the neighboring parish to satisfy the duties of her devotion. On her way back home, in the same place, the same apparition appears to her, in the presence now of more companions, those who had gone to [94] Mass with her. This second apparition contributed much to the news' spreading through all the woods. There was much talk, but in quite different tones. Some were awed, others mocked, but no one yet believed that the Blessed Virgin could have had anything to do with a girl whom they were accustomed to regard as in every way similar to any other. Even so, many resolved to accompany her on her next journey and judge for themselves. That was soon to take place.

Having made her confession, heard holy Mass, and received communion, Adèle Brice took her usual way back, to return to work at her parents' farm. But this time she was accompanied by a much larger group of people, among whom there happened to be some men. On the way each was discussing the topic that was causing such commotion throughout the woods; each was promising to examine it carefully if it should happen again and expressing his opinion on the subject. Opinion was naturally very divided. The devout woman was calm and trusting. She had prayed deeply during [95] Mass and abandoned herself to divine Providence. Whether the idea had been given to her by someone or this idea had been inspired from on high, she had resolved to question this beautiful Lady if she appeared before her.

They arrive at the place on the way where the Lady had shown herself twice already before. Suddenly, she appeared again, but more beautiful, brighter, more smiling than the other times. The devout woman falls to her knees and begins a long conversation with this majestic Lady, who, far from instilling in her any fear, inspires her on the contrary with great confidence. I will recount only the part that is necessary to my subject.

She said to her, "Good mother, what do you want of me?"

"I want you," the Lady responded, "to instruct my children. You have just received my son, and you have done well, but these poor children receive him without knowing what they are doing and are growing up in ignorance of Religion. I want you to instruct them and above all to prepare them for their first communion."

"How will I do that, good mother? I [96] am but a poor ignorant woman myself."

"Go and fear nothing. I will help you."

From that moment onward, faithful to her mission, this girl was seen going from village to village, through the woods, in snow, in rain, and in hot weather. Neither fatigue nor the mockery she heard from many could stop her. She gathered as many children as she could and when she finished her lesson in one place, she went to another. Arduous and thankless work, which she continued for many years. A good priest was finally found for this settlement. This priest advised the devout woman to collect from the wider world an amount of money sufficient to help her build a school that would allow her to gather the children around her, instead of wearing down her health hiking after them herself through the woods. She took this wise advice.

Today she holds two things most dear: a school big enough to accommodate more than a hundred children who each year are prepared for their first communion and a small chapel built over the place where the Holy Virgin appeared to her and in which as a relic she [97] keeps the tree over which the apparition took place. These two buildings are of wood, plain, but clean and comfortable. Around the two structures stretch six acres of land, which were given over to the devout woman and which she herself gave over to his Excellency the Bishop of Green Bay. These six acres are enclosed by a board fence, around which winds a little path along which passes the solemn procession that takes place each year at two fixed times, a procession that attracts more than four thousand pilgrims from the area.

The work that Adèle Brice could do alone at the beginning advanced considerably and now would be beyond her own efforts. Providence sent her help. Five or six young girls, as pious as she, came to join her and share her devoted work.

Chapel of Our Lady of Good Help (1881) and school, Robinsonville, Wisconsin in 1885. Diocese of Green Bay.

So, this is the place and these the circumstances that made things what they are today. Now the event of which I wanted to speak and that will demonstrate the protection of the Blessed Virgin over those who have confidence in her.

[98] On October 8, 1871, the whirlwind of wind and fire fell also on this Belgian colony, causing as well great destruction of farms and forests, extending over many leagues, though without the same loss of life as in Peshtigo. When the firestorm broke, those devout women said to one another, "If the Blessed Virgin still needs us, she will know how to protect us, if not, she will let us burn with the others." Motivated by these feelings of confidence, they run into their chapel, take the statue of the Blessed Virgin, and on their knees carry it in procession all around their beloved Sanctuary while reciting the Rosary. When the wind and the fire blew too strong on one side of the chapel for them to go forward without exposing themselves to

asphyxiation, they waited for the firestorm to lessen or change direction while continuing to pray and to hope.

So passed for them the long hours of that terrible night. I would not be certain whether, humanly speaking and with their natural powers alone, they would have been able to stay alive [99] in the midst of this hurricane, but I do know well that, barring a miracle, they would not have been able to in Peshtigo.

Come morning, the appalling effects of the conflagration became visible. All the houses and fences in the neighborhood had been burned, every one — except the school, the chapel, and the fence that encloses those six acres of land consecrated to the Blessed Virgin. This fence had been singed and damaged in many places, but, as if the fire had known what it was doing, even as it proceeded to cut down or consume everything in its reach, so to speak, the fire had stopped right there and the path that goes all around the property is not more than eight or ten feet wide. This place, sanctified as it had been by contact with the Mother of God, looked like a verdant island in the midst of a sea of ashes.

Assumption day procession at Our Lady of Good Help, August 15, 1953. Diocese Green Bay.

From that time, these pious daughters of Mary have continued their work of devotion among the poor Belgian people, with even more courage and confidence because they had one more proof that such is the will of the Blessed Virgin.

Important reflection

By relating [100] the preceding event I have absolutely no intention of calling it a miracle, any more than I am calling a miracle the preservation of my tabernacle in the midst of the Peshtigo fire. Each of these events edified me and as I retell them here I have no other aim than to edify others.

Nor do I presume to pass official judgement on this apparition of the Blessed Virgin and the acts of pious pilgrimage that have resulted from it. Ecclesiastical authority has said nothing yet; without making a pronouncement it allows the good to go on, while awaiting a proof more irrefutable and striking before making its judgement. Obviously, it is not my place to anticipate this episcopal decision.

I add but one word: if any of my readers has the opportunity I urge him to take himself to the very spot and go visit this humble place of pilgrimage, which is still unique, I think, in the United States and which is just at its beginning. There he will see and be able to ask questions of the devout woman, Miss Adèle Brice, who is, without having wished it, the soul and heroine of a good work that goes ahead day by day and I am sure that he, as I have and as all [101] persons have who go there with right intention, will return edified and glad of heart, if not convinced of the reality of the apparition.

THE END

Commentary

Approbation

Ignace Bourget (1799-1885), Catholic bishop of Montreal (1840-1876). Bourget had designated May 24 the patronal feast of Notre-Dame de Bon Secours in Montreal (Our Lady Help of Christians on the Catholic calendar). To have dated the approbation **May 24, 1874** acknowledged a sympathetic link to the religious community of Robinsonville, Wisconsin.

Preface

The **two distinguished bishops** likely were St. Louis Archbishop Peter Richard Kenrick (1806-1896, (arch)bishop 1841-1895), whose diocese hosted Pernin during his post-fire stay in St. Louis the first seven months of 1872, and Herbert Vaughan (1832-1903), bishop of Salford, England from September 1872, eventually Cardinal Archbishop of Westminster, whom Pernin would have met there in January 1872 as Vaughan traveled through the American south to support Catholic missionary outreach to African-Americans.

two articles "Filling Up the Waste Places," and "Catholicity in Marinette, Wis." *Freeman's Journal* June 28, 1873 and January 31, 1874. (The complete articles are found in the Appendix.) Pernin understandably changed the title of the first to "Un désert qui refleurit de nouveau (A desert blooms again)." These passages, here as published, in Lovell 1874 are a retroversion into English of Pernin's translation into French.

"A. Druiding, St. Louis, Mo., architect(e)," is added to the text of the list, present in the *Freeman's* publication of the Latin dedication document but omitted from its English translation and then by the 1874 Senécal and 1874 Lovell. Adolphus Druiding (1838–1899) was a German emigre architect who became the most prolific builder of German Catholic churches in America. Pernin met him in St. Louis and for a fee of $100 engaged him to design the new Our Lady of Lourdes church. Use of economical materials and willingness to scale a project to what the client could afford were part of a business plan that appealed to parishes even of modest means. Pernin's commission came early in Druiding's extensive work in the diocese of Green Bay and Pernin could have been involved as mediator when Bishop Melcher engaged Druiding to design the new Green Bay cathedral, initially called St. Mary's, the next year, 1873. (*Proceedings of the Annual Convention* 33 (1899) American Institute of Architects, Druiding memorial minute page 243; Hampton. $100 fee: *Eagle* November 21, 1874.)

A survey of the 1874 Sadlier's *Catholic Directory* confirms Pernin's claim to have **dedicated the first church in the United States** to Our Lady of Lourdes.

Menominee means "people of the wild rice," which the tribe considered a manna-like gift. A native Wisconsin Ojibwe couple harvests wild rice. Marquette University.

Chapter 1

Indians Pernin here calls the native Menominee "*Indiens*" and twice elsewhere "*sauvages*" (translated "savages"), conventional locutions. The Menominee were the indigenous Americans of north central and eastern Wisconsin and the south-central Upper Peninsula of Michigan. Around what became Marinette, Wisconsin is the sacred site understood by their traditional religion, Mitāēwin, as the place where the Creator transformed the supernatural bear into the first Menominee human being and where was located the original main village, at the mouth of the Menominee River, Menekaunee. While in the end resisting removal from Wisconsin entirely, in steady steps ending with treaties in 1854 and 1856, the Menominee had been resettled on a reservation 40 miles west of Oconto around Keshena Falls. (Beck 1-45)

Menominee were among Pernin's parish supporters in Marinette and on January 6, 1874 celebrated the anniversary of his ordination. Catholic Menominee of a later generation celebrate ceremonial events on the reservation. Marquette University.

There were Menominee who had intermarried with the French and been Catholic from the mid 17th century, through the years of a Jesuit mission 1669-1707, though when Catholic missionaries were again among the Menominee in the 1820s, there had been a gap in attendance of more than a century. As Marinette pastor Pernin had responsibility for Menominee on his side of the Menominee River.

Sugar Bush There were three farming communities of about 300 families known as the Sugar Bushes, now in the town of Grover, Wisconsin: "Lower Sugar Bush... extending for about seven miles west of Peshtigo on the road leading to Oconto, Middle Sugar Bush ... along a road running to the southwest, and Upper Sugar Bush ... along what was known as the Lake Noquebay Road." (Haywood [3] from Frank Tilton, *Sketch of the Great Fires*.) **pleasant hunt for pheasant**, trying to reproduce Pernin's pun *faisant la chasse aux faisans*.

Article on the September 24 fire "P.," "Great Fire at Peshtigo" Green Bay *Advocate*, October 5, 1871 (dated Wednesday September 27). Lovell 1874 has a retroversion into English of Pernin's translation into French. Here as originally published, with the five passages Pernin omitted marked by ellipses. Those passages:

"On Friday I came through from Oconto, and we were compelled to run our horses some distance, with fire above us, and on either side of us, and barely escaped being singed." (apparently repetitious the anecdote of his own similar experience just told)

"while we were sitting in the church prepared to listen to an interesting sermon, the minister having just announced his text and launched out under "firstly," the steam whistle of the factory blew a wild blast, which told us that there was danger from terrestial (*sic*) fires more immediately pressing than from those infernal, and we incontinently left the minister there and rushed out to see what was the matter."

"Mr. Ellis, Supt. of the Peshtigo Co., with Messrs. Shepard, Beebe, Hempstead, Burns and others of our citizens, labored incessantly."

"Monday the factory was shut down to give the men rest, and Tuesday it was only partially run. The fire swept round the town and burned over the marshes between this and Marinette, destroying large quantities of hay. The whole force of two hundred hands were out at the Harbor to keep off the fire from the marsh where the Company has hundreds of tons of hay and they barely succeeded in saving it."

"There is a case of small-pox reported in town—precautions are taken to prevent the spread of the disease. The few green leaves left here are fast putting out their beautiful autumn colors. Respectfully, P."

Pernin had been in **Peshtigo** for nearly two years, appointed missionary rector of Assumption of the Blessed Virgin Mary, Peshtigo, and of St. Patrick's, Marinette, in December 1869, under the authority of vicar general Edward Daems, diocesan administrator in the absence of Bishop Joseph Melcher, who was in Rome attending the Vatican Council. Assumption church was at the corner of Oconto and Ellis Avenues. The pre-fire church faced Ellis Avenue. When rebuilt the church would be reoriented more prominently to face Oconto Avenue. Pernin's house and stable were across Ellis Avenue. (1871 and 1881 Bird's Eye Views. reorientation: *Eagle* May 17, 1873.)

Peshtigo Company Saw Mills, 1867. Pioneer photographer John Carbutt (1832-1905) traveled with an excursion party to document the progress of the Chicago and North Western Railway extension in June 1867. New York Public Library.

Peshtigo, eight miles up the Peshtigo River from Peshtigo Harbor on Green Bay, had been developing as a lumber center for more than 30 years. By 1871 the town had a school house, jewelry shop, several hotels, Lutheran, Congregational, Presbyterian, and Catholic churches, and a lodge of Odd Fellows, and, to serve the transient population of lumberjacks, loggers, railroad workers, and salesmen (50 to 100 newcomers a week), a number of saloons and brothels. Peshtigo was "half wild, half civilized." (Gess and Lutz 9, 7-17)

In 1871 Peshtigo was a company town. The **Peshtigo Company** was the investment of William G. Ogden (1805-1877), first mayor of Chicago, and Wisconsin businessman and future senator Isaac Stephenson (1829-1918). Its establishments included the Peshtigo Woodenware Factory, claimed the largest at the time in the world; a saw mill; a sash, door, and blind factory; foundry; grist mill; Company boardinghouses; and Company dry goods store. The Harbor was developed to export the lumber coming from the rich, untouched forests of the Wisconsin interior along the riverine highway. Value was added to the lumber that stopped in Peshtigo at the woodenware factory by manufacturing it into buckets, tubs, axe and broom handles, barrel covers, and clothespins. (Gess and Lutz 8-28)

Both as a city and a Catholic parish, **Marinette** began a few years later than Peshtigo, but with its bigger business center and harbor and twin city across the Menominee soon became predominant. By 1871 Pernin thought the Marinette parish "much more important" and the population about double that of Peshtigo. This was not quite true; Marinette's population grew from 470 (1860) to 1334 (1870) to 2544 (1875), while Peshtigo's was 562 (1860) and 1749 (1870). (US Census 1860, 1870, Wisconsin State Census 1875, Boatman1 348)

Marinette, town and eventually county, was named for Marie Chevalier Jacobs Farnsworth (~1793-1865), daughter of a Menominee mother and a French Canadian trapper, wife in turn of two fur traders, known as "**Queen Marinette**." It may have been that her mother was the daughter of a Menominee leader or that she was named or nicknamed for Marie-Antoinette, last French queen before the Revolution, guillotined in 1793 around the time she was born. But as a formidable operator of a trading post on the Menominee

River, intermediary between Menominee natives and traders, logging companies, and US officials from the 1850s, and someone whose wood frame house, first in the area, was a central charitable resource for people in need, she was certainly "queen of the city." Her son John B. Jacobs, Jr. was first chairman of a board of supervisors, platted the town of Marinette, and succeeded his mother as a Menominee translator and trade mediator. At least once, in 1875, he planned to accompany Pernin on a missionary trip up the Menominee River. Queen Marinette was a Catholic mainstay eventually buried in Allouez Catholic Cemetery outside Green Bay when she died in 1865. In 1987 her remains were ceremoniously reinterred in the town named for her. ("Marinette, Queen" wisconsinhistory.org; Boatman1 18-20, 66, 147-8. unsuccessful missionary trip: *Eagle* August 14, 1875; Boatman1 354-5.)

Cedar River, Michigan is 26 miles north of Marinette, Wisconsin along Green Bay, at the mouth of another logging riverway. Crossing the state line between Wisconsin and Michigan at the Menominee River took Pernin across another boundary into the adjoining diocese of Sault Sainte Marie and Marquette. Pernin would minister in someone's house; the first mission church in Cedar River dates from 1887 (Rezek2 328-9). Rezek knew Martin A. Fox (1825-1881) as the first to attend Cedar River, a German priest of Sault Sainte Marie and Marquette whom Bishop Frederic Baraga had recruited in Paris, ordained, and set to work in upper Michigan. But before the diocesan boundary became less fluid in 1872 Pernin from Marinette was taking responsibility for Menominee and Cedar River, Michigan. Fox in 1872 organized for Menominee its own parish and pastored it for several years. He was a dignitary at Pernin's Lourdes church cornerstone ceremony in Marinette June 8, 1873. (Rezek1 380-83, Walling and Rupp, findagrave)

The **Drees** family were Catholic Prussians. (Pernin spelt the name phonetically, Dress, in his church register and in his memoir.) Jeanne Catherine Drees (1807-1877) was six years the widow of Thomas Drees (1800-1865) and lived with the three youngest of their six adult children, including Edward (1841-1888) and wife. Mrs. Drees was a pillar of the parish, collecting money for rebuilding in the fire aftermath. Edward arranged for the post-fire $200 church organ and later billed Pernin $50 for a cutter (small sleigh) Pernin destroyed while making his way through a forest collecting money from lumber camps. Pernin had officiated at Edward's marriage to Mary Allgeier, December 21, 1869. Drees family members still live in Peshtigo: Henry Drees (1910-2001) was mayor (1968-1990) for the fire centennial in 1971, the recipient of a letter from President Richard Nixon on the occasion now displayed in the Peshtigo Fire Museum. (US Census 1860, 1870; Lourdes register; Lourdes church accounts *Eagle* November 14 and 21, 1874; findagrave.)

Grave of Queen Marinette, Forest Home Cemetery, in the town named for her.

Chapter 2

The 1870 US Census shows a **Tyler** family in Peshtigo: Mary Jane Bowers Tyler (1833-1927), 36, wife of Loren Tyler (~1828-1904), 43, mill engineer, and three daughters, Clara, Ida, and Jennie, 13, 9, and 6. After the fire, they would relocate to Oshkosh. (US Census 1870, 1880, 1900; findagrave; familysearch)

filled all day with drunkards Pernin's censoriousness of saloon patrons here apparently betrays his temperance sentiments, which he certainly had to have espoused later in his career in Minnesota. He would not otherwise have been appointed first vicar general of Winona, Minnesota, as he was in 1891 under Bishop

Joseph Cotter and St. Paul Archbishop John Ireland, two vehement temperance crusaders. Being French made Pernin an easy ally of Irish temperance, at least politically and culturally, as against German anti-assimilation and anti-temperance.

Ireland first learned of anti-alcohol at Meximieux, as influenced by Mathias Loras, fourth superior of Meximieux (1817-1824) and eventually bishop of Dubuque who became an exemplary total-abstainer. Pernin understood early that temperance was an appropriate value for the American missionary frontier and knew that also from Charles Chiniquy's popularity as a temperance evangelist in Montreal, as once supported by his own supporter Ignace Bourget, and in Illinois.

Philibert Crud once required a temperance oath before baptizing someone on the 1860s Door Peninsula. Auguste Bessonies (1815-1901), with whom Pernin shared the voyage to America in 1864, French missionary priest to Indiana, vicar general of Vincennes/Indianapolis from 1872-77 and 1878-1901, "probably the best-known Catholic clergyman in the West" according to his New York *Times* obituary, February 23, 1901, became "the Old Wheel-Horse of Temperance in Indiana," an important figure in the Catholic Total Abstinence Union locally and nationally, and Ireland's acquaintance and ally, from 1873. (French temperance in Minnesota: Reardon 1908, Villerbu 2014 228-234. Crétin support for teetotalism, Ireland learns temperance at Meximieux: O'Connell 105-7, Crozier 28. oath: Voyé 51. "Old Wheel-Horse: Gibbs 60, 196.)

railroad under construction: the northern extension of the Chicago and North Western Railway from Fort Howard to the Menominee and onward to Escanaba and the iron mines in the Upper Peninsula of Michigan. (Pernin 1999 60, note 5; Gess and Lutz 24-7)

housekeeper, named Delia Borman, Belgian, 18, if she was the same as Pernin's housekeeper in June 1870. (US Census 1870) **ran as far as the †second store†** *courut jusqu'au †2e magasin†* Lovell 1874 supplies "neighboring store" for the obscure phrase.

irresponsible Eucharistic custody 1917 Code of Canon Law 1265.3, reflecting earlier law, held: *Nemini licet sanctissimam*

Eucharistiam apud se retinere aut secum in itinere deferre. "No one is allowed to keep the Blessed Sacrament on his person or to carry it with him on a journey," let alone display the tabernacle at a riverbank for two days, as Pernin did (72), under the admittedly unusual circumstances.

better to moisten than to burn, *il valait mieux se mouiller que de brûler*, a droll allusion to 1 *Corinthians* 7.9, "It is better to marry than to burn (*il vaut mieux se marier que de brûler.*).”

Chapter 3

I have a big church there The Catholic diocese of Milwaukee (then Green Bay after 1868) expanded its Catholic parishes northward up the Bay's shoreline as the logging towns of Oconto, Peshtigo, and Marinette developed in the 1860s. As early as the late 1840s, circuit riders had attended Catholics in the Marinette area. They said Masses on boats in the harbor or in houses, some, by 1862, in the area of the Old Catholic Cemetery (on Pierce Avenue, between Cleveland and University Avenues) in Menekaunee, the area east of downtown Marinette. This perhaps reflected the proximity of Menominee Catholics; the word *menekaune* anyway means "village" in Menominee, the traditional site of the original Menominee settlement.

Antoine M. Mazeaud, while attending Marinette in 1865, his first year as Peshtigo pastor after an unsuccessful year 1864-5 on the Menominee reservation, built a small chapel, St. Patrick's, near the cemetery and instituted the first regular Catholic pastoral service in Marinette. This chapel burned in 1868. In summer 1868, as a site for a new St. Patrick's church, along the river in Menekaunee, Mazeaud acquired a block of property, bounded by Main, Water, and 9th Streets and Terrace Ave.

The property was a gift of Jesse Spalding (1828-1904), though not a Catholic. Spalding was early on his way to becoming a prominent Chicago lumber baron and was developing Menekaunee with the purchase (1861) and rebuilding (1870) of a lumber mill there and a two-story store in 1864. He would balance the heritage of lumber exploitation with communitarian projects such as a memorial library to his son in his hometown of Athens, Pennsylvania and a school in Chicago that, by the standards of its day, mainstreamed disabled children.

In 1870 and 1871 Pernin was further developing the property with the addition of a rectory, where he intended to live, and school.

The Menekaunee Catholic block, originally donated by Jesse Spalding, seen in a postcard ~1905: Our Lady of Lourdes church and the St. Mary's Institute.

The ambition to erect a school building was in keeping with the priorities of the First Plenary Council of Baltimore (1852) for the establishment of parochial schools and the Second (1866) for developing catechesis for public school students, especially those preparing for the sacraments. Pernin had at the same time almost finished the new Peshtigo church. (early Marinette Catholicism: Rezek 314-7, Boatman1 110, 156 (though church is St. Patrick's, not yet Our Lady of Lourdes, and pastor is Mazeaud, not Pernin), Dorner. Mazeaud: Long *IHV*, Beck 16-18. Spalding: Boatman1 104-5, 156, 191; findagrave.)

fire from your church to the Bay The fires mostly bypassed downtown Marinette and Menominee, Michigan, but went eastward to destroy Menekaunee as well as northward to Birch Creek, Michigan. St. Patrick's parish buildings burned at the edge of a zone in Menekaunee including 50 others: 35 houses, sawmills, flour mill, two hotels, a million feet of lumber. Jesse Spalding lost the new saw mill he built the year before on stilts in river water, thinking it so fireproof he had not taken fire insurance. (Hough 234; Boatman1 191, 204.)

motionless men on iron hoops Haygood, Pernin 1999 60 note 6, solved the mystery from information in a July 1927 survivor's letter: iron barrel hoops were being used to transport bodies.

"Can it be? ...to Marinette!" Pernin's words belong to the colloquy, not to his narrative voice, on the evidence of 1874 Senécal, which lacks the opening quotation marks but has the closing ones. 1874 Lovell lacks both.

General state of feeling in Marinette and Menominee This passage does not occur in the 1874 Senécal. (The equivalent subheading in 1874 Senécal is *Repos (Rest)*.) It is an expansion written for the 1874 Lovell English edition. Perhaps Pernin was made to realize that it was poor salesmanship to present so little material on Marinette while trying to raise funds for the Marinette church and added the material for his English readers, even though he wasn't an eyewitness (as his title had promised) and could speak only from hearsay. Assuming the passage is a translation of what he submitted in French, I have edited it lightly, particularly its archaic 19th century words, to make it less inconsistent with the rest of the translation.

Frank R. Garon (1840-1872), living in Menominee, Michigan, a shoemaker, younger brother of Joseph Garon, a successful Green Bay lumber baron from the area of Trois Rivières, Québec. (1870 US Census, findagrave)

prayed without human respect In post-Tridentine Catholic understanding, human respect (*respect humaine*) is the sin of excessive concern for the opinion of others and social conformity at the expense of witnessing the Catholic faith, see Boutry, Philippe "Le respect humain" «*Alla Signorina*». *Mélanges offerts à Noëlle de La Blanchardière*. Rome : École Française de Rome. Publications de l'École française de Rome 204 (1995).

à l'étouffée braised, that is, as meat fried lightly and stewed slowly for a long time. After **"... or an electric current had crossed it."** the 1874 Senécal in translation reads "—Many in fact noticed a trembling of the earth when everything was shaking on the surface under the fury of the whirlwind. —", set apart by dashes, a passage I omit. The sentence is logically out of place, as acknowledged by the additions in the 1874 Lovell: "Whilst touching on this subject we may add that many felt a shock of earthquake at the moment that ever[y]thing on the surface of the earth was trembling before the violence of the hurricane." It was either misplaced in the text or escaped an intended editorial deletion.

Over there, one of them was a father, moving the awkwardly placed *me dit l'un d'eux* to the previous sentence. Pernin's **Towsley** is C. R. Tousley in the official victims list, *Journal of Proceedings of the Wisconsin Legislature Assembly* 1873, 170. Pernin's spelling of names is automatically suspect, but Towsley and Tousley have equal distribution as a Wisconsin family name. The Towsleys lived and died in the Lower Sugar Bush. The "implication here that the bodies were found in Peshtigo," which Haygood corrected in note 8 of the 1971 Wisconsin Historical edition (repeated in 1999 61), arises only from the loss of accurate quotation marks. "One of the workers…" is spoken by an interlocutor.

hanged on the spot Lynching was an occasional form of adjudication in 1870s Wisconsin logging towns. In the spring of 1871 a bouncer hired to protect from roughnecks the Sunday night dance at a saloon dancehall in Oconto had the errant marksmanship to shoot instead the most popular young man in town and won the "manila necktie." In 1880 in Menominee two brothers were abducted by a mob from prison and dragged to death in nooses in vengeance for having stabbed to death a Menominee métis in a bar fight. In September 1872, the pimp of a brothel in Menekaunee shot an unruly john and was nearly lynched by a mob before the sheriff prevented it. (1871 and 1880: Nelligan 38-41; 1872 Boatman1 248-9, *Eagle* September 14, 21, 1872)

surplice, a white vestment worn over a cassock for a service that is not Mass. **stole**, a long fabric strip worn over the shoulders by someone ordained, symbolic of conferring sacraments. **sacramentary** (*rituel*), the book from which sacramental formulas are read, not "breviary," the text of the Divine Office recited by priests, as in Lovell 1874. **ostensorium, ciborium, chalice, paten** vessels used in

Catholic liturgy, made of gold or other precious metal. Within Pernin's tabernacle, the ceremonial box in a Catholic church that holds the consecrated hosts of unleavened bread, were two vessels that held Eucharistic hosts: an ostensorium (*ostensoire*), a transparent pyx, holding a large host, which could be inserted into a larger ostensorium or monstrance for display and worship, and a ciborium (*ciboire*), a gold or silver cup-like container with a lid that held the smaller hosts routinely reserved in a tabernacle. (Not impossibly by ostensorium Pernin means a small monstrance itself, small enough to fit inside the tabernacle.) A chalice is a ceremonial wine cup and a paten a ceremonial plate for the host both used at Mass.

I learned of Chicago's fate So Pernin learned that his niece Zoé, her husband Victor Lassagne, and their one-year-old son Victor, were at risk. The three did survive the Chicago fire, but may have lost the jewelry store at 61 W. Kinzie St. that was Victor's commercial step forward from peddling fruit. The fire crossed Kinzie Street around midnight and the family may have proceeded with everyone else north to the lake or west to the river. Many jewelers buried their property. ("Personal Experiences during the Chicago Fire" Frank J. Loesch Chicago 1925) Maybe Lassagne did too, the same night Pernin buried his ecclesiastical treasures and headed for his river.

In advertising copy 16 years later, Lassagne wrote: "In the great fire of October, 1871, [Victor Lassagne] suffered a very severe loss, his place of business being then located where now the Pacific house stands. Nothing daunted, however, he at once re-established himself, and as soon as practicable secured his present central and eligible premises." (*1887 Business Tour of Chicago* E. E. Barton Chicago 1887) In a 1968 oral history their daughter Zoé remembered: "The Chicago fire of 1871 spared his jewelry store in Kinzie St.; a southwest wind blew the fire to the north side."

THE FAR WEST.

Cholera Increasing in the Frontier Settlements—A Panic and Stampede of the People—Horrible Tragedy on the Santa Fe Road—Bishop Lamy and Ten Priests Murdered and Mutilated—Six Sisters of Charity Prisoners in the Hands of the Savages.

[Special to Cincinnati Commercial.]

LEAVENWORTH, July 18.—The number of cholera cases are increasing at Fort Harker, Ellsworth, Salina and Fort Riley. There is a panic at Fort Harker, and many of the people are leaving.

Intelligence has been received of a terrible tragedy on the Santa Fe road, near Fort Larned, on the 15th instant. A train was captured by the Indians, and among the passengers was Bishop Lamy, of Santa Fe, ten priests and six sisters of charity. The men were all killed and horribly mutilated, and the females were reserved for another fate.

The intelligence was brought in by an escort that tried to overtake the train to protect it, but was too late.

BOGUS INDIAN NEWS.—The special dispatch to the *Herald* announcing the massacre of Bishop Lamy and ten sisters of charity by the Indians proves, like three-fourths of the Indian news, to be utterly without foundation. In fact, the Indian news, as well as the Indian war, is in the main manufactured by dishonest speculators, who make profit out of the military movements on the Plains. There is nothing they dread more than peace, and there is nothing the rest of the people so much desire.

Bogus news 1867. The Lamy massacre as reported in the Ohio Statesman *July 20 and debunked in the Buffalo* Courier *July 26.*

Antoine Vermare (1835-1920), was a French missionary priest, pastor of St. Peter's, Oconto, where Pernin had briefly been pastor, August to December 1869, before his appointment to Peshtigo and Marinette. Vermare, from Les Sauvages (Rhône), after studies in Paris at the Séminaire des Missions étrangères had been ordained in 1865 at 29 for Santa Fe, New Mexico by Bishop Jean-Baptiste Lamy. In July 1867 serving in Trinidad, Colorado, he got word, as reported in newspapers all over the country, of the death of Lamy in a massacre of ten priests and abduction of six Sisters of Charity by Indians who captured their train. Vermare wrote letters of consolation to family and friends in France and said a requiem Mass for the departed bishop in his mission chapel. When Lamy and party arrived in Denver, it emerged that the report had been malicious fake news in support of native American genocide. Vermare transferred to the diocese of Green Bay in 1869, where he remained for 14 years, including one on the Menominee reservation, 1870-71, and twelve in Oconto, 1871-1883. Vermare spent his last 38 years on the Upper Peninsula of Michigan in the diocese of Sault Sainte Marie and Marquette. (Long *IHV*, findagrave, Audet. Menominee missionary: Beck 193. Lamy massacre: Horgan 344, 349.)

Vermare's name was spelled correctly in the 1874 Senécal, 77, then incorrectly in the English versions thereafter: Vermore Lovell 1874 80, Vermore 1918 289, corrected incorrectly "Vermore [A. Vermere]" 1971 [24], perpetuated in 1999 52.

All Saints' Day Philibert Crud had invited Pernin to come down from Peshtigo to preach in French for the feast of All Saints, November 1, 1871, at the "French church" he pastored from August 1870 to March 1875, St. John the Evangelist, Green Bay. As pastor Crud took the opportunity to build a landmark, new St. John's dedicated in November 1872, the grandest Catholic church in Green Bay before the completion of the cathedral in 1881. (Door County *Advocate* July 27, 1871.) The twin towers and façade with triple arches of Crud's new church were features of its design so memorable that they would be echoed, when it burned in 1911, in the successor church that stands today, finished in 1915.

Philibert Crud commissioned St. John the Evangelist, Green Bay (1872) (top) of Green Bay architect David M. Harteau, a future Fellow of the American Institute of Architects. Henry A. Foeller (1871-1938), another prominent Green Bay architect, echoed the earlier design in the current St. John's (1915) (bottom).

St. Louis Bishop Joseph Melcher would have recommended Pernin to friends and connections in the diocese where he had spent 28 years before coming to Green Bay in 1868 and been vicar general. In his roughly seven months in St. Louis ending July 1872, Pernin had a carte de visite taken at Cramer, Gross & Co. (1264 S. Fifth Street, Between Convent and Rutger, Below the French Market), made many friends, and found supporters who contributed $2000 to the new building going up in the Catholic block in Marinette to replace the parish buildings lost in the fire, intended to be a Catholic school, a Sisters of Charity hospital, and temporarily the parish church. In December 1872 these friends bolstered Pernin with a letter attesting that the money had been donated to him personally, to be used at his discretion. He filed the letter in the offices of the Marinette and Peshtigo *Eagle* as defense against allegations of embezzlement.

Writing *Finger* of *God* was suggested to him in St. Louis by his host Archbishop Kenrick and Herbert Vaughan, who visited in January 1872. Pernin met there also architect Adolphus Druiding, based in St. Louis, whom he engaged to design the new Our Lady of Lourdes church.

In the last week of March Pernin preached three times daily a Holy Week mission in French at the Cathedral of St. Louis, King of France. On the octave day of Easter, April 7, he sermonized in French at the cathedral on "Infidelity." During that Holy Week, the cousin who had brought Pernin to Meximieux, Denis Maîtrepierre, died at 72, March 29, 1872, Good Friday, at a Marist house on the Mediterranean coast, Notre-Dame de Montbel (Var).

A mission, later in the spring, to the French community of Carondolet, was scheduled for ten days but Pernin's popularity as a preacher warranted an extension to three weeks. A petition signed reportedly by eight hundred Carondolet Catholics asked the Archbishop to keep Pernin there, but Pernin was determined to return to Marinette and Peshtigo.

On Saturday July 20, the Marinette and Peshtigo *Eagle* was politely "glad" to report Pernin's return from St. Louis and its "hope he may remain with us in future." He held his first services in the new Catholic building in Marinette on Sunday July 21, Mass and five baptisms of babies born between late April and early July. ("Mission

Française à la Cathédrale," "Infidelity" Missouri *Republican* March 24, April 7, 1872; Green Bay *Weekly Gazette* June 1, 1872; *Eagle* May 18, July 20, 1872; Green Bay *Press-Gazette* July 27, 1872. Maîtrepierre last years: Monfat 338-346.)

Today's estimated **death toll** is 1500 to 2500. **may I have finished my church** Our Lady of Lourdes, Marinette was completed and dedicated in 1876. Pernin had by then been replaced as pastor; the new church was dedicated by his successor, John Chebul. **my turn will also come** Pernin would have 35 more years to live, dying in Rochester, Minnesota, October 9, 1909 at age 87.

St. Louis Cathedral (1834), on Walnut Street, St. Louis, looking east, seen ~1848 in a daguerreotype by Thomas M. Easterly. Pernin preached Holy Week sermons there in March 1872. Missouri Historical Society.

Conclusion

Terre Haute is a detail lost from the 1874 Lovell translation, perhaps in confusion over the toponym. "Pendant que je passais à Terre Haute (Indiana)" became "Whilst passing through Indiana on my way to St. Louis...," Lovell 1874 90. The lecture was "Great Fires of the World and Their Results," Friday evening, December 15, Dowling Hall, Terre Haute, given by Rev. John L. Gay, rector of St. James Episcopal, Vincennes, Indiana. Pernin is gratified that in the lecture Gay twice cited articles of his own, as if they had already appeared before December 1871. If while writing in 1874 he is not referring in confusion to the *Freeman's* pieces that appeared in 1873 and early 1874, after this event, I am unaware what he could be referring to, perhaps an empty boast.

Et nunc reges intelligite Pernin cites the Vulgate version of *Psalm* 2.10 and then paraphrases its last three verses, 10-12. 1874 Lovell here represents Pernin's paraphrase with the more literal Catholic English 1749 version, Challoner's revision of Douay-Rheims:

And now, O ye kings, understand: receive instruction you that judge the earth.

Serve ye the Lord with fear, and rejoice unto him with trembling.

Embrace discipline, lest at any time the Lord be angry, and you perish from the just way.

When his wrath shall be kindled in a short time, blessed are all they that trust in him!

Appendix

Colony of Belgians From 1853 to 1857 the wave of emigration to Green Bay from Holland, Belgium, and Germany made for the largest community of Belgians in the United States. Edouard Daems, OSC (1826-1879), a priest of the Order of Canons Regular of the Holy Cross, eventually first vicar general of the Diocese of Green Bay at its establishment in 1868, is credited with bringing Belgians to the Door Peninsula. In 1855 Daems founded a Crosier community at

Bay Settlement at the invitation of Milwaukee Bishop John Henni. He built Holy Cross Church at Bay Settlement, was the first resident pastor, and from there also founded and attended some 14 congregations on the Door Peninsula among them those at Robinsonville and Thiry Daems, half named for him. Daems had started a one-room school for his parish in Bay Settlement in 1865 and asked Dominican Sisters of Racine to staff it, the beginnings of the Franciscan Sisters of the Holy Cross at Bay Settlement. (Long *IHV*. Sisters of St. Francis: "Founders" and "Community"; Bay Settlement *Glimpse* 32.)

Adèle Brice (1831-1896) was 43 in 1874. Pernin phonetically spells the family name Brisse; Brice is the spelling on her birth certificate and tombstone (and that of Philibert Crud). So, though the variant Brise is common and used standardly in the writings on Robinsonville, I will use the spelling Brice here. Marie Adèle Joseph Brice, with her parents Lambert and Marie Catherine Pierard Brice, two sisters, and a second cousin, joined the Belgian emigration, in 1855, to the village of Red River, Wisconsin from Dion-le-Val, a village in Brabant, and settled on a 240 acre farm they bought. Adèle had decided on religious life in Belgium, but, sad to leave, deferred to the wishes of her parents and came with them to Wisconsin. The **neighboring parish** she attended was Daems' Holy Cross, Bay Settlement. (Dominica 16-17)

For Adèle and members of her community Pernin uses the word *fille* (girl, daughter, unmarried woman), a word difficult to translate for its range of literal meanings, which also can encode sexist denigration.

Wanting neither to disguise Pernin's use of a traditional locution nor misrepresent the word's range, I translate it according to context: "*fidèle à sa mission, on vit cette fille...,*" "faithful to her mission, this girl was seen..." (96); "*cinq ou six jeunes filles,*" "five or six young girls [Adèle's religious recruits]," (97); "*fille, âgée aujourd'hui de quarante ans environ,*" "an unmarried woman, today about 40" (92); "*que la Sainte Vierge put avoir quelque chose à faire avec une fille...,*" "that the Blessed Virgin could have had anything to do with an (ordinary) girl..." (94), *fille* being part of the skeptical disparagement of the 28 year old woman. "*Pieuse fille*" (seven times of Adèle and twice of her sisters), while not entirely devoid of sexism, is something else, a term of spiritual respect that I translated "devout woman/women," rather than "pious girl/s," except for *"pieuses filles de Marie,"* "pious daughters of Mary." (99)

Sister Marie Adèle Joseph Brice (1831-1896). Diocese of Green Bay.

no resident priest, ...good priest finally found, who advised
It was Philibert Crud, whom Pernin mentioned by name earlier as pastor of St. John's, Green Bay, but leaves unnamed here, who ten years before, by late November 1864, had come after a pastorate at Bourbonnais Grove, Kankakee County, Illinois in the diocese of Chicago, to become pastor of St. Joseph's, Robinsonville (after 1890 renamed Champion), Brown County, Wisconsin, then in the diocese of Milwaukee. Pernin succeeded Crud as pastor of St. Joseph's, Robinsonville from December 7, 1868 to September 6, 1869 and took on attending the Belgian and other communities of the 600 square miles of the Door Peninsula.

St. Joseph's, Robinsonville became Adèle Brice's parish and Crud a spiritual support, encouraging her as she developed a community of sisters and a school at the Chapel of Our Lady of Good

Help, facilities such that children could come to her, rather than she travel to them. Crud sent her out to fundraise accompanied by an English-speaking companion and fortified by his letter of recommendation. The companion was Marie Marguerite Allard (1851-1890) of Bay Settlement, "Sister Maggie," a mainstay of Adèle Brice's congregation and her beloved assistant for 19 years before death at 39. She was the older sister of Zoé Allard (1853-1932), who would become Philibert Crud's lifelong companion and partner in his orthopedic institutes in France. (Marguerite: Dominica 24-5, 48, 55. Zoé: Voyé.)

apparitions of the Virgin Pernin's 1874 account here is the second published account of the 1859 Robinsonville Mariophany and the first of the putative fire miracle of 1871.

The official history of Adèle Brice, her visions, and the Robinsonville chapel, shrine, and school that came in the aftermath is Sister M. Dominica Shallow, OSF (1898-1966), *The Chapel: Our Lady of Good Help* (1955, slightly revised 2014). Her fundamental source for the apparitions were the unpublished manuscripts, two of which dated 1907, of Sister M. Pauline LaPlante, OSF (~1846-1926), founding member of the Franciscan Sisters, original teacher at the school Edward Daems founded at Bay Settlement, and someone who knew the story from Sister Adèle herself.

Eliza Allen Starr (1824-1901) wrote the first published account of the Robinsonville Mariophany. Wikimedia Commons.

Before Sister Dominica's there were three published versions of the apparition: those in Eliza Allen Starr's *Patron Saints* (1871), in Pernin's 1874 account here, and in Philibert Crud's memoir as told to Antonin Voyé, *L'abbé Crud et la nouvelle Orthopédie* (1912). (Starr's and Crud's versions are found in the Appendix.) Starr (1824-1901) was a Catholic convert and writer, living in Chicago, recipient in 1885 of Notre Dame's Laetare medal, who met Adèle in Chicago in about 1871 in the course of her fundraising, encountering Crud's letter of recommendation written "in choice French," and heard the story from Adèle through Sister Maggie's translation. (Starr 298)

Philibert Crud had returned to France in 1882 and would establish himself as a nationally notorious charismatic orthopedic healer. Antonin Voyé (1828-1920) was a conservative Catholic priest of the diocese of La Rochelle-Saintes writing under the secular, liberal, state and scientific establishments of the Third French Republic, which were hostile to Catholicism, to defend Crud's right to practice anti-science, uncredentialed faith healing, inspired in part by Lourdes, in the face of civil requirements for medical licensure.

Pernin might have given the Franciscan Sisters for their library a copy of the 1874 Lovell edition of *Finger of God*. Sister Dominica drew from Starr and Pernin as well as Sister Pauline; Voyé's Crud was unknown to her. Pernin writes about Adèle and the apparitions partly from the personal experience of his 1868-69 pastorate. The official history is unaware of it and assumes his material came from a post-fire visit (Dominica 17).

Pernin's account of the apparitions diverges from Starr's and from the official history (Dominica 19-21) in a few ways large and small. His distance of "two and a half leagues" (some seven and a half miles) between the Brice farm and Bay Settlement is somewhat more accurate than Sister Dominica's "eleven miles" (which agrees with Starr). Pernin has Adèle on the morning of the third vision and colloquy making sacramental confession before, not after Mass, as in the official history, and he does not know (95) what Sister Dominica reports, that Adèle was advised by the confessor to ask the vision, "In God's name, who are you and what do you want of me?"

Pernin's chronology of the visions is an important discrepancy: he has three appearances occurring over three succeeding Sundays as Adèle returned home from Mass. The official version has three appearances within a week: the first on an unspecified day early in October 1859 on her way to the grist mill; the next, a few days later, "on the following Sunday," October 9, 1859, on the way to Sunday Mass; and the final, climactic vision the same day, on the way home. Starr's version (297-301) has three appearances, the first, on a Sunday, returning from Sunday Mass "one summer day," which Adèle kept to herself, and the second and third before and after Mass another Sunday, "a few weeks after," with the Marian colloquy that inspired her work on the third.

Pernin's version allowed him to narrate the buildup over two weeks of accompanying witnesses and the talk and opposition they provoke. Sister Dominica moved Pernin's account of derogatory reaction to a second apparition to the time after the third. Sister Dominica's

> The people were astonished when they heard the news. Most of them believed it, but there were some who thought Adele demented. (21)

drew from Pernin, in the 1874 Lovell version she was reading,

> This second mysterious appearance was greatly commented on, and viewed in different lights by different people. Some wondered, some laughed; but no one really believed that the Blessed Virgin had manifested herself to a girl but little different in most things from girls of her station. (96)

Also in another place Sister Dominica, narrating Adèle's dogged work after the visions:

> Faithful to her mission she was seen going through the woods as far north as Little Sturgeon, some fifty miles distant from her home. Rain, snow, or heat did not prevent her from accomplishing her work; neither did fatigue or ridicule have any effect upon her—she was showered with an abundance of both. (22)

drew without acknowledgement from the 1874 Lovell:

> From this moment, Adèle Brisse, faithful to her mission, was to be seen going through the woods from village to village, through rain, snow or heat. Neither fatigue nor ridicule made any impression upon her. She assembled as many children as possible in one place, and, her instructions concluded, she went to another wearisome and often ungrateful task, which she nevertheless faithfully performed for many years. (97-8)

Sister Dominica cited Starr for Starr's meeting with Adèle, who was carrying Crud's fundraising recommendation, but did not attempt to resolve the discrepancy between her version and Starr's on the matter of witnesses and the spreading of word of mouth. Starr remembered from Adèle that after the first vision "full of joy, [she] kept the vision in her heart, telling no one of the heavenly consolation given to her." Starr, the earliest published witness to Robinsonville, mentioned neither companions nor a challenged community: the vision was a personal, private revelation that inspired Adèle's educational work.

Most importantly, Pernin reports a shorter Marian colloquy, telling, to be sure, "only the part that is necessary to my subject." He omits, if he knew them, the Virgin Mary's castigation of Adèle's laziness, "What are you doing here in idleness, while your companions are working in the vineyard of my son?" and her request to pray for the conversion of sinners. That request in the official version includes the minatory words: "If they do not convert and do penance, my Son will be obliged to punish them." (Dominica 21) The official version itself abbreviates the version of these words that one of Sister Pauline's manuscripts reports: "If they do not convert and do penance, my Son will be obliged to punish them. I can hardly hold his avenging Arm." (There are as many as five written versions of Sister Pauline's account of the apparition that are attributed to her. Of the two dated August 25, 1907, one attests the words "I can hardly hold his avenging Arm." in the colloquy and one lacks these words. (Wendt communication)) (Park 7).

For understanding Robinsonville, Karen Park recognized the relevance of the Marian apparition of September 19, 1846 at La Salette near Grenoble (Isère), which would have influenced Adèle as a teenager in Belgium from age 15. Park notes parallels between La Salette and Robinsonville: Mary appears as an adult woman dressed in white and yellow; the message of both Robinsonville and La Salette was one not of physical healing, but of warning to a people dechristianized by negligence of Catholic duty, particularly of catechesis; and the threatening words are strikingly similar, "If my people will not submit, I shall be forced to let go the arm of my Son. It is so strong, so heavy I can no longer hold it." The "arm of my Son" was an important motif in materials popularizing devotion to Our Lady of La Salette. To Park, La Salette is more relevant to accounting for Robinsonville than the 1858 Marian apparition of Lourdes. (Park 9-15)

Park emphasized the possible influence of the patterns of La Salette on the narration of Robinsonville and also the divergences between official versions and archival evidence (particularly on the matter of Adèle's charging school fees and a history of diocesan resistance to popular devotion at the Shrine (Park 16-25)). But there have been divergences in the story from the beginning, as you would expect in a tradition transmitted at first orally before being written down by Starr, Pernin, LaPlante, and Crud. The reminiscences of Milo P. Smits, O. Praem. (1883-1971) are also part of the oral tradition that Sister Dominica had to work with, a Norbertine Father, pastor of St. Joseph, Champion (Robinsonville) from 1908 to 1951 who knew Sister Pauline for the first eighteen of those years (Dominica 58). Adèle herself left no written account.

All who have written on Robinsonville shaped their narrative to their themes. Starr's comparatively peaceful and merciful version supported her proposition that holiness of life is not only for Europeans, but even Americans: "Our good American girls try to be like Italian and French saints, instead of trying to be, simply, saints of God; of God, who created them, in whatever country He has seen fit to place them."

Green Bay Bishop David L. Ricken also omitted the minatory words, "If they do not convert and do penance, my Son will be obliged to punish them. I can hardly hold his avenging Arm." from the official decree (2010) that declared the apparition worthy of belief. When I asked for comment he kindly answered that the reason for this was:

> the words were not seen as essential to the apparition's message, which was included in a redacted form in the original 2010 decree, typical of such documents. Also, their exclusion acknowledges that the original sources (Sister Pauline's writings) only include the minatory words ["I can hardly hold his avenging Arm."] in one of her written accounts and not in the others. While the minatory words remain an important part of Mary's message, their meaning, along with the entire message, are only properly understood in light of the constant magisterial teaching of the Church.

(Girotti communication) (see also Park 7, note 12).

Sister Dominica's official Shrine history (1955) attests the minatory words, drawn not from Pernin but from one of Sister Pauline's memoirs (1907), and their authority could have been influenced not only by La Salette, but by then also by the Marian visionaries of Fatima in Portugal in 1917 who reported from their dire experience of the Virgin Mary, "If men do not change their ways, Our Lady will send the world a punishment..."

Even before Fatima, the version of Robinsonville in Voyé's *Crud* (1912) had included a version of the minatory words, "You will tell the world to convert if it wants to avoid the wrath of my Son. (43)" La Salette, which Crud never mentions, would have echoed agreeably to Voyé's conservative French Catholic audience. But Crud through Voyé for his own purposes was assimilating Robinsonville to Lourdes. Crud claimed Robinsonville for a healing shrine like Lourdes from its earliest days and Crud's association, then, became an origin of his own miraculous healing ministry in France 30 years later.

Official Green Bay diocesan versions have long associated Robinsonville (1859) with Lourdes, which took place the year before (1858). For Sister Dominica, Robinsonville confirmed the decrees of the First Plenary Council of Baltimore that mandated Catholic catechesis (1852), as the Virgin's words at Lourdes confirmed the papal declaration of the doctrine of the Immaculate Conception (December 8, 1854) (Dominica 19 and Looney). Bishop Ricken's dating his Robinsonville decree December 8, 2010, was an implicit link to Lourdes. (Bishop Bourget had found another association, dating his approbation of *Finger of God* to May 24, 1874, Our Lady of Good Help in Montreal.)

Starr's early impression of the Robinsonville apparition was reminiscent of Lourdes ("...as one sees the Blessed Virgin represented in pictures of the Immaculate Conception"). Even clearer association of Robinsonville with Lourdes dates back to Pernin in *Finger of God*, who does not mention La Salette, but shaped his narrative of Robinsonville to assimilate it to the Lourdes event, which comprised 18 appearances, spread over six months, provoking interest and attracting crowds, and subjected the visionary Bernadette Soubirous to ridicule. In *Finger of God* Pernin gave to Adèle at

Robinsonville in 1859 some of the experiences of Bernadette at Lourdes in 1858 and connected that with his opportunity as pastor in 1872 to plan a new church, the first in the United States, dedicated to Our Lady of Lourdes and with the name of the town of Marinette, "Little Marie," in which he found a providential, Marian significance.

(In September 1846 for La Salette Pernin was in Autun in his last months of major seminary before his ordination in December. The year 1858 falls in the blank decade in Pernin's Autun diocesan record (1853-63), so we have no idea how his devotion to Lourdes originated.)

Academics speak in terms of negotiation at margins of contestation. A Mariophany might well represent challenge to male hierarchical church authority by a female visionary empowered by unmediated access to the divine, claiming her own authority on behalf of a dispossessed, marginal immigrant community. (That is roughly how in 1912 Philibert Crud identified Edward Daems' interpretation of it, "...an act of revolt against authority" (Voyé 44), though Crud was motivated by personal animus towards Daems.) More conservative historiography would assume of two contradictory versions that one (if that) is true and another is false and seek to determine which is which. (For example, Pernin's chronology, apparently amplified by the influence of the Lourdes story, is not arguably correct as against that of the official history. Or for another, exactly what minatory words if any did the Virgin Mary utter?)

Yet even a conservative Roman Catholic model can account for how subjective appropriation, by the visionary herself and by subsequent chroniclers, will defeat elusive attempts to establish an objectively true account of a Mariophany. Apparitions of the Virgin Mary, indeed any private supernatural revelation, according to this view, can be received only within the limits of the subjectivity of the visionary. The Virgin Mary is heard by visionaries in language they can understand, not with a trained theologian's sophisticated nuance, which would allow for a more balanced expression of doctrine in light of the totality of Catholic understanding.

Attempting to dampen the vengeful theology and conservative conspiracy theories that surround reception of the Fatima apparitions, Cardinal Tarcisio Bertone wrote:

> "Interior vision" is not fantasy ...but it also has its limitations... The visionary ...sees only in so far as [she] is able, in the modes of representation and consciousness available to [her]... the subject shares in an essential way in the formation of the image of what appears. [She] can arrive at the image only within the bounds of [her] capacities and possibilities. Visions... are influenced by the potentialities and limitations of the perceiving subject. (Bertone 146)

And among many cautions concerning private revelation, Benedict Groeschel, CFR credited the notion that the subjective element in authentic revelations can occasion "misunderstanding and even error" because of the "tendency to use revelation to write history rather than to use it symbolically," "the tendency of the visionary to mix subjective expectations and preconceived ideas with the action of divine grace," "a subsequent altering or amplification of the testimony after the revelation," and "errors made in good faith by those who record the testimony." (Groeschel 50-51)

The role of Adèle's companions as she experienced her visions would seem a clear example of such "amplification": the narrative's progress from Starr's three visions within a few weeks that she kept to herself, no companions (1871); to Sister Pauline's three visions in a week with two companions and skepticism thereafter (1907); to Pernin's three visions over two weeks that attracted a buildup of more and more companions and skepticism before the period of the visions was concluded, a scenario influenced by the Lourdes story (and written, after all, by someone with Collège training in *amplification*) (1874); to Crud's version in which two companions are joined by an apostate Protestant who miraculously returns to the faith and it is not a supportive Belgian community that opposes Adèle but the villainous diocesan authority Edward Daems (1912).

Potentially another example of subsequent amplification by "subjective expectations" is the Virgin Mary's castigation of Adèle, "What are you doing here in idleness, while your companions are working in the vineyard of my son?" appearing in the official version (Dominica 21), but not in Starr, Pernin, or Crud, which would have been provoked by Adèle's guilty feeling that she did not keep a commitment to pursue religious life in Belgium and obeyed her parents' wish to accompany them to Wisconsin rather than the New Testament injunction to hate her parents (*Luke* 14.26).

If Pernin knew from Adèle the request to pray for the conversion of sinners and the minatory words "If they do not convert…," it is unaccountable that he omitted them, since they would have suited perfectly his theology of the fires. The phrase and idea of "his terrible avenging arm" actually occurs in both Pernin's Marinette expansion for the Lovell translation and Bishop Bourget's Approbation of the work. The words did suit Sister Dominica, who in the official history herself suggested that the 1871 fires were their fulfillment: "What was it the Queen of Heaven said? 'If they do not amend their lives and convert themselves, my Son will be obliged to punish them.' We do not propose to pass judgment on the reasons for this catastrophe, but we know that twelve years later almost to the day, the great calamity fell." (Dominica 30)

The stated subject of *Finger of God* was, in part, God's vengeance. Even if limiting himself to "only the part that is necessary to my subject," Pernin need not have excluded the minatory words from his version of the colloquy and reported only the Virgin Mary's prompting of Adèle's catechetical work, as also did Starr, the other of the two earliest published accounts of the colloquy. Pernin's account is evidence that the minatory words in Sister Dominica's official version are themselves possibly "subsequent altering or amplification" or "error made in good faith" by those who later recorded the testimony. In any event, an account of the Mariophany that lacks the language "I can hardly hold his avenging Arm." would conform more easily to the Mariology of the Second Vatican Council's *Lumen Gentium* (1964), which emphasized Mary's "subordinate role" (62) as "there is one mediator between God and humankind" (1 *Timothy* 2.5), and to the emphases of recent popes, as from John Paul II's "*Dives in Misericordia*" (1980), who have asked that God's justice be thought less his punishing vengeance than his mercy.

Source Notes

(Sources for the material in the Commentary are noted there.)

Preface

"dealing largely, "religious reflections Pernin 1918/1919 158, 293.
"cachet as 'forgotten Pyne in Pernin 1999 8.

Introduction

The life and times of Peter Pernin

The documentary foundation of **Pernin's life** lies in the civil record of his birth in Flacey-en-Bresse (Saône-et-Loire); the records of his education, ordination, and postings in the dioceses of Belley (now Belley-Ars) and Autun; his (meager) diocesan files in Green Bay, St. Paul, and Winona; the continuous series of semi-official annual Sadlier's *Catholic Directories*; and his sacramental registers, which are extant for all his parishes in America. In his own hand in the late 1890s or early 1900s he filled out an autobiographical questionnaire for an intended "Biographic Cyclopedia—Diocese of Winona." **Pernin's extended family** Flacey Actes d'État Civile, Birth, Marriage, and Death, and the quinquennial Censuses, Recensements.

Evidence for **Pernin's birth date** is contradictory. For the "Biographic Cyclopedia" Pernin wrote February 22, 1822, also the date in his Autun diocesan ordination record ("Registre des inscriptions") and on his tombstone. In the baptismal record of February 26, 1822 (Parish register, St. Martin, Flacey-en-Bresse), the birth is recorded as occurring the day before, February 25. A birth date of February 24 is given by the Flacey civil birth record, recorded May 13, 1822; Autun diocesan personnel record, *"Registre matricule du Personnel,"* 339; and the "État Des Mutations" submitted by the diocese to the *département* in 1863.

Maîtrepierre Belley archives personnel *fiche*; Alloing 725; Monfat 269, 323-46. The two shared a grandmother. **Meximieux history** Alloing 724-27; Rochet 324-25; O'Connell 42-45, 50-56. **Tailland** Autun diocesan "Registre matricule"; "Notice" Tailland Migne 9-10; Fouilheron 419-423. **Collège d'Autun** Gady; de Fontenay 462-471; *Centenaire*, especially Vernier "Discours."

Van de Velde letter *Annales de la propagation de la foi* 22 (1850) 313-4; Price 46-7. **French missionaries** Ireland 59, Essertel. **missionary literary culture** that "only partially captured the unromantic experiences of personal suffering," Pasquier 92; 91-4, 105-111. **Devie, Loras, Crétin network** Villerbu 2014 84-6, 175-180. **networking and recruitment** Villerbu 2009, 2014; particularly in the early nineteenth century, Pasquier 95-99, 100-105. **Chanel friends' missionary intention** Nicolet 49-55, 60, 123. **Chanel's will** Nicolet 542.

Duggan efforts Garraghan 181-3. **Chiniquy** Price, Brettell. **Duggan spoke French** Chiniquy 1886 809 ch. 66. **annihilated** "French Catholic Meeting in Chicago" Chicago *Tribune* January 26, 1857 (reprinted in Chiniquy, ch. 63). **nieces "heart-broken** Lassagne oral history.

Crud career Belley Bishop's register; Schianchi communication; letter Paroissiens August 18, 1862. **Duggan asked help** Gingras to Baillargeon, 10 November 1862; Ducroux to Baillargeon, December 3, 1862. Crud sometimes went by a *dit* name Ducroux. **Gautherin** (died 1877) societyofmaryusa.org

clerical rights Trisco and McKenna narrate the story of the progress to canonical rights for American Catholic clergy. **Duggan illness** one account, by a participant in the crisis, is McMullen, edited by McGovern.

Crud dismissal from Chicago Côté to Baillargeon, November 7, 1864. **Door Peninsula** "Baptizavi apud Belgas," as Crud wrote, St. Joseph, Champion register, December 4, 1864. **Pernin replaces Crud 1868** St. Joseph, Champion register; Ratajczak "St. Joseph Catholic Church" and communication.

Berger Pernin wedding Iroquois County, Illinois Marriage Records, LDS microfilm #1321548. I thank Norma Meier for this reference. **Pierre Joseph Berger** (1828-1900) obituary Clifton *Comet* November 17, 1900. **Maria-Berthe Pernin Berger** obituary Clifton *Advocate* September 1941. **Zoé Lassagne teacher, Dearborn, jeweler** *Chicago City Directory* Richard Edwards 1870. **Victor Lassagne** (1826 -1900) Lassagne oral history. **Restaurant Français** *1887 Business Tour of Chicago* E. E. Barton Chicago 1887.

Ireland O'Connell. **"Meximieux is** Ireland 1916 201. **ecclesiastical reorganization** O'Connell 260-4; Crozier 87-102. **chosen vicar general** Crozier 137; Hokah *Chief* October 15, 1891. **appointed chaplain** St. Mary's *Annals* April 1, 1898. Rochester *Post* April 29, 1898. **87th birthday** Pernin to Zoé Lassagne, March 8, 1909. **illness, death, obituaries** Rochester *Post and Record* and Olmsted County *Democrat* October 8-15, 1909.

The Finger of God

Melcher (1806-1873) catholichierarchy.org; archstl.org; Long *IHV*. **Vaughan in St. Louis** Ochs 44. New Orleans Archbishop Antoine Blanc, for one, had defended slavery in a pastoral letter "Slavery and True Freedom" (1852) and many post-war southern Catholics were uninterested in the needs of former slaves, Pasquier "Slavery, Civil War, and Southern Catholicism," 166-202. **replacement** *"...Rev. father Galweiler meus vicarius pro tempore...,"* **"the very last days** Lourdes register 37. **Nicholas Gällweiler** (Gaellweiler) (1842-1882) Long *IHV*, findagrave.

Senécal Michon *DCB*. **Lovell** Parker *DCB*. **Bourget, "authoritarian, Chiniquy crusade** Sylvain *DCB*. **Bourget and Bon Secours** *Manuel;* Simpson 89-99. **temperance and submission to ecclesiastical authority** Noel 1990. **Jules Marion** (1851-1878) Karel 538. **not long after** The French copy digitized on Internet Archive, for example, was inscribed by its first owner June 11, 1874. **Lovell procedure** Parker communication.

Joseph Schafer (1867-1941) LaLande. **editor** Pernin 1971 [4]. **"Fortunately,** "**dealing largely** Pernin 1918 158, **"religious reflections** Pernin 1918 293. **"no writer** Pernin 1971 [4].

Amateur scientist, ironist, theodicist

Autun history, monuments, lore Thévenot; Nixon and Rodgers 4-10, 145-150. **first edition Pectorius inscription** Pitra.

Meximieux curriculum and Pernin prize winning *Distribution Solennelle*; O'Connell, for Ireland's time, 45-48, 50-53. Rochet 301-11 provides extensive details for the contemporary curriculum of another Belley minor seminary, Petit séminaire de Belley. **"Sailor** "Le navigateur et le pêcheur" Meximieux 1841, Delacour 13-17, a commonplace subject for composition in *Abeille française* vol. 1 1828, 214. **Apostrophizing a lamp** is itself a Classical trope (Aristophanes fragment 573, Palatine Anthology 5.8, Dante *Paradiso* 21.73 "...sacra lucerna...").

"I" taken mistakenly Gess and Lutz 49, 58-60. **Haywood's footnote 8 "implication"** Pernin 1999 61. **"The way is open** ("Le chemin est ouvert) (42) l'Abbé Pellegrin *L'Imitation de Jésus-Christ, mise en cantiques spirituels* Nicolas Le Clerc 1727, canticle 32, 65: "Le chemin est ouvert / lui-même il nous le trace."; Ahern 116.

Lovell religious publishing Parker *DCB*. **meaning of Lovell format** Parker communication. **"power of God** John P. Meier 463, note 48. **As God is the truth** Tailland 131-2.

"a positive judgment John P. Meier 514. **"Whether we were** Gess and Lutz 53.

Peshtigo paradigm Pernin 1999 8. **Faverney** Marchal and Tramaux. **surviving house** Pernin 1999 60 note 7. **"hysterical with fear** Nelligan 42-3. **Abram Place** (1818-1891) Boatman1 204-5; Gess and Lutz 93-5. **"questions like** Weinberg, Steven "Eye on the Present - The Whig History of Science" *New York Review of Books* December 17, 2015. **"all prosperity** Calvin *Institutes* 17.8 (trans. Beverage). **itinerant preachers; Sunday September 24 preaching** Gess and Lutz 45, 47, 230; 57.

Gay "old school" *Journal of the Annual Convention of the Diocese of West Missouri*, Volumes 12-17, 41-2. **lecture** Terre Haute *Gazette* December 2, 7, 13, 15, 18, 1871. Gay gave the lecture twice in Vincennes, and in Sullivan, Evansville, and Terre Haute, Indiana.

Balzac critique Lowrie 44-52. *La Rabouilleuse* from *Un Ménage de Garçon* (earlier title) Houssiaux Paris 1853, Honoré de Balzac *Scènes de la vie de province*, Volume 6 of *Oeuvres complètes* **"filled with deeds** 64, **"There's a God after all** 290 (my translations). **practical joke** Nelligan 101-2. **"snufflings of pietistic** *Freeman's Journal* October 21, 1871. **Aquinas on fire** *Summa Theologiae* 1 Q. 49 Art. 1; *divina providentia Summa Contra Gentiles* 3.72. **"how fearfully** Cotton Mather, "The Terror of the Lord" (1727) via nationalhumanitiescenter.org/pds/becomingamer/ideas/text1/god earthquakes.pdf.

"There was a general impression Nelligan 44. *Homo sum* Monfat 333, Terence *Heauton Timorumenos* 77, a commonplace of clerical humanism: Bishop Devie linked it to the golden rule as a basis for Christian *politesse*, Devie 32. **Devie importance** Boutry 1988 213. **Devie adopts Liguori** Larcombe 162-4; Boutry 1986 415-6; see Guerber, Jean SJ *Le Ralliement Du Clergé Français a la Morale Liguorienne; L'abbé Gousset Et Ses Precurseurs (1785-1832)* Rome Analecta Gregoriana 1973. **"When it is** Liguori *Sermon* 3, 270 "...il attend, il avertit, il multiplie les avertissemens..." (my translation of French version, including the Vulgate version of *Amos* 3.7). **"up to a certain** "à un certain point au-delà duquel il laisse agir sa justice" *Sermon* 3, 268. **"God never tires** *Evangelii Gaudium* 3.

Diocesan and parish politics

Daems Long *IHV.* **obtained and filed letter** *Eagle* November 14, 1874. **"I left unfortunately** Lourdes register 16.

cornerstone day *Eagle* June 7, 1873; *Freeman's Journal* June 28, 1873. **concentration of Menominee population** Beck xxiii. **silver wedding and Indian dinner** *Freeman's Journal* January 31, 1874. The *Eagle* reported on the similar Epiphany celebration in 1886, "always a great day" for Catholic Indians, *Eagle* January 9, 1886; Boatman2

448. **devout and gracious** according to missionary Marianus Glahn in 1881, Beck 36, 208. Pernin's third form music teacher at Meximieux, Antoine-Marie Garin (1810-1889), on the other side of the world came to feel similarly about the Maoris with whom he spent the last 49 years of his life as Marist missionary in New Zealand. Garin, who had pastored in Salavre and Chalamont in Ain, corrected himself on his preconceptions of Maori savagery: "The natives are not, as one might expect, living in the woods like animals... the people are of an unparalleled intelligence and self-awareness... They are well above the people of our [French] countryside... more teachable and civilized." (Larcombe 145-9)

White new pastor Lourdes register 100-102, beginning August 15. "**Leaving Rev. father Galweiler** Lourdes register 37, 39. "**Jus**" **hanged** Trisco 168. "**house as a** Lourdes register 39.

"**Dear Sister** Sister Pauline in Dominica 36. "**Some people came here** Brice to Krautbauer, July 20, 1875 (I thank Olivia Wendt for a scan of this letter.); Dominica 36, Park 22-3. Erasmus Eusébius Leccia (1847-1923) was pastor of St. Joseph's, Robinsonville 1874-77 (Sadlier's; Long *IHV*), mentioned in Daems' will for a substantial sum (Door County *Advocate* March 13, 1879). **Krautbauer resumed, allows larger chapel** Dominica 36, 44. **Crud on Daems' opposition, This extraordinary movement** Voyé 44-6 (my translation). Crud does go on to claim that Daems publicly recanted his skepticism of Adèle at a solemn dedication of the Sanctuary of Our Lady of Good Help, August 15, 1866. (Voyé 47) His account is absurd and anachronistic in many ways, but, to limit ourselves to one falsehood, Daems could not have been in Robinsonville that day, as he was in Green Bay dedicating St. Patrick's Church. (Martin, Deborah Beaumont *History of Brown County, Wisconsin: Past and Present*, Volume 1 S.J. Clarke Chicago 1913, 254.) **Laus Mariophany, Lambert recantation** Juge 146. "**fact undisputed** Park 21; Dominica 33-5, 72. **same that Crud claims** Voyé 45.

White changes parish name In late summer 1874 White with diocesan approval reported himself to Sadlier's *Catholic Directory* as pastor of Sacred Heart of Jesus, Marinette for inclusion in Sadlier's 1875, 205. (Directory listings for a year in Sadlier's represented the status of early the previous fall. Ideally, Sadlier's envisaged that the publisher circulate questionnaires in July, they be filled out in August in the dioceses for September 1 or late September at the latest, and for the next year's directory to appear in November. (Sadlier's 1865, iii)) Sadlier's 1875 "Additions and Corrections" (page 4) lists the late-breaking item, "Page 205—Marinette, omit Rev. William White." **Crud suspended** *Daily State Gazette* March 8, 1875.

      tabernacle "Tabernacle's journey part of Peshtigo Fire lore" *The Compass* October 5, 2011. Grellinger, Bishop John B., *The* (Green Bay diocesan) *Spirit* October 8, 1976. **deliberately diverse mix** Crozier 135-45. **Leschak "trying** 7; **"On the banks** 260, after *North American Review* 105 (July 1867) 249.

English translation

translation of Garneau Morley *DCB*.

Appendix: Some relevant writings

1. The earliest published account of the Robinsonville apparition
Eliza Allen Starr *Patron Saints* (1871) 297-301.

...Half of the piety in the world is lost, so far as its fitness to the
everyday necessities is concerned, by these very causes. Our good
American girls try to be like Italian and French saints, instead of
trying to be, simply, saints of God; of God, who created them, in
whatever country He has seen fit to place them, with the intention of
having them become types of their race in the order of sanctity, and
benefiting their race by the exercise of natural virtues in a
supernatural degree. I wish you all to think about this, and believe
that sanctity is the same in all nations; as the soul of man is the same
among all nations; but, like that soul, clothed upon by the
peculiarities of race and clime, which peculiarities are not to be forced
upon other races in other climes, any more than dress and social
habits.

A charming example of what I wish to make you understand
about this occurs to me as I write, and I shall give you the story with
its real names.

On one of the warmest days of this last summer, coming into
my little parlor, I saw two women seated there, dressed in black serge
gowns and cloaks, and in bonnets exactly like the cape-bonnets that
many little girls still wear, made of a straight piece of black barège,
with narrow strips of pasteboard run in, to make them stand out from
the face. You have all seen these cape-bonnets made of pretty colored
cambric. Those worn by the two women in black dresses and cloaks,
as I have said, were of black barège, and they gave an air of the most
rustic humility to their costume. I welcomed them as "Sisters," of
some Order unknown to me, and found that only the youngest one
[Maggie Allard] could speak English; but a letter in choice French,
from Rev. Father P— [Philibert Crud] of Robinsonville, near Green
Bay, in Wisconsin, gave me a clue to the mystery before me. It
introduced to me Sister Adèle, a humble Belgian woman, to whom
had been granted, undoubtedly, an apparition of Our Blessed Lady,

leaving her to tell me, through her young interpreter, the story of her graces and of her labors.

Twelve years ago [from Starr's writing in 1871], Sister Adèle, living in the same neighborhood as now, was in the habit of going to mass every Sunday, though she could do this only by walking eleven miles to the place where mass was celebrated. One summer day as she was returning through the dense woods from mass, she saw a bright, luminous atmosphere in the woods around her, and from this luminous atmosphere there came forth the figure of a most lovely lady, white and shining, her face covered with a veil, her robe falling over her feet, and her hands joined, as one sees the Blessed Virgin represented in pictures of the Immaculate Conception. Our good, humble sister Adèle, recognized the Virgin Mother, and full of joy, kept the vision in her heart, telling no one of the heavenly consolation given to her. A few weeks after, as she was on her way to mass, the same lovely apparition made her step light and her heart joyful; and that same afternoon before sunset, as she was returning, the same white and shining figure stood before her. This time, encouraged by its repeated appearance, she spoke in her humble way, to the veiled Vision, saying, "Dear Mistress, what do you wish me to do?" Good Sister Adèle did not think that the Blessed Virgin was thus appearing to her, repeatedly, for her spiritual consolation, alone; she knew that something was wanted of her. Our Blessed Lady's reply was, "Gather around you the neglected children in this wild country, running idle about the woods, and teach them what they should know for salvation." "Gladly would I gather them in, dear Mistress," said Sister Adèle, "but how shall I teach them, who know so little myself?" "Teach them," said the radiant visitor, "their catechism, how to sign themselves with the sign of the cross, and how to approach the sacraments. This is what I wish you to do;" and the beautiful vision, with its luminous atmosphere, disappeared, and left the dense woods as solemn as before, while dear Sister Adèle walked on to her own humble home with her heavenly commission in her heart. You may believe that Sister Adèle did not put off doing what our Blessed Lady had asked of her, but began to collect the children running wild about the woods and living in the log cabins of the neighborhood. Sister Adèle had no "price," for teaching, no tuition bills to make out to her pupils, even at the end of a whole year; and their parents, finding the school a free school, were glad to send their children. Once started, there was no lack of scholars; and very soon Sister Adèle found that her room was too small for her school. Then this courageous woman undertook to beg, from more favored communities, the money necessary for building a large school-house, then a chapel, and, finally, to raise a home for the religious, whom she hoped to persuade to assist her in her great work. It was on this errand that she had come to our city, where churches, and schools, and sisterhoods, flourish, and there were few hearts on which her appeal fell unheeded. Every year, on the Feast of the Assumption of Our Lady, a religious procession celebrates the appearance of the Blessed Virgin to Sister Adèle; thus keeping in mind the origin of her humble school of instruction for these wandering lambs of the fold of Christ, which has changed this wilderness into a garden of delights to the Saviour of souls. Sister Adèle does not yet belong to any religious Order, but if she ever does, I hope she will wear her simple cape-bonnet, as a memorial of the rustic garb in which she met the Queen of angels and of saints, and received her commission to teach the little ones of the 'household of faith."

Sister Adèle's vocation is one very liberally distributed among the Catholic women of America; and if not always attended by such impressive circumstances, the same zeal, courage and cheerfulness, are the dispositions required in fulfilling it.

2. The two *Freeman's Journal* articles cited in *Finger of God*

Our Lady of Lourdes church cornerstone ceremony, June 8, 1873

"Witness" and P. Pernin, "Filling Up the Waste Places," *New York Freeman's Journal and Catholic Register* June 28, 1873 vol. 34 no.15

Filling Up the Waste Places
Marinette, Wisconsin
Editor Freeman's Journal:

Sunday, June 8th, was a day long to be remembered by the Catholics of Marinette, Wisconsin. It was the occasion of a visit from their Bishop, Rt. Rev. [Joseph] Melcher, of Green Bay, for the purpose of laying the corner-stone of the new Church that is to supply the place of the one destroyed by the devastating and memorable fire of 1871.

There were four masses celebrated by the Fathers present, at one of which the Rt. Rev. Bishop received a number of girls as members of the Sodality of the B[lessed] V[irgin] Mary. High Mass was celebrated by Rev. G. N. [Thomas J.] Ackley. The Rt. Rev. Bishop delivered two short sermons, one in French and the other in German, the merits of which are highly commended by those understanding the language. Father Ackley then delivered a sermon in English on the subject of the day, the B[lessed] Trinity, which was eloquent and impressive.

The ceremony of laying the corner-stone took place in the afternoon. It was performed by Rt. Rev. Melcher, assisted by Rev. Fathers [William] Corby, of Watertown, Ackley, of Green Bay, [Martin A.] Fox, of Menominee, and our esteemed pastor, Rev. Father Pernin. It was impressive, and witnessed by a vast assemblage of people. The sermon for the occasion was delivered by Very Rev. Corby. It was suitable, listened to with marked attention, and, to say the least, worthy of high commendation.

The service of the day closed with a lecture in the evening, at the National Hall, by Very Rev. Corby, SS. C. — subject, "The Church as she is, and as she is not."

The Rev. lecturer engaged the closest attention of his audience for the space of two hours.

He was loudly applauded, and the highest encomiums were bestowed on him by all who heard him. Too much cannot be said in praise of the success of his effort. The degree of satisfaction may be understood from the fact that many of his auditors have since offered to pay $2 per ticket for a repetition of the same by the Rev. gentleman, and some of his dissenting hearers remarked "that they would never speak so badly of the Catholic Church again."

All this is the index of the endeavors of our esteemed Pastor, Rev. Pernin, to promote the welfare of his people.

The parish, although laboring under disadvantages from the loss of their Church and property in the late fire, promises, under his energetic direction, to be one of the most flourishing in this part of the country.

With his zeal and labor he cannot fail to win the love and esteem of his parishioners, and advance the cause of holy religion in this place.

WITNESS

DOCUMENTUM.

Pio Nono, summo pontifice,

Josepho Melcher, Diocesis Episcopo,

Admodum Domino Gulielmo Corby SS. C., concionatore,

U.S. Grant, statuum foederatorum praesidente,

C.C. Washburn, Wisconsini Status Gubernatore,

A. Druiding, St. Louis, Mo., Architect[o],

P. Pernin, pastore Ecclesiae Catholicae Marinette,

Pluribus Sacerdotibus assistentibus et coram magna astantium corona

ab ordinario Sinus Viridis consecratus est iste angularis lapis Ecclesiae aedificandae in honorem B. M. V. apud Lourdes et in plurimorum salutem.

Ista nova Ecclesia aedificanda est in loco prioris quae destructa fuit in terribili et devastante igne qu[i] totam istam regionem in desolationem reliquit Anno Domini Millesimo Octogintesimo Septuagesimo primo, Die autem Octobris octava.

Datum Marinette, Die octava Junii, Anno Domini Millesimo Octogintesimo Septuagesimo tertio, MDCCCL[XX]III

P. PERNIN

Translation in English.

DOCUMENT.

Pius the Ninth being Pope,

Jos. Melcher, Bishop of the Diocese,

Very Rev. W. Corby, SS. C., Preacher

U. S. Grant, President of the United States,

C. C. Washburn, Governor of the State of Wisconsin,

[A. Druiding, St. Louis, Mo., Architect,]

P. Pernin, Pastor of the Catholic Church of Marinette,

Many priests being present, besides a vast concourse of people,

this corner-stone was blessed by the Ordinary of the Diocese of Green Bay for this Church, which is a building in honor of the Blessed V. M. of Lourdes, and for the salvation of many.

This Church is to replace the former one, destroyed by the great and devastating fire which left this whole country in ruin, in the year of our Lord Eighteen Hundred and [Seventy]-one, October the eighth.

Given at Marinette, this eighth day of June, in the year of our Lord Eighteen Hundred and Seventy-three.

A tin and sealed box, laid in the corner-stone, contained, besides this document, a few specimens of our present currency and some silver and copper pieces.

P. PERNIN

Feast of Epiphany in Marinette: Pernin's silver wedding celebration and the Annual Indian Dinner, January 6-7, 1874

"A Witness," "Catholicity in Marinette, Wis." *New York Freeman's Journal and Catholic Register* January 31, 1874 vol. 34 no. 46.

Catholicity in Marinette, Wis.
Marinette, Oconto Co., Wis., Jan. 18, 1874.
Editor N.Y. Freeman's Journal:

The Catholics of Marinette suffered severely during the fearful fires that about two years ago devastated Upper Michigan and Wisconsin. Their church was destroyed, and they have been struggling ever since to replace it. Their good Pastor, Rev. P. Pernin, has been working very hard, and, with the limited means at his command, has until now only succeeded in getting the new church about half finished. Father Pernin, although laboring under many disadvantages, did not forget the wants of the children under his charge, and after the most strenuous efforts has succeeded in erecting a parochial school. The zeal of the Pastor has been generously assisted, not only by the Catholic, but by the Protestant portion of the inhabitants; but they have been able to accomplish very little in consequence of the heavy losses they sustained by the fire. The school is not yet open for want of means, but it is hoped that assistance will soon come from some unexpected quarter.

Even in this far-off section of our country God does not forget the good missionary, and not infrequently sends him consolations. Father Pernin has just been blessed with one of these pleasing incidents in missionary life. On January 6th Marinette was in commotion.

Besides celebrating the Feast of the Epiphany, the good people were going to celebrate a holiday of their own. Their Pastor was about to celebrate his *silver wedding*—he was going on this day, with the Kings of the East, to place at the feet of the Infant Saviour, the labors of twenty-five years of service in the priesthood. The people were hastening to the church in their holiday attire to rejoice with their Pastor and to thank God for this auspicious day. The Rev. Clergy from the neighborhood, ten in number, came also to congratulate their faithful co-laborer. Solemn High Mass was celebrated by Father Pernin, assisted by Deacon and Sub-deacon, and three sermons were preached, one in English, by Rev. Edward [Edmund] Walsh, of Fort Howard; one in French, by Rev. L[ouis] Cornelis, of Oshkosh; and one in German, by Rev. N[icholas] Juli, of De Pere. The Rev. Celebrant was the recipient of numerous congratulations from his parishioners, who vied with each other in supplying their good Pastor with all he required for this occasion. The visiting clergy fully entered into the spirit of the appreciation manifested by the congregation for their Pastor, and in their turn presented their faithful co-laborer with a beautiful testimonial of their esteem and respect. Great satisfaction was evinced by all who participated in this joyous occasion.

On the following day, another very interesting event took place. It was the occasion of the *Annual Indian Dinner*.

There are in Marinette about fifty Indian Catholic families, good, simple, and pious people. In accordance with an old and deeply cherished custom, established by the early French Missionaries, they assemble every year at a grand and general dinner. For this dinner a large cake is prepared, and in it are placed three beans. The cake is distributed among the guests and the persons getting the pieces containing the beans are elected "Kings," an honor which permits them to provide the dinner for the following year.

All the Priests invited were present at the dinner. As soon as their approach was noticed some two hundred Indians arranged themselves in two long lines and knelt down on the snow and allowed the Black Gowns to pass through them. The dinner was a source of great joy to all present. The Indians were overjoyed to see so many Priests among them. The oldest chief, rising, asked permission to say a few words. Through an interpreter he expressed his joy at seeing such a large number of Black Gowns at their festival; he felt as if he was in heaven, and he regarded it as a sign that God did not forget His red children, however poor and miserable they might be.

After the speaking, which was participated in by the Rev. Clergy, the cake was cut and to the intense delight of the Indians the first bean fell to the lot of Rev. C[harles] B[e]yerle, of Duck Creek. He was at once proclaimed an Indian King, and was decorated with the insignia of his office, the star and ribbons, which the Indians attached to his coat. After a prayer of Thanksgiving the Priests retired, leaving to the simple children of the wood a blessed remembrance that will long be cherished by them.

A WITNESS.

3. Philibert Crud in 1912 on Adèle Brice, the Mariophany of Robinsonville, and the enmity of Edward Daems

Antonin Voyé L'Abbé Crud et la nouvelle orthopédie (1912) 42-46.

L'apparition de 1859

Adèle Brice, âgée de trente ans, fille pieuse et de grand coeur, avait suivi ses parents en Amérique, non sans un vif regret de la Belgique, sa terre natale. Etablie avec sa famille à une lieue de Robinsonville, elle se rendait le dimanche aux offices religieux de Bay-Settlement, à trois lieues de sa demeure ; Robinsonville n'avait pas encore le service régulier du dimanche.

Dans les premiers jours d'octobre 1859, elle suivait dans la forêt le sentier de Robinsonville, où elle devait faire quelques emplettes, quand tout à coup, sur un tertre entre deux érables, apparut une dame d'une ravissante beauté. Adèle Brice, saisie d'une violente émotion, s'arrêta ; la dame disparut. Rentrée à la maison, Adèle raconta toutes les circonstances de l'apparition à ses parents, gens simples et craignant Dieu, qui furent vivement touchés.

Le dimanche suivant, 9 octobre 1859, la jeune fille, accompagnée par sa soeur et une femme du voisinage, se rendait aux offices de Bay-Settlement. Auprès du lieu de l'apparition elle dit à ses compagnes : « Là, entre ces deux arbres, j'ai vu la belle dame. » Subitement pâle et tremblante, elle s'arrêta, et la dame disparut. A Bay-Settlement, Adèle se confessa, entendit la messe et communia.

Dans l'après-midi, en revenant chez elles, les trois femmes rejoignirent un Belge qui, depuis son arrivée en Amérique, s'était fait protestant. Elles racontèrent à cet homme l'apparition du matin. Adèle, silencieuse, sentait l'émotion l'envahir à l'approche du lieu béni. Près des deux arbres la belle dame apparut soudain, mais cette fois la jeune fille redevenue calme s'avança vers l'apparition et s'agenouilla. La dame dit :

— « Je suis la Reine des Cieux et je prie pour la conversion des pécheurs.

— « Chère dame, dit Adèle, que demandez-vous de moi ?

— « Vous devez instruire les enfants pour leur première communion.

— « Chère dame, je suis moi-même si peu instruite !

— « Vous leur apprendrez la prière et le catéchisme.

— « Oui, chère dame.

— « Vous direz au monde de se convertir s'il veut éviter la colère de mon Fils. »

La Dame disparut.

Le récit de l'apparition fit grand bruit. Connues et estimées, les femmes témoins de ce fait extraordinaire trouvèrent créance parmi la population belge. L'apostat qui les accompagnait le publia comme elles, fit abjuration publique et rentra dans le sein de l'Eglise, qu'il avait abandonnée. La foi et la piété se réveillèrent parmi ces pauvres émigrés délaissés, que l'indifférence déjà gagnait. On se rassembla sur le lieu de l'apparition, on pria, on baisa cette terre sanctifiée, on chanta des cantiques d'action de grâce et on décida de construire une chapelle sur le lieu où la Sainte Vierge s'était montrée. Dès le lendemain de cette décision les hommes revinrent en habits de travail. Les plus beaux sapins furent coupés, équarris, entassés les uns sur les autres en forme de murs. Une chapelle couverte d'ardoises de bois fut élevée, et avec la scie on ouvrit la porte et les fenêtres nécessaires. Sous la direction de là voyante, qui ne quittait pas les travailleurs, on érigea l'autel, sur lequel fut placée une statue de la Sainte Vierge et qui fut, comme toute l'église, orné de guirlandes. Belges, Allemands, Autrichiens, Irlandais accoururent à l'envi au pèlerinage, bannière en tête, à l'occasion de toutes les fêtes de la Sainte Vierge, et plus particulièrement le 9 octobre, anniversaire de l'apparition.

L'épreuve

Ce mouvement extraordinaire de la population catholique de toute la contrée attira l'attention du missionnaire de Bay-Settlement, le R. P. Daems, chargé de la mission de Robinsonville. Il savait que l'autorité épiscopale ignorait l'existence du pèlerinage pour lequel aucune autorisation n'avait été demandée. Il crut devoir intervenir pour réprimer ce qu'il considérait comme un acte de révolte contre l'autorité. Sans tenir compte de l'ignorance des règles canoniques qu'il était sage de supposer chez cette population livrée à elle-même, il la traita avec une sévérité que pouvait seul expliquer un acte de révolte consciente. Ce n'était pas le cas. L'enthousiasme et la piété avaient inspiré l'ignorante population dans tout ce qu'elle avait fait. Elle se scandalisa des reproches que lui adressa le missionnaire pour l'érection de la chapelle et du doute qu'il fit planer sur la réalité des apparitions. Le mécontentement éclata avec une extrême violence quand le P. Daems choisit un jour de fête pour venir défendre aux pèlerins de prier dans la chapelle du pèlerinage élevée par Satan comme un étendard contre celui du Christ et quand il annonça que la voyante serait privée des sacrements aussi longtemps qu'elle n'aurait pas rétracté ses mensonges.

Désastreux pour le missionnaire, ce discours n'arrêta pas le concours des pèlerins. La voyante, elle-même, ne pouvant déclarer faux ce qu'elle savait être vrai, s'abstint de revenir à Bay-Settlement afin d'éviter de nouveaux scandales, et, fidèle à sa promesse, se livra avec plus d'ardeur à l'instruction religieuse des enfants. Son ascendant sur la population belge ne fit que grandir et les hameaux où elle devait séjourner lui ouvraient leurs portes avec empressement.

L'apostolat de la Voyante

Le passage d'Adèle Brice dans un hameau était une sorte de mission. Les réunions du matin et du soir avaient lieu dans la chapelle, là où il y en avait une, ou dans la maison particulière qui lui donnait l'hospitalité. Elle présidait les prières et, le soir, on chantait des cantiques ; elle racontait l'apparition et les faits merveilleux qui se passaient à la chapelle du pèlerinage et profitait des soins qu'elle donnait à l'instruction religieuse des enfants pour raviver dans l'esprit de ses auditeurs les vérités oubliées ou obscurcies de la foi chrétienne et les devoirs que l'Eglise impose à tous ses enfants.

C'est à ce moment, octobre 1865, que M. Crud arriva à Robinsonville. Mgr Henni, évêque de Milwaukee, prévenu par les rapports du P. Daems, n'avait chargé M. Crud d'aucune recherche au sujet du pèlerinage et n'avait pas cru nécessaire de lui parler de cette affaire. M. Crud voulut étudier sur place toutes les circonstances de l'apparition, interroger la voyante et les témoins ; il constata leur bonne foi et le dévouement et la piété d'Adèle Brice. Dans ses courses à travers la grande mission il rencontra les principaux malades dont la guérison était attribuée à la Vierge apparue et il les interrogea, eux, leurs parents et les témoins de la guérison. Il enquêta particulièrement sur le cas du jeune François Abe, guéri, à la chapelle du pèlerinage, d'une tumeur au genou dont il souffrait depuis quatre ans et qui le privait de l'usage de sa jambe.

Dès qu'il eut appris l'apparition et l'érection de la chapelle, le jeune François Abe fut saisi d'un désir invincible d'y aller pour demander sa guérison. Mais il fallait faire quatre lieues dans la forêt par des chemins impraticables aux voitures. Ses supplications amenèrent enfin ses parents à atteler les boeufs de la ferme, et, assis sur la lourde charrette, conduisant lui-même l'attelage, il arriva par les sentiers des bois à la chapelle, après une demi-journée de voyage. Il se fit descendre et porter dans le sanctuaire où il commença une prière ardente. Elle n'était pas achevée que déjà du genou malade coulait une quantité de matières putrides ; la tumeur se vidait et les douleurs avaient cessé. Il retourna à pied, conduisant son attelage.

Muni de renseignements précis, indiscutables, M. Crud alla exposer lui-même à Mgr. Henni la vérité telle qu'elle lui apparaissait. Il reçut de l'évêque l'autorisation de bénir la chapelle et de construire un couvent où se ferait la préparation des enfants à leur première communion, afin de réaliser ainsi la volonté de la Vierge apparue et de rendre possible et efficace la mission qu'avait reçue Adèle Brice de se consacrer à cette oeuvre.

Translation in English.

The apparition of 1859

Adèle Brice, thirty years old, a devout woman with a big heart, had followed her parents to America, not without bitter regret, from Belgium, her native land. Settled with her family one league from Robinsonville, on Sundays she went to religious services at Bay Settlement, three leagues from her house; Robinsonville did not yet have a regular Sunday service.

In the first days of October 1859, she was on the Robinsonville forest path, where she had to do some shopping, when suddenly, on a mound between two maple trees, appeared a lady of stunning beauty. Adèle Brice, seized with a violent emotion, stopped; the lady disappeared. Adèle returned home and told the whole story of the apparition to her parents, simple and God-fearing people, who were deeply moved.

The following Sunday, October 9, 1859, the girl, accompanied by her sister and a woman from the neighborhood, went to services at Bay Settlement. Near the place of the apparition she said to her companions: "There, between these two trees, I have seen the beautiful lady." Suddenly pale and trembling, she stopped, and the lady disappeared. At Bay Settlement, Adèle went to confession, heard mass, and received communion.

In the afternoon, while returning home, the three women were joined by a Belgian who, since his arrival in America, had become Protestant. They told this man the story of the appearance that morning. Adèle, silent, felt emotion come over her as she approached the blessed place. Near the two trees the beautiful lady suddenly appeared, but this time the girl, once again calm, advanced towards the apparition and knelt. The lady said:

"I am the Queen of Heaven and I pray for the conversion of sinners."

"Dear lady," said Adèle, "what do you ask of me?"

"You must educate the children for their first Communion."

"Dear lady, I am myself so poorly educated!"

"You will teach them prayer and catechism."

"Yes, dear lady."

"You will tell the world to convert if it wants to avoid the wrath of my Son."

The Lady disappeared.

The story of the apparition caused a big stir. The women who witnessed the extraordinary event were known, respected, and credible to the Belgian population. The apostate who accompanied them told it as they did, publicly abjured Protestantism, and returned to the bosom of the Church, which he had abandoned. Faith and piety arose among these poor forsaken emigrants, whom religious indifference had long ago defeated. People gathered at the place of the apparition, prayed, kissed this sanctified land, sang hymns of thanksgiving, and decided to build a chapel on the place where the Blessed Virgin had appeared. The day after this decision, the men returned in work clothes. The finest firs were cut down, squared, piled on top of each other to form walls. A chapel with slate roof was erected and with a saw the necessary door and windows were opened. Under the direction of the visionary, who did not leave the workers, an altar was built, on which was placed a statue of the

Blessed Virgin and which, like the whole church, was decorated with garlands. Belgians, Germans, Austrians, Irish came again and again as pilgrims, holding banners high, on the occasion of all the feast days of the Blessed Virgin, and more particularly on October 9, the anniversary of the apparition.

The trial

This extraordinary movement of the Catholic population throughout the whole area attracted the attention of the Bay Settlement missionary, Rev. Father Daems, charged with the Robinsonville mission. He knew that episcopal authority was unaware of the existence of the pilgrimage for which no authorization had been requested. He thought it necessary to intervene to stop what he considered an act of revolt against authority. Without taking into account that this people lacked knowledge of the canonical regulations that it would have been wise to suppose that they left to themselves, he treated them with a severity that could only imagine that it was an act of conscious revolt. This was not the case. Enthusiasm and piety had inspired these ignorant people in everything they had done. They were scandalized that the missionary reproached them for building the chapel and the doubt he cast over the reality of the apparitions. Discontent flared violently when Father Daems chose a feast day [1864 or earlier] to come and forbid the pilgrims to pray in the pilgrimage chapel built by Satan as a standard against that of Christ and when he announced that the visionary would be excluded from the sacraments for as long a time as she refused to retract her lies.

Disastrously for him, the missionary's speech did not stop the pilgrims from coming. The visionary herself, unable to declare false what she knew to be true, refrained from returning to Bay Settlement in order to avoid new scandals, and, faithful to her promise, dedicated herself with more zeal to the religious instruction of children. Her influence over the Belgian population only grew and the villages where she went to stay eagerly opened their doors.

The visionary's apostolate

When Adèle Brice visited a village, it was a kind of mission. Morning and evening meetings took place in the chapel, where there was one, or in a private house that offered hospitality. She presided over prayers and, in the evening, hymns were sung; she told the story of the apparition and the marvels accomplished in the pilgrimage Chapel and took advantage of the efforts she made to give religious instruction to children to revive in the minds as well of those who heard her the forgotten or obscured truths of the Christian faith and the duties that the Church imposes on all her children.

It was at that point, October 1865 [1864], that Father Crud arrived in Robinsonville. His Excellency Bishop Henni of Milwaukee, put off by Father Daems' reports, had not made Father Crud responsible for investigating the pilgrimages and had not believed it necessary to speak to him about this matter. Father Crud wanted personally to look into all the circumstances of the apparition and question the visionary and the witnesses. He recognized their good faith and the devotion and piety of Adèle Brice. In his travels across his wide mission territory he met the important sick persons whose healing was attributed to the Virgin who had appeared and he questioned them, their parents, and witnesses to the healing. He investigated in particular the case of a young man named François Abe, who was healed at the pilgrimage Chapel of a knee tumor from which he had suffered for four years and which deprived him of the use of his leg.

As soon as he learned of the apparition and the building of the chapel, young François Abe conceived an overwhelming desire to go there to ask to be healed. But he had to make it through four leagues of forest trails impassable to carriages. His pleas finally persuaded his parents to harness their farm oxen, and, seated on the heavy cart, he drove the team himself and got to the chapel on paths through the woods, after half a day's journey. He was taken off the cart and carried to the sanctuary where he began to pray ardently. Before his prayer was even finished, from the sick knee there flowed a quantity of putrid matter; the tumor was emptying, and the pain had stopped. He returned on foot, leading his team.

Now armed with information precise and indisputable, Father Crud went to put the truth before Bishop Henni as it appeared to him. He received the bishop's authorization to bless the chapel and build a convent where children would prepare for first communion, in order to fulfill the wish of the Virgin's apparition and to make possible and effective the mission that Adèle Brice had received to devote herself to this work.

Works Cited

Editions of *Doigt de Dieu*

L'abbé Pernin, Missionnaire aux États Unis, *Le Doigt de Dieu Est Là!: Ou Episode Emouvant d'un Évènement Étrange Raconté par un Témoin Oculaire* Eusèbe Senécal Montréal 1874.

Rev. P. Pernin, United States Missionary, *The finger of God is there!, or, Thrilling episode of a strange event related by an eye-witness* John Lovell Montreal 1874.

Reverend P. Pernin, "The Finger of God is There" *The Wisconsin Magazine of History* 2.2 (December 1918) 158-180 and 2.3 (March 1919) 274-293.

Reverend Peter Pernin, "The Great Peshtigo Fire; An Eyewitness Account," *Wisconsin Magazine of History* 54: 246-272 (Summer 1971) and booklet reprint 1971.

—— "The Great Peshtigo Fire; An Eyewitness Account," Wisconsin Historical Society Press; second edition, 1999.

Primary Sources

Public documents

Actes d'État Civil — Saône-et-Loire, Jura, Ain

Recensement de la population, Flacey-en-Bresse (Saône-et-Loire) 1836, 1841, 1846, 1851.

"Diocèse d'Autun, Département de Saône-et-Loire, État Des Mutations survenues parmi les MM. vicaires de paroisse pendant le 1er trimestre 1863" ; and "--1er trimestre 1864," Saône-et-Loire departmental archives.

United States Federal Census 1860, 1870, 1880, 1900

Wisconsin State Census 1875

Hough, Franklin B. *Report on Forestry*, Volume 1 Washington, Government Printing Office 1882.

Ricken, Most Reverend David Laurin, "Decree on the Authenticity of the Apparitions of 1859 at the Shrine of Our Lady of Good Help" Diocese of Green Bay December 8, 2010.

Diocesan archives ordination and personnel records

"Acta Episcoporum Ecclesiae Aeduensis, Cabillonensis, et Matisconensis et Nivenensis Liber 1us"

"Registre des inscriptions des séminaristes, 1836-1873" (also called "Livre Ordonnance") and "Registre matricule du personnel" (undated, after 1888), Autun diocesan archives.

Bishop's sacramental register, Belley-Ars diocesan archives.

"Biographic Cyclopedia – Diocese of Winona" undated [1890s] questionnaire, Green Bay diocesan archives.

Pernin's sacramental registers in America

St. John the Baptist, L'Erable 1856-1879, kept at Assumption of the Blessed Virgin Mary, Ashkum, Illinois.

St. Joseph, Champion, Baptisms, fiche 1862-8, Green Bay diocesan archives.

St. Peter, Oconto, Combined Register, fiche 1860-69, Green Bay diocesan archives.

Our Lady of Lourdes, Marinette, Baptism and marriage, fiche 1869-1875, Green Bay diocesan archives.

St. Peter and St. Paul's Church, Wisconsin Rapids, Wisconsin Volume III, 1875-1878.

Church of the Crucifixion, La Crescent, Minnesota "Parish Ledger 1878-1909."

St. Patrick's, Brownsville, Minnesota, Book A 1870-1936.

St. Bridget's, Simpson, kept at St. Bernard's, Stewartville, *Registrum Baptizatorum, Registum Matrimoniorum*, Record of Interments.

St. Joseph's, Rushford, *Registrum Baptizatorum, Matrimoniorum, Defunctorum* 1885-1913.

Diocesan ordos, clerical directories, and almanachs

Breve Aeduense seu Ordo divini officii recitandi, sacrique peragendi ad usum Ecclesiae Aeduensis pro anno 1828-1895.

La France ecclésiastique : almanach du clergé Ed. Gaume frères 1844-1856.

Sadlier's Catholic directory, almanac and ordo 1865-1878.

Letters

Paroissiens de Saint-Cyrille, L'Islet, August 18, 1862, St-Cyrille, I : 18, Archives of Diocese of Sainte-Anne-de-la-Pocatière.

Gingras to Baillargeon, 10 November 1862; Ducroux to Baillargeon, December 3, 1862; Côté to Baillargeon, November 7, 1864, 7 CM, États-Unis, VII, Archives of Archdiocese of Quebec.

Pernin to Zoé Lassagne March 8, 1909, author's material.

Oral history

Oral history interview of Victor Francis Lassagne and Zoé Lassagne Mercier by Theodore Hawley Lassagne March 9-10, 1968 La Jolla, California, author's material.

Writings

Abeille française : ou Archives de la jeunesse Lyon volume 1 1828.

Audet, Leo "Antoine Vermare: A Biography" [undated (~1980), unpublished manuscript], Green Bay diocesan archives.

Centenaire du Collège d'Autun 1803-1903 L. Marceline Autun 1903.

Chiniquy, Charles *Fifty Years in the Church of Rome* Fleming H. Revell Chicago 1886.

Delacour, Avit *Poésies* (Précédé d'une notice biographique par J.-B. C.) Milliet-Bottier Bourg-en-Bresse 1853.

Devie, Alexandre-Raymond Devie *Correspondance d'un ancien directeur de séminaire avec un jeune prêtre sur la politesse* L. Lesne 1842.

Distribution Solennelle des Prix du Petit Séminaire Episcopal de Meximieux Pélagaud et Lesne Lyon 1837-1842.

Oeuvres complètes du Bienheureux Saint Alphonse-Marie De Liguori, Tome 15 *Neuf Sermons à Prêcher dans les temps de Calamité*, 249-338 Parent-Desbarres 1836.

Manuel du pèlerin de Notre-Dame de Bon-Secours à Montréal Lovell et Gibson Montréal 1848.

Nelligan, John Emmett *A White Pine Empire; The Life of a Lumberman* North Star Press St. Cloud, Minnesota 1969 (first edition 1929).

St. Mary's Hospital Annals 1897-1909.

Starr, Eliza Allen *Patron Saints* J. Murphy & Co. Baltimore; Catholic publication society New York 1871.

Tilton, Frank *Sketch of the Great Fires in Wisconsin at Peshtigo, the Sugar Bush, Menekaune, Williamsonville, and Generally on the Shores of Green Bay: With Thrilling and Truthful Incidents by Eye Witnesses* Robinson & Kustermann Green Bay 1871.

Vernier, M. C. "Discours prononcé le 8 novembre 1903 par M. C. Vernier, professeur de rhétorique" in *Centenaire*.

Voyé, Antonin *L'Abbé Crud et la nouvelle orthopédie* Masson fils La Rochelle 1912.

Newspapers

Chicago *Tribune* 1857

Clifton *Advocate* 1941

Clifton *Comet* 1900

(Green Bay) *Daily State Gazette* 1875

(Green Bay diocesan) *The Spirit* 1976, *The Compass* 2011

Hokah *Chief* 1891

Marinette and Peshtigo *Eagle* 1871-1875

New York Freeman's Journal and Catholic Register 1871-1874

Olmsted County *Democrat* 1909

Rochester *Post, Daily Post & Record* 1898, 1909

(Saint Louis) Missouri *Republican* 1872

Terre Haute *Gazette* 1871

Maps

Bird's Eye view of Peshtigo, Wisconsin Sept. 1871 Madison, Wis.: T.M. Fowler & Co. 1871. Retrieved from loc.gov

Bird's Eye View of Peshtigo, Wisconsin 1881 Madison, Wis.: J.J. Stoner 1881. Retrieved from wisconsinhistory.org

Bird's Eye View of Marinette, Wisconsin 1881 J.J. Stoner 1881. Retrieved from wisconsinhistory.org

Secondary Sources

Ahern, Patrick *Maurice and Therese: The Story of a Love* Doubleday 1998.

Alloing, Louis *Le Diocese de Belley ; Histoire Religieuse des Pays de l'Ain* Chaduc Belley 1938.

Beck, David *The Struggle for Self-Determination: History Of The Menominee Indians Since 1854* University of Nebraska Press 2005.

Bertone, Tarcisio *The Last Secret of Fatima: The Revelation of One of the Most Controversial Events in Catholic History* Crown 2013.

Boatman, John F. *"...And the River Flows On..." Memories from a Wisconsin-Michigan Border Town: the Marinette, Wisconsin Area. Vol. 1. From Ancient Times Until the Creation of Marinette County in 1879.* University of Wisconsin - Milwaukee 1998.

—— Vol. 2. *From the creation of Marinette County until Marinette becomes a city in 1887.* University of Wisconsin - Milwaukee 1998.

Boutry, Philippe *Prêtres et paroisses au pays du Curé d'Ars* Cerf Paris 1986.

—— "'Vertus d'état' et clergé intellectuel : la crise du modèle 'sulpicien' dans la formation des prêtres au XIXe siècle" in *Problèmes d'histoire de de l'education* 207-228 Publications de l'École française de Rome 1988.

Brettell, Caroline B. *Following Father Chiniquy: Immigration, Religious Schism, and Social Change in Nineteenth-Century Illinois* Southern Illinois University Press 2015.

Crozier, William L. *Gathering a people: A history of the Diocese of Winona* Diocese of Winona 1989.

Sister M. Dominica, OSF *The Chapel: Our Lady of Good Help,* De Pere, Wis.: Journal Publishing Co., 1955; second edition: *The Shrine of Our Lady of Good Help: A History* The Shrine of Our Lady of Good Help 2014.

Essertel, Yannick *L'aventure missionnaire lyonnaise, 1815-1962* Cerf Paris 2001.

de Fontenay, Harold, Anatole de Charmasse, *Autun et ses monuments* Dejussieu Autun 1889.

Fouilheron, Joël "Vu de Saint-Flour. Et s'il etait auvergnat ?" 359-432 in André Mandouze, Joël Fouilheron, eds. *Migne et le renouveau des études patristiques : actes du colloque de Saint-Flour, 7-8 juillet 1975, Théologie historique* 66 Editions Beauchesne 1985.

Gady, Éric "Histoire du Lycée Bonaparte." Retrieved from lyceebonaparteautun.fr [dead link].

Garraghan, Gilbert Joseph *The Catholic Church in Chicago, 1673-1871: An Historical Sketch* Loyola University Press 1921.

Gess, Denise and Lutz, William *Firestorm at Peshtigo: A Town, Its People, and the Deadliest Fire in American History* Macmillan 2003.

Gibbs, Joseph C. *History of the Catholic Total Abstinence Union of America* Philadelphia 1907.

Groeschel, Benedict J., CFR *A Still Small Voice: A Practical Guide on Reported Revelations* Ignatius 1993.

Hampton, Roy A., III "German Gothic in the Midwest: The Parish Churches of Franz Georg Himpler and Adolphus Druiding," *U.S. Catholic Historian* 15 (1997) 51-74.

Horgan, Paul *Lamy of Santa Fe* Wesleyan University Press 1975, 2003.

Ireland, John "Life of the Rt. Rev. Joseph Cretin, First Bishop of the Diocese of St. Paul" *Acta et Dicta* 4 (1916) 187-218 and 5 (1917) 3-66 and 170-205. Catholic Historical Society of St Paul.

Juge, Henri-Cyrille-Adrien *Sœur Benoîte ou cinquante-quatre ans d'apparitions de la très sainte Vierge à la pieuse bergère du Laus: Esquisse historique* Josserand 1869.

Karel, David *Dictionnaire des artistes de langue française en Amérique du Nord; peintres, sculpteurs, dessinateurs, graveurs, photographes, et orfèvres* Presses Université Laval 1992.

LaLande, Jeff "Joseph Schafer (1867-1941)" *The Oregon Encyclopedia.* Retrieved from oregonencyclopedia.org

Larcombe, Giselle "Antoine Marie Garin: A Biographical Study Of The Intercultural Dynamic In Nineteenth-Century New Zealand" PhD thesis University of Canterbury (2009).

Leschak, Peter M. *Ghosts of the Fireground: Echoes of the Great Peshtigo Fire and the Calling of a Wildland Firefighter* HarperOne 2003.

Long, Sister Brideen, OSF *In his vineyard, 1868 to 1983: A series of life sketches of the bishops and priests, and permanent deacons of the Green Bay Diocese* Franciscan Publishers, Pulaski, Wisconsin 1983. (*IHV*)

Looney, Edward "Called to Evangelize: The Story of Adele Brise and the Mariophany that Changed her Life," *Marian Studies*: Vol. 62, Article 10 (2011). Retrieved from udayton.edu

Lowrie, Joyce O. *The Violent Mystique: Thematics of Retribution and Expiation in Balzac, Barbey, d'Aurevilly, Bloy, and Huysmans* Librairie Droz Geneva 1974.

McGovern, James J. *The Life and Writings of Right Reverend John McMullen, DD First Bishop of Davenport, Iowa* Hoffman Brothers Chicago 1888.

McKenna, Kevin E. *The Battle for Rights in the United States Catholic Church* Paulist Press 2007.

Marchal, Corinne and Tramaux, Manuel (eds.) *Le miracle de Faverney (1608); L'eucharistie : environnement et temps de l'histoire* Presses universitaires de Franche-Comté 2010.

Meier, John P. *A Marginal Jew; Rethinking the Historical Jesus*, vol. 2 *Mentor, Message, and Miracles* Doubleday 1994.

Michon, Jacques "Senécal, Eusèbe" *Dictionary of Canadian Biography.* Retrieved from biographi.ca

Morley, William F. E. "Bell, Andrew" *Dictionary of Canadian Biography.* Retrieved from biographi.ca

Monfat, A. *Dix années en Mélanésie: étude historique et religieuse* E. Vitte Lyon 1891.

Nicolet, R. P. *Vie du bienheureux Pierre-Louis-Marie Chanel* E. Vitte Lyon 1890.

Nixon, C.E.V., and Rodgers, Barbara Saylor *In Praise of Later Roman Emperors: The Panegyrici Latini* University of California Press 1994.

Noel, Jan "Dry Patriotism: The Chiniquy Crusade" *Canadian Historical Review* 71 (1990) 189-207.

O'Connell, Marvin R. *John Ireland and the American Catholic Church* Minnesota Historical Society Press 1988.

Ochs, Stephen J. *Desegregating the Altar: The Josephites and the Struggle for Black Priests, 1871–1960* LSU Press 1993.

Park, Karen E. "The Negotiation of Authority at a Frontier Marian Apparition Site: Adele Brise and Our Lady of Good Help" *American Catholic Studies* 123 (2012) 1-26.

Parker, George L. "Lovell, John" *Dictionary of Canadian Biography* Retrieved from biographi.ca

Pasquier, Michael *Fathers on the Frontier: French Missionaries and the Roman Catholic Priesthood in the United States, 1789-1870* Oxford University Press 2010.

Pitra, Jean-Baptiste-François "Inscription chrétienne des premiers siècles de l'Église, confirmant plusieurs de nos croyances, par M. l'abbé Pitra professeur au séminaire d'Autun" *Annales de Philosophie Chrétienne* 19 (1839) 195-200.

Price, W. J. "Aux origines d'un schisme : le centenaire d'une réconciliation avortée" *Revue d'histoire de l'Amérique française* 12 (1959) 517-534 and 13 (1960) 45-78.

Reardon, James Michael "The Beginning of the Catholic Total Abstinence Movement in Minnesota" *Acta et Dicta* 1 (1908) 199-209. Catholic Historical Society of St Paul.

Rezek, Rev. Antoine Ivan *History Of The Diocese Of Sault Ste. Marie And Marquette Containing A Full And Accurate Account Of The Development Of The Catholic Church In Upper Michigan* (Vols. 1 and 2) M. A. Donohue & Co. Chicago 1907.

Rochet, Sylvain *Histoire du collège-séminaire de Belley* E. Vitte Lyon 1898.

Simpson, Patricia et Louise Pothier *Notre-Dame-de-Bon-Secours; une chapelle et son quartier* Fides Montréal 2001.

Sylvain, Philippe "Bourget, Ignace" *Dictionary of Canadian Biography*. Retrieved from biographi.ca

"Notice sur Claude Tailland" 9-10 and *Oeuvres Complètes de Claude Tailland*, curé de Saint-Pierre de Macon, 11-909 of Jacques-Paul Migne, ed., *Collection intégrale et universelle des orateurs sacrés du premier et du second ordre* volume 80, Imprimerie catholique 1856.

Thévenot, Émile *Autun ; Cité Romaine Et Chrétienne, Histoire, Monuments, Sites* Autun 1932.

Trisco, Robert "Bishops and Their Priests in the United States" 111-292 in John Tracy Ellis *The Catholic Priest in the United States: Historical Investigations* St. John's University Press Collegeville 1971.

Villerbu, Tangi "Une histoire culturelle du missionaire: Julien Moulin du diocèse de Rennes au Nord-Ouest canadien, 1830-1878" *Annales de Bretagne et des Pays de l'Ouest* 114 (2007) 7-34.

——— "'Ramener une colonie de bons missionaires': le recrutement de prêtres européens pour les Etats-Unis au 19ème siècle" *Revue d'histoire moderne et contemporaine* 56 (2009) 33-65.

——— "Early Catholic Minnesota, New sources and New questions" in Atkins, Annette, Deborah L. Miller (eds.) *The State We're in: Reflections on Minnesota History* Minnesota Historical Society 2010.

——— "Missionnaires catholiques français aux États-Unis, 1791-1920" *Histoire et missions chrétiennes* 17 (2011) 5-14.

——— *Les missions du Minnesota : Catholicisme et colonisation dans l'Ouest américain, 1830-1860* Presses Universitaires de Rennes 2014.

Walling, Regis M. and Rupp, N. Daniel (eds.) *The Diary of Bishop Frederic Baraga: First Bishop of Marquette, Michigan* Wayne State University Press 2001.

Parish and local histories and websites

Bay Settlement Historical Society *A Glimpse Into The Past - A History Of The Town Of Scott* New Franken, Wisconsin 1976, 2007.

Dorner, Joseph E., "Welcome to Holy Family Parish," Holy Family, Marinette (undated).

Pat Ratajczak, St. Joseph, Champion, St. Kilian, New Franken, St. Thomas the Apostle, Sugarbush, "St. Joseph Catholic Church" Retrieved from ssjosephkilianthomas.com

Sisters of St. Francis of the Holy Cross "Community Founders" and "Community celebrates 130th anniversary" Retrieved from gbfranciscans.org

Society of Mary History. Retrieved form societyofmaryusa.org

Internet websites, encyclopedias, and libraries

Archdiocese of St. Louis archstl.org

Catholic Hierarchy.org catholic-hierarchy.org

Dictionary of Canadian Biography biographi.ca/en

Diocese of Green Bay gbdioc.org

Door County Library Newspaper Archive
    doorcountynewspapers.org

FamilySearch familysearch.org

Find A Grave findagrave.com

Gallica gallica.bnf.fr

Google Books books.google.com

HathiTrust hathitrust.org

Internet Archive archive.com

Wisconsin Historical Society wisconsinhistory.org

Personal communication

Rev. John Girotti

Norma Meier

George L. Parker

Pat Ratajczak

Carlo Maria Schianchi, SM, Marist Archives, Rome

Olivia Wendt, Green Bay diocesan archives

Acknowledgements

This work depended on the kindness of archivists and librarians who granted me access to their treasures. I am very grateful, but an urgent reminder: responsibility for all opinions expressed is my own and not that of anyone I thank here.

From the Diocese of Green Bay, I thank Archivist Olivia Wendt for much generous assistance even under circumstances made difficult by the pandemic, Kris Matties, and Archivist John LeDoux (1955-2013), Very Rev. John Girotti, and Rev. Joseph Dorner, one of Pernin's successors as pastor in Marinette.

My thanks to Archivist Paul Cattin and Rev. Christian Josselin of the Diocese of Belley-Ars; Autun diocesan Archivist Agathe Pajor and Corentin Durand; Isabelle Vernus, director, and Sylvie Delorme, Saône-et-Loire departmental archives, Mâcon; Franck Métrot, Mâcon municipal archives; Carlo Maria Schianchi, SM, Marist Archives, Rome; Gaétan Godbout, Communications, Diocese of Sainte-Anne-de-la-Pocatière; Archivist Pierre Lafontaine, Archdiocese of Quebec; Mariel Carter, Stephenson Public Library, Marinette, Wisconsin; Mary Jane Herber, Brown County Library, Green Bay, Wisconsin; Lori B. Bessler, Wisconsin Historical Society Library, Archives and Museum Collections; Amber Polzin, Anuta Research Center, Menominee, Michigan; Mark Thiel, Marquette University Archives; Sean Eisele, Vigo County Public Library, Terre Haute, Indiana; and JoEllen Dickie, Newberry Library, Chicago, Illinois.

Thanks also to Rev. Francisque Bruel, Msgr. Pierre Calimé (1933-2015), Éric Gady, Norma Meier, George L. Parker, and Andrew Walther (1974-2020).

Mary Norris and Tessa Nunn generously read the manuscript, made many contributions, and saved me from many errors. Jonathan Valleau designed the maps. I thank Fabrice Jaumont for his belief in the project.

Final thanks to Ronald Rainey for sharing the joys of ecclesiastica; Bernard and Christiane Barré, who keep the memory of

Philibert Crud at their Maison d'Aviler in Sens (Yonne), once the quarters of Crud's Institut Orthopédique; Liliane Goulut, who stimulated this work at an early stage and gave memorable hospitality in Lons-le-Saunier (Jura); and my wife Wendy for ceaseless loving interest and support, not to mention skillful driving on several continents.

Photo credits

Wikimedia Commons: Peshtigo Harbor 1871, Peshtigo *Times*; Collège d'Autun, MarcJP46, Autun Lycée Bonaparte PA00113150 01 JPM.JPG (2013); Bourget photo, William Notman, 1862, I-4562.0.1, Notman Photographic Archives, Musée McCord, Montreal; Starr photo, from James J. McGovern *Life and Letters of Eliza Allen Starr* (1905).

Diocese of Green Bay: Melcher portrait, photos of Crud, Daems, Sister Adèle, Robinsonville chapel and school 1885, Assumption day procession 1953.

Archdiocese of Chicago's Joseph Cardinal Bernardin Archives and Records Center: Healy portrait of Duggan.

New York Public Library: John Carbutt, 1867, Mill dam and sash factory, Peshtigo, Wis. b11707595; The excursion party at Peshtigo saw mills, Wis. b11707595, Robert N. Dennis collection of stereoscopic views, Miriam and Ira D. Wallach Division of Art, Prints and Photographs.

Marquette University Archives, Bureau of Catholic Indian Missions Records: rice harvesters ID 1219, parish celebrants ID 1207, 07458a.

Missouri Historical Society: Thomas M. Easterly, ~1848, Old Cathedral, Walnut Street looking east from Third Street, N17074, Thomas Easterly Daguerreotype Collection.

Vigo County (Indiana) Public Library Archives: Dowling Hall, Ulyssean Debating Society minutes clipping file, SM DC 45 A, Folder 1.

Manitowish Waters (Wisconsin) Historical Society: logging railroad car Voss Photos, 2018.2.76.

City of Merrill, Wisconsin: Wisconsin loggers.

All others from author's material.

About the Author

Charles Mercier is professor of Classics at College of Humanities in Cheshire, Connecticut, the college seminary of the Legionaries of Christ, a Roman Catholic religious congregation of pontifical right. He holds BA and PhD in Classics from Columbia University and has wide experience teaching Classical and European Humanities and Greek and Latin language and literature. Charles has cultivated an interest in performance of ancient Greek and Roman poetry and drama in both productions and academic publications. In journalism for Catholic news sources he has written on topics such as nineteenth century American Catholic history, the Chaldean Catholic archdiocese of Erbil, and the notion of purification of memory promoted by John Paul II and what it implies for Catholic humanities education.

After a trip to Zambia in 2001, he produced a documentary short about the life of AIDS orphans in Lusaka and a CD compilation of songs by street kids with an edition of their lyrics in Town Bemba and Nyanja. He has translated previously, from Latin, *Terence Brothers* (1997). Charles is the great grandson of Zoé Pernin Lassagne (1842-1892), one of the two nieces who accompanied Jean-Pierre Pernin from France to Illinois in 1864.

About TBR Books

A Program of The Center for the Advancement of Languages, Education, and Communities (CALEC)

TBR Books is a program of the Center for the Advancement of Languages, Education, and Communities. We publish researchers and practitioners who seek to engage diverse communities on topics related to education, languages, cultural history, and social initiatives. We translate our books in a variety of languages to further expand our impact. Become a member of TBR Books and receive complimentary access to all our books.

Our Books in English

Immigrant Dreams: A Memoir by Barbara Goldowsky

Salsa Dancing in Gym Shoes: Developing Cultural Competence to Foster Latino Student Success by Tammy Oberg de la Garza and Alyson Leah Lavigne

Mamma in her Village by Maristella de Panniza Lorch

The Other Shore by Maristella de Panniza Lorch

The Clarks of Willsborough Point: A Journey through Childhood by Darcey Hale

Beyond Gibraltar by Maristella de Panniza Lorch

The Gift of Languages: Paradigm Shift in U.S. Foreign Language Education by Fabrice Jaumont and Kathleen Stein-Smith

Two Centuries of French Education in New York: The Role of Schools in Cultural Diplomacy by Jane Flatau Ross

The Clarks of Willsborough Point: The Long Trek North by Darcey Hale

The Bilingual Revolution: The Future of Education is in Two Languages by Fabrice Jaumont

Our Books in Translation

La Rivoluzione bilingue: Il futuro dell'istruzione in due lingue by Fabrice Jaumont

El regalo de las lenguas : Un cambio de paradigma en la enseñanza de las lenguas extranjeras en Estados Unidos de Fabrice Jaumont y Kathleen Stein-Smith

Rewolucja Dwujęzyczna: Przyszłość edukacji jest w dwóch językach by Fabrice Jaumont

Le don des langues : vers un changement de paradigme dans l'enseignement des langues étrangères aux États-Unis de Fabrice Jaumont et Kathleen Stein-Smith

Our books are available on our website and on all major online bookstores as paperback and e-book. Some of our books have been translated in Arabic, Chinese, English, French, German, Italian, Japanese, Polish, Russian, Spanish. For a listing of all books published by TBR Books, information on our series, or for our submission guidelines for authors, visit our website at

www.tbr-books.org

About CALEC

The Center for the Advancement of Languages, Education, and Communities is a nonprofit organization with a focus on multilingualism, cross-cultural understanding, and the dissemination of ideas. Our mission is to transform lives by helping linguistic communities create innovative programs, and by supporting parents and educators through research, publications, mentoring, and connections.

We have served multiple communities through our flagship programs which include:

- TBR Books, our publishing arm; which publishes research, essays, and case studies with a focus on innovative ideas for education, languages, and cultural development;

- Our online platform provides information, coaching, support to multilingual families seeking to create dual-language programs in schools;

- NewYorkinFrench.net, an online platform which provides collaborative tools to support New York's Francophone community and the diversity of people who speak French.

We also support parents and educators interested in advancing languages, education, and communities. We participate in events and conferences that promote multilingualism and cultural development. We provide consulting for school leaders and educators who implement multilingual programs in their school. For more information and ways, you can support our mission, visit

www.calec.org

CPSIA information can be obtained
at www.ICGtesting.com
Printed in the USA
FSHW010645110521
81252FS